# Love & War
as never before

# Love & War
## as never before

World War II through the eyes of a young boy
and in the letters of a loving family

### George Wilson Morin

Copyright © 2010 by George Wilson Morin

Library of Congress Control Number: 2010915686
ISBN:    Hardcover    978-1-4568-0108-3
         Softcover    978-1-4568-0107-6
         Ebook        978-1-4568-0109-0

All rights reserved. No part of this book may be reproduced or transmitted in any form or by any means, electronic or mechanical, including photocopying, recording, or by any information storage and retrieval system, without permission in writing from the copyright owner.

This book was printed in the United States of America.

**To order additional copies of this book, contact:**
Xlibris Corporation
1-888-795-4274
www.Xlibris.com
Orders@Xlibris.com
85974

# Contents

## 1941

1. Citadel Street — 11

## 1942

2. The Family Gathers — 19
3. Pritchard Street — 22

## 1943

4. Finally . . . — 29
5. The Grown-Up War — 32
6. Love to All, Write Soon — 37
7. New Neighbors — 47
8. Marauders at Work — 50
9. Blackout and Black Market — 57
10. No Letup — 60
11. War Hits Home — 64
12. War Around the Edges — 66
13. The Bradleys — 78
14. New Assignments — 82
15. General MacArthur — 92
16. Hope for the New Year — 94

## 1944

| | | |
|---|---|---|
| 17. | Getting Ready | 105 |
| 18. | Eyes Front, No Talking | 147 |
| 19. | In the Calm | 149 |
| 20. | D-Day on Pritchard Street | 157 |
| 21. | In My Mind and Prayers | 159 |
| 22. | The Man of the House | 182 |
| 23. | Pushing On | 184 |
| 24. | Centre and Craig | 211 |
| 25. | News, News, News | 215 |
| 26. | Getcher Paper Here | 223 |
| 27. | Before the Storm | 226 |
| 28. | The Oakland Boys | 244 |
| 29. | Counterpunch | 249 |

## 1945

| | | |
|---|---|---|
| 30. | The Beginning of the End | 261 |
| 31. | Doomsday | 272 |
| 32. | The President's Last Chapter | 274 |
| 33. | Over the Wall | 298 |
| 34. | V-E | 301 |
| 35. | Now We Know | 338 |
| 36. | P.S. | 342 |
| 37. | Ball Hawk | 344 |

Acknowledgments   347

In loving memory of my mother,
Dorothea Wilson Morin
1903-1977

*1941*

## Chapter 1

### Citadel Street

According to my big sister Jane, we once lived in a large white house high on a terrace overlooking Pittsburgh's Chartiers Avenue. But the first house I remember was a small orange-brick row house on Citadel Street, down the hill from a city firehouse.

It was the second in a row of eight connected two-story houses. Each had its own porch, a green and white awning and a bacon strip of grass next to the sidewalk. I lived there from age four to six with my mother, grandmother and two sisters.

Jane, eleven years older than me, had straight brown hair that she held back with barrettes. She wore sweaters buttoned down the back, pleated skirts, white socks, and brown and white shoes. Her face was sprinkled with freckles and one of her front teeth had a corner chipped off.

She did anything and everything to make me laugh. When I'd giggle at the goofy face she made, she'd tickle my ribs until I collapsed squealing. She took me swimming, read me stories, and showed me how to print my name even before kindergarten. She also took me up the hill to the white brick firehouse on the corner. All the firemen knew her. One said, "Hi Janie, back to see your plaque again are ya?"

"Yeah, it's time I showed it to the man of the house," she said, pointing to me, barely five years old. She led me past the giant red fire engines and the thick brass pole and pointed to large marble plaque high on the wall with lots of words on it.

"See," she said, pointing to the name JOHN M. MORIN, "that's our grandfather." I could only read "Morin," my last name. Jane said Grandfather's name was carved in marble because he had been Pittsburgh's Director of Public Safety when the firehouse was built many years before.

My other sister, Nellie, was only two years older than me. She had a spray of dark reddish curls and a chubby freckled face and always shoved and pushed and tried to tell me what to do. I got even by chanting, "Who hit Nellie in the belly with a can of Spam?" and then running to safety behind my grandmother.

Nellie and Georgie

My favorite thing to do was walking up Chartiers Avenue past the firehouse, the gas station, the 5 & 10 and Kroger's grocery to the movie house my aunt and uncle owned. Aunt Ruth, my mother's sister, was in the ticket booth. I'd ask her for a "nick," my word for *nickel*. She'd give me one so I could buy a box of Good 'n' Plenty's at the candy counter. Then I opened the door to the darkness and found my way to the front row. There I watched the movie until Grandmother or Jane came to take me home.

Everyone called our mother Dot, but her real name was Dorothea. She worked during the day and Nellie and I couldn't wait for her to come home. Her ride would drop her at the corner. As we ran to greet her she'd break into a smile. She was very thin with dark brown hair and pale green eyes and worked in accounts payable at the Dravo Corporation, a company that built ships on the Ohio River.

On payday she'd arrive home with a roll of pennies and sit in the middle of the sofa between the two of us with her green pack of Lucky Strikes and a glass of beer. She'd peel the paper from the coins and split the contents in two, one stack for each of us, our allowance for the month.

The best day on Citadel Street was when the strawberry man came. He sat atop a horse-drawn wagon loaded with boxes of strawberries. I could hear him before I could see him. "Strawberrieees. Strawberrieees." I'd run to my grandmother, she'd run to her purse, and I'd run back to the strawberry man clutching Grandma's coins. Grandmother's gray hair was neatly held together by bobby pins and a hair net. Her eyes hid behind the reflection of her glasses. She had a wide smile and heavy body. I grew up with the certainty that she would do anything I asked her to do.

With the strawberries rinsed and cut, my afternoon was spent stamping out circles in Grandmother's dough with the rim of a water glass. When the biscuits were brown from the oven, she'd pour the cream from the top of a milk bottle into a bowl and whip it with the eggbeater. Dessert that night was juicy red berries over warm biscuits topped with fluffy mounds of cream.

But it wasn't always summer. One winter day, when the snow was stacked high on the railings and steps of the back porch like I'd never seen snow before, the backyard looked like a white cloud come to earth. I pleaded with Grandmother to let me go out in it. Finally, she gave in, wrapped me in snow clothes, and let me out the back door. I took two steps down into the yard and was up to my neck in snow. "Grandma!" I screamed.

She was right behind me, dressed for the mission, and lifted me to safety.

On a cold and sunless Sunday, Mother, Jane, Nellie, and I went to eleven o'clock Mass at the Church of the Holy Innocents. It always seemed to be a long walk, and longer when with the wind whipped up so even when you put your head down into the wind your ears froze numb and your cheeks ached. The church was warm relief as we went down the aisle. Mother waited for me, Nellie, and Jane to genuflect and make the sign of the cross before entering a pew halfway down the aisle. Then Mother would genuflect and follow us in. She had to convert to Catholicism to marry my father – and was now the most devout Catholic of all. I loved the music and the incense and couldn't wait to make my first Holy Communion.

Grandmother didn't come to church with us because she was a Presbyterian and didn't like Catholics – but she always had bacon, pancakes, butter, and syrup ready when we returned. After we ate, I spread out the metal beams of my erector set in front of the living room fireplace. My high socks and wool knickers fought off swirls of cold air on the floor. Coals in the fireplace glowed yellow and red with tiny tongues of blue dancing around the edges.

I was on my knees screwing in the top beams of my building when I noticed Mother, Grandmother and Jane huddled around the living room radio looking at the orange light behind the dial. Nellie, on the sofa, had stopped coloring in her book.

*"Shortly before 8 a.m. Honolulu time, without warning, Japanese aircraft attacked American ships and military installations on Pearl Harbor,"* the radio said.

"Where's Pearl Harbor?" Jane asked. "I never heard of it."

I kept building, not much interested in what grown-ups listened to on the radio. A little later, Aunt Ruth and Uncle Charles came in the front door and took off their hats, coats, and galoshes. Mother and Grandmother kissed and hugged them, but no one was laughing or talking loud as they usually did. Aunt Ruth asked, "Has anyone heard from Martin?" Martin was my uncle who I knew from his and my Uncle Bill's West Point photographs on the mantel.

Uncle Charles was a head higher and a foot wider than anyone in the room. He combed his hair back with a sharp part on one side. He didn't talk much.

Aunt Ruth always wore lots of red rouge and a big smile, but she wasn't smiling now. She knelt down and gave me a kiss on my cheek. She smelled nice. In the past, she'd slip me a nick, but not this time.

The radio was still on. The couch filled up with Mother, Uncle Charles, Aunt Ruth, and Grandmother. The talking continued. Glasses and bottles of beer were passed out. Cigarettes lit. Ashtrays pushed closer to the smokers.

Aunt Ruth asked Mother, "What will John do?" John was my father, a man I had yet to meet.

"He'd better join the Army," Mother said. "Get this damn war over before this one," pointing to me, "grows up."

"I'll bet Martin will be in it."

"Poor man, he's already in it, in Washington."

The radio continued, *"American battleships West Virginia, Oklahoma and Arizona were sunk or mortally damaged . . ."*

"Oh, it's just awful, you know what they did in China," said Aunt Ruth.

My mother said, "That damn Roosevelt got us into this."

"Oh, Dot, you can't mean that," Ruth said.

*The battleship Nevada has been beached and cruisers Honolulu, Helena and Raleigh have been sunk. Many U.S. destroyers have also been put out of action."*

"I forgot about Davy Foster in the Navy," Jane said.

"My God," Ruth said, "We're all going to have someone – "

"Jack Darr will be drafted," Mother said.

"Not with that eye," Uncle Charles said.

Aunt Ruth sipped her beer and said, "Why do you need two eyes to fight?"

*"Within minutes of the first attack, battleships next to Ford Island suffered bomb or torpedo hits . . ."*

"I can't stand this. I'm getting another beer," Mother said.

Uncle Charles added large lumps of coal to the fireplace. Grandmother stirred bowls and rolled dough in the kitchen. Jane and Nellie set the table. The radio continued in the background. Sometimes, everyone would stop talking to listen. And then go on talking. I took down my building and put the pieces back into the box that said "Fun for Junior Engineers" on the cover.

After dinner, after Nellie and I took our bath and I was in bed, Mother came into the dark room to kiss us good night. I asked about the word I had wondered about all day, "Mommy, what does *war* mean?"

She kissed me again and left the room without answering.

A few weeks later, it was Christmas Eve. Nellie and I tacked our long bright-red Christmas stockings to the mantel over the fireplace. As we went up the stairs to bed, I looked back at the sagging stockings, the only color in the drab and empty room.

I crawled into my bed and vowed to stay awake until Santa Claus came. I watched the shadows float across our bedroom ceiling each time a car drove up or down Citadel Street. As long as I watched the shadows, I thought, I would stay awake.

The next thing I knew, Nellie was shaking me. "Get up. Santa Claus came."

Just a hint of morning light shone through the windows as we eased down the staircase into the dark living room. At first all I saw was a faint twinkle of icicles on the tree. Then, in the shadows under the tree, I made out stacks of packages. The red stockings on the mantel were now plump, overflowing with candy canes and popcorn balls.

Jane came down the steps putting on her bathrobe, smiling like someone who knows a wonderful secret she can't wait to tell. She turned on the tree lights and our little living room exploded into a glittering wonder room. She stood before us, touching our shoulders, her eyes sparkling from the lights.

"Father was here. He brought the tree – and presents."

He was here, I thought. "Why didn't he stay?" I asked.

"He had to go," is all she said.

I spent the morning examining my new toys and wondering which ones came from him.

The first day of school after Christmas vacation, Sister Agnes Vincent waited until we were all in our seats and quiet before she said, "I hope all of you had a happy and blessed Christmas."

Someone coughed and a chair leg scraped the floor. "We all can do our part to win this awful war. The enemy will stop at nothing, as they have in China. We must pray for the missionary priests and nuns in China and around the world.

"On the corner of my desk, there's a Mite box to help the Catholic Missions. You can put in pennies, nickels, dimes, and quarters. Each week, we'll empty it and count how much this class has contributed.

"You can also bring in canned food and clean, used clothing for people made homeless by the war. Girls, make sure your mother saves bacon grease. It's needed to make ammunition. Boys, you should flatten empty tin cans to help with the war effort. But most of all, you should pray."

Patricia Connors marched up to the Mite box and put a coin in, and then Ralph Broder got up and did the same thing. Then other kids got up and pulled coins from their pockets or purses and put them in the box. All I had was my weekly milk money in an envelope, and I couldn't give that.

The war meant that Nellie and I saw less and less of our mother. She left for work earlier in the morning and came home later at night. Then she'd eat the dinner Grandmother saved, smoke her Luckies, drink her beer, and go to bed. Sometimes she worked on Saturday. Her company was now building ships for the Navy.

One cold, snowy morning, Jane told Nellie and me that we wouldn't be going to school that day, not because of the snow, but because we had to go downtown to buy new clothes. Something awful had happened.

*1942*

# Chapter 2

## The Family Gathers

I had never seen a dead person before.

The casket rested between two tall candles with golden caps under steady flames. The wall was blanketed with bursts of crimson, white, and yellow flowers. The man lying in the dark suit with his hands folded was my grandfather. I edged closer and knelt on the soft red velvet cushion. His fingers were entwined with worn rosary beads.

He looked asleep. I watched his red tie and white shirt closely for a hint of breathing. Then I reached out and touched his hand – and quickly pulled back. He felt like cold chicken.

I lowered my head and whispered a Hail Mary and turned away to my mother behind me. Walking from the somber candle lit room overflowing with flowers; we entered a bright room alive with relatives I had never met. They were sitting in wide chairs or on long couches – or standing near the long linen-covered table with lines of green, brown and white bottles surrounded by glasses of all shapes.

"Well, Georgie, did you pay your respects to your grandfather?" The voice came from behind my right ear and I turned to see smiling, bushy-browed blue eyes in an army uniform.

"This is your uncle Martin," Mother said.

"Gosh, you've grown," he said. "I remember when your grandfather held you up for the priest to pour water on your head. It's too bad he can't see you now. He'd be very proud."

He had gold oak-leaf pins on each shoulder and a thin row of colorful ribbons on his chest.

He turned to my mother and said, "Dot, how's everything with you? You getting along?"

"Oh, you know me, Mart. Laughin' 'n' scratchin'. Just get this damn war over before . . ." Her eyes again tilted down to me.

They went on talking as I looked over the other people in the room. Nellie and Jane were sitting on one of the couches talking with two women who had the reddish-blond look of Martin. Jane saw me and said, "Come over here."

I went over, cautiously, never sure of what to expect. I felt good in my new blue suit, even if it did have short pants.

"Meet your aunts," Jane said. "This is your aunt Margaret."

"Just call me Margy," Aunt Margaret said. She sat very straight on the edge of the couch and held a small purse and a pair of white gloves on her lap. "How old are you?"

"Six," I said.

"And what grade are you in?"

"First."

While Aunt Margy went on asking me questions, I couldn't take my eyes off the other aunt. She was leaning back on the couch smiling at me with her whole face – blue eyes twinkling, teeth gleaming, and the spread of red lips dimpling her cheeks. Her light blondish hair framed a picture that even a six-year-old first grader knew was beautiful.

Jane said, "And this is your aunt Mary Eleanor."

"That'll be Aunt Nell to you," she said as she reached over and smoothed my hair and pinched my cheek.

"Aunt Nell and Margy are joining the Red Cross," Jane said. "To help people in the war."

"Let's not bore the boy with that," Aunt Nell said.

I didn't think it would be boring, but before I could say so, Jane turned to Margy and asked, "What will Uncle Bill do?"

"He'll get his commission back. After that, it's anybody's guess," Margy said. Uncle Bill had graduated from West Point but was now out of the army.

"He told me the airborne," Nell said.

"Oh, God," said Margy. "Anything but that."

The next aunt I met was Aunt Rose. I knew who she was. Every year she sent me a birthday card with a dollar in it. She was smaller than her sisters and had brown hair and a little scar on the lid of her eye. I don't know if the scar had anything to do with it, but she had a way with her eyes. After she'd make a joke or tell a story, she fluttered her eyes very fast as she laughed. She was the oldest of the sisters, sort of the family camp counselor.

Aunt Rose

Grandfather's sons and daughters who weren't at the funeral home when I was there were Aunt Biz, Aunt Anne, Aunt Patsy, Uncle Bill and, my father, John.

While Nellie stayed next to Jane listening to all the grown-ups talk, I wandered out of the room to the long ramp that we walked down when we came in. The ramp had a wall on one side and on the other side panels of glass that looked out onto a garden, now white with snow. I took to walking up to the top of the ramp and running down – as fast as I could – again and again. After a while I heard people say the mayor was coming and a man told me to stop running and stand to the side. A group of men came down the ramp. Two in front, two in back and one smaller, rounder man in the middle.

The next day Jane came home with the newspaper. It had a picture of the man in the middle. Jane read the story out loud. He came from New York to Pittsburgh for Grandfather's funeral because they had been friends since they were in Congress together. But he had to take a train home instead of a plane because the Pittsburgh airport was snowed in. When the reporter asked what he would do if he were mayor of Pittsburgh, he said, "Shovel the snow at the airport."

He had a funny name: Fiorello LaGuardia.

# Chapter 3

## Pritchard Street

The last thing the movers put on the truck was the refrigerator. The gray-haired man inside the truck shouted to the large bald man on the porch behind the refrigerator, "Hold it. Take it easy. Now push, push, push." After the last grunt, they slammed the truck door closed and hopped in the cab.

I watched the big yellow crate of a truck turn and lumber up the hill to Chartiers Avenue, Jane waving from the front seat. Aunt Ruth waited in her Plymouth coupe at the curb. Mother and Grandmother got in the front seat. Nellie and I got in our prized rumble seat that folded outside in the back. The wind blew our hair and made us squint as we laughed up the avenue past the firehouse, Aunt Ruth's movie theater, the gas station, Kroger's, the Sheraden Tavern and all the other stores until the car made a hard left up one steep hill and a sharp right up another, all the way to the top, where the moving truck waited at the gray and white house on the corner of Pritchard and Fredette Streets.

Nellie and I hopped out of the rumble seat, scrambled up the steps, ran across the porch and burst into the empty house. Our voices echoed as we raced through the rooms on the first floor and then up the stairs to the second. We knew the bedroom in the front would be ours and we gazed out the window over the red brick house across the street, the wooden city steps that marched down the hill, and a neat green garden dotted with red tomatoes next to the steps. "A real victory garden," I said.

Downstairs the movers were filling the rooms with furniture and boxes. I went out to the porch to survey my new domain – as fresh and exciting as it was frightening. I sat on top of the cement steps that led down a small terrace to the sidewalk.

I saw four boys around my age come down the alleyway across the street between the big white house and a building that looked like a garage or something.

They crossed Fredette Street to the sidewalk between the moving truck and my house. They looked at me through the corners of their eyes and I didn't know what to do. They looked tough, especially the biggest one. My knees started to shake. So I said, as tough-sounding as I could, "What are you looking at? Get off my sidewalk." The biggest one said something to the others – and they all laughed. Then my hands shook too.

But it didn't take long before I became friends with those boys I tried to chase away. We all had one thing in common – we loved to play war. They were Tommy and Bobby Bradley, Dickie Roberts and Frankie Newman.

The smallest and friendliest was Frankie: dark red curly hair and freckle-covered nose. His red brick house on Fredette Street was catty-corner from my house on Pritchard. Dickie had straight blond hair, a soft voice and never seemed to get dirty. His house was next to Frankie's and overlooked the woods covering the hill next to the city steps – and Mr. Clancy's victory garden, who lived in the red brick house across the street for ours.

Tommy was the oldest and biggest. In the summer, he wore bib dungarees over his bare chest. His brother, Bobby, around my age, wore glasses so tight he had ridges in his skin from his eyes to behind his ears. And he always needed a haircut.

Frankie's father was in the Army and Dickie's in the Navy. Tommy and Bobby's dad was a policeman and had been in World War I. Tommy and Bobby had their father's World War I helmet and gas mask to prove it. I never talked about my father, and no one asked.

Playing war was an easy game to learn. One side would be the Germans or the Japs, the other would be American soldiers, marines or, sometimes, British commandos. Once we settled who was who, one side would turn their backs and the other side would run and hide. The battleground included the high bushes around Frankie Newman and Dickie Roberts's front yards and the woods over the wall from Dickie's yard.

The action was fast and brutal. As one side would advance on the other, a kid would pop up from behind a hedge with an imaginary tommy gun in his hands with an *ahk-ahk-ahk-ahk-ahk-ahk-ahk*. The kid who was shot would fall down dead – for about two heartbeats – and then leap up declaring, "I'm a new man," and deliver a lethal *poom-poom-poom-poom-poom* from his imaginary weapon and the other kid would then fall, splayed on the ground until he too became a "new man" armed with deadly imagination and endless endurance. The battle would rage behind the hedges and over the lawns and spill down into the woods and under and over the city steps.

A variation pitted one side on the wall of Dickie's yard and the other side in the woods below. The wall side lobbed grenades disguised as pebbles on the forces below. Once, when I was defending the woods against Dickie Roberts's onslaught, a blue, pebble-size shard of glass arced from behind the wall and hit the center of my bare chest.

Blood poured out.

I ran home to Grandmother fearing for my life. At first glance, she feared for it, too, but after some cleansing she saw the wound was no deeper than my breastbone. She patched me up and sent me back into battle – now seasoned with a taste of reality.

When we weren't playing war, we studied war, comparing the profiles of the B-17 Flying Fortress and the P-51 Mustang with the profiles of German bombers and Japanese Zeros. Instead of doing homework, I spent hours drawing airplanes with guns blazing and bombs exploding.

We also knew the ranks in the Army, Navy and Marines – privates, seamen, corporals, petty officers and sergeants; ensigns, lieutenants, captains and majors; colonels, generals and admirals.

Everything else we knew about war came from the movies. We learned how they fought World War I in *Sergeant York*, where Gary Cooper licked his thumb to wet the sight at the end of his rifle before picking off a trench load of Germans, last man first, just like he picked off geese on the wing back home.

We learned how the United States Marines fought against great odds in *Wake Island* and shuddered as a satanic Nazi pilot parachuted into the rose garden of the brave and vulnerable *Mrs. Miniver*.

In the movie newsreels we saw American battleships, carriers, cruisers and destroyers churn through the waves; our tanks, artillery and troops push forward over dusty roads and pitted terrain.

We also learned about war with music:

"This Is the Army Mr. Brown," "Praise the Lord and Pass the Ammunition," "Flying Home on a Wing and a Prayer," "When the Lights Come On Again," and "We'll Meet Again."

*1943*

# Chapter 4

## Finally . . .

It was a warm day near the end of April. I trudged up Pritchard Street with a deck of books under my arm, heading for the side door of our house. Inside, as I slogged up the stairs, I glimpsed a man's tan trousers in front of the living room fireplace. I scampered to the top and stopped at the doorway.

I don't know how, but I knew. "Dad!" I yelled and leaped into his arms. He caught me, backing up against the mantel. I could feel the stubble of his beard against my cheek.

"Well, hello, Buster," he said, as he lowered me to the floor.

*Buster! That's not my name*, I thought. *Why did he call me Buster?*

Jane came over and said, "Father is going overseas, Georgie. He wanted to see us before he went."

I looked him over. He had captain bars on the epaulets of his dark brown jacket and an Army Air Corps shoulder patch. His tan trousers had sharp creases, his shoes glistened. His hair, short and wavy. Jane once told me he looked like Jimmy Cagney – and he did – a little.

"What are you going to do in the war?" I asked.

He sat on the edge of the couch., "Well, I'm going to help show the pilots where to drop their bombs."

I had seen movie newsreels showing bombs falling out of bomb bays and the clouds of explosions when they hit the ground. I climbed up on the couch, a cushion width between us.

"Are you going to fly in the airplanes?"

"Sometimes. My main job will be on the ground, studying maps and photographs so I can brief pilots and their crews."

He had two campaign ribbons on his jacket. "How did you get your medals?," I asked.

"This is the World War I victory medal."

"You were in World War I?"

"No, but I was at West Point before it ended and the Army gave me a medal. The other medal is for being in the Army now."

Nellie, who had hurried home before me, was sitting in a chair in the corner with a book open on her lap.

"Have you ever been in a Flying Fortress?," I asked.

"Yes, I have," he said. "What do you know about them?"

"I like to draw them, and P-51s, and Flying Tigers."

"Do you draw the B-26 Marauder?"

"No, I never heard of it."

"It's smaller and faster than the Flying Fortress. It's what my bomb group flies."

"Will you see Uncle Martin and Margy and Nell when you get overseas?" Jane asked.

"I don't know where they are. The censors won't let us say where we are in our letters."

Nellie said, "Aunt Nell wrote me. She's serving donuts from a Red Cross Clubmobile somewhere in England."

"That's okay to say it that way. I'll be sure to keep my eyes open for her, and her donuts."

"Father, you should know," Jane said, "Nellie is at the head of her class."

"That's wonderful, dear. After the war you're going to need a good education to get anywhere. That goes for you, too, Georgie."

"He never does his homework," Nellie said.

"I do too," I said, lying.

"He tries hard," Jane said as she handed him the opened magazine from the coffee table. "Here's an article about me in *Outlines*. You can read it on the train."

"What a wonderful picture of you. I can't wait to read it." He looked at his watch and said, "It's time I leave."

I looked at the clock on the mantel. It was almost time for Mother to come home. He kissed Jane and Nellie and shook my hand. Then he put on his officer's hat, like the one I saw Clark Gable wear in a movie newsreel, and was out the door, across the porch and down the steps. I watched from the doorway as he disappeared into the city steps next to Mr. Clancy's house on his way to the streetcar stop below.

As I walked to school the next morning I told Tommy and Bobby Bradley my dad was a captain in the Army Air Corps and was going overseas – but he couldn't say where because it was a secret. After school I saw Frankie Newman and Dickie Roberts and also told them. Now we all had dads in wars. I was dizzy thinking mine was a *captain* in the Army Air Corps.

# Chapter 5

## The Grown-Up War

While me and my pals played war, my relatives were fighting it. Perhaps the staunchest warrior was Aunt Rose, who waged the battle from the family's apartment on East 86 Street in Manhattan's Yorkville. Her brothers, sisters and cousins overseas sent her hand-written letters, which she would type on a manual typewriter in quadruplicate and then send the copies to the other siblings and relatives. Often a hand-written letter from the most prolific of her sisters required three, four or more pages of single-spaced typing.

More than 400 pages like these were typed in quadruplicate by Aunt Rose on her circa 1935 typewriter.

I inherited this trove of methodically numbered and dated letters after my father died at age 93. Some 400 pages covering 1943, '44 and '45 were yellowing in a crushed cardboard box in the corner of his garage. In addition to Rose, the letters were from his sisters Margy and Nell in the Red Cross; his brother Martin, a lieutenant colonel in the Army; his cousin Alvin "Pat" Mente, also an Army lieutenant colonel; and his brother-in-law Tom Hanson, a lieutenant commander in the Navy.

With the permission of the children and sisters of the writers, I have edited the letters here for conciseness and readability.

The head of this family had been my grandfather, John M. Morin. He was born in 1868 to Irish immigrants in Philadelphia and moved to Pittsburgh with them four years later. He ran a saloon in the Oakland district of Pittsburgh, entering politics at the turn of the century, first as a member of the Pittsburgh City Council, then as the Director of Public Safety, and ultimately as a Member of Congress and Chairman of the Military Affairs Committee. His three sons attended the Military Academy at West Point. Two graduated.

My grandfather was said to be "stern." All the photos I've ever seen of him would back that up. The record shows he also knew how to get things done. As a former saloon keeper, he had a hand in ending Prohibition with his House colleague Fiorello LaGuardia and helped push through Social Security when he was the Grand Worthy President of the Fraternal Order of Eagles. F.D.R. sent him a letter of thanks.

My father, John M. Morin, Jr., the first son, left the military academy after a year and a half. The family buzz was he turned 21 and could then legally defy his father and elope with my mother. However, on his application for an Army commission after Pearl Harbor, he said he had left because of illness.

My father's career after West Point included heading up a traveling vaudeville act, managing movie theaters, and selling glass facades for movie theaters for Pittsburgh Plate Glass. He separated from my mother some months before I was born in January 1936.

He received his Army Air Corps commission in 1942 and was trained as an intelligence officer. Assigned to the 8th Army Air Force on his arrival in England on May 11, 1943, his duties at times included flying with bomber crews as an observer. On September 5, 1943, he was on a B-26 Marauder named *Lady Luck II* going to France when one of the plane's two engines failed, causing it to crash near Honington, England. He suffered a shattered arm and was awarded the Purple

Heart. After the war he stayed in the Air Force as a master sergeant, retiring in 1955.

Uncle Martin, Martin J. Morin, the second son, graduated from West Point and had a distinguished career in the Army, retiring as a major general. During World War II he was a lieutenant colonel and battalion commander in the 41st Armored Infantry, 2nd Armored, "Hell on Wheels," Division of Patton's Third Army. He fought in North Africa, Sicily, Normandy, France and Belgium. He was awarded the Silver Star and the Bronze Star with four oak leaf clusters.

My trove of letters was sent to my father, so I have none from him – and none from Uncle Bill, William A. M. Morin, who also graduated from the Military Academy. When the war started he was called back to duty and assigned to teach the cadets at West Point. He and his fellow officers at The Point believed the Army was holding them back for the assault on Japan after victory in Europe.

Aunt Margy, Margaret Fleming Morin, an accomplished pianist and music teacher, joined the American Red Cross Social Services to help refugees and other civilian victims of war as fighting progressed through North Africa, Sicily, Italy, France, Belgium and Germany. While the Battle of the Bulge was raging, the Red Cross sedan in which she was riding made a wrong turn and found itself in the middle of an artillery barrage on the outskirts of Bastogne. On orders from a startled G.I., they got out of there fast.

Aunt Nell, Mary Eleanor Morin, a social worker in New York, signed on with the Red Cross and worked in England on a Clubmobile team.

L to R: Dulcie Langman and Aunt Nell in their Clubmobile.

She and a crew drove through the English countryside visiting military outposts to hand out coffee, sandwiches and doughnuts to the troops. She was later assigned to Red Cross Clubs in London. As the war progressed, she went into Civilian Relief and followed the troops to Red Cross facilities from France to Belgium to Germany, enduring the ever-worsening conditions through war-torn Europe.

Cousin Alvin "Pat" Mente, also a West Point graduate, was a lieutenant colonel in the 7th Armored Division. In the Battle of the Bulge, after escaping capture by the Germans, he approached the American lines and was confronted by an American soldier who asked a question to which all Americans were supposed to know the answer. He failed the test and got a bullet in each leg because of it. His wounds took more than a year of difficult treatment and therapy to heal, but he never complained, always referring to the wounds as strokes of luck.

Uncle Tom Hanson was the husband of Aunt Patsy, the youngest of the nine Morin children. Tom had been in the Secret Service assigned to the White House before the Navy came calling. He served as a lieutenant commander in the Philippines and weighed in with letters about the bloody fighting there.

The other members of the Morin clan included Aunt Anne, married to Bob Brown and raising a family in California; and Aunt Biz, Mary Elizabeth, who lived in New York with Rose and worked as a secretary with the Cunard Steamship Line. She helped Rose fill the deluge of shopping requests from Margy and Nell.

There was also a small Morin contingent still living in Pittsburgh – my mother, my sisters and me.

# Chapter 6

## Love to All, Write Soon

Aunt Rose wrote to John as he left New York for England aboard an overcrowded Queen Elizabeth. He arrived with the 453 Squadron of the 383 Bomb Group in Horham, England on May 11, 1943. His job was described as "Intelligence Staff Officer, Combat."

> Rose Mary Morin
> 425 East 86th Street
> New York City
> May 4, 1943
>
> Dear John:
> Congratulations on your promotion. We were sorry we missed your call, especially since you had to stand in line so long to make it. Biz had gone to Washington and I stayed downtown to see the circus.
> When you go across you could pop in on one or several of our kinfolk. Lord knows they are in all parts of the globe.
> Martin is in North Africa. Margy is in Algiers and Nell somewhere in England, but apparently near London since she writes of seeing shows and having tea at the Savoy on her days off.

Bill has been ordered to duty with the troops at West Point. Pat Mente is an instructor at the Armored Force School in Fort Knox.

Nell is with a Red Cross Clubmobile. They go from camp to camp serving doughnuts and coffee. If you find yourself in London, inquire at Red Cross headquarters at 12 Grosvenor Square. She has been hoping someone would bring her a civilian outfit. She went off in such a hurry she took nothing but uniforms.

Margaret has been promoted to Asst. Program Director and likes the work exceedingly. Martin is with 41st Armored Infantry, 2nd Armored Division. Outside of "Somewhere in North Africa" he never gives an inkling of his whereabouts.

We still hope we'll hear from you by telephone. If not, au revoir, happy landing, good luck and a safe and soon return.

Much love from Biz and I, ROSE

L to R: Martin, Margy, John and Nell.

After the Italian and German surrender in North Africa on May 13, 1943, Margaret looked to Rose to do some clothes shopping for her – and prepared for a reunion with Martin.

Margaret F. Morin
American Red Cross
Somewhere in North Africa
June 19, 1943

Dear Rose and Biz:

I received your May 27th letter about two days ago and your May 19th letter today. You can see how mixed up the mail can be.

Have you received any of my pleas for clothes? I've asked for summer dresses, toeless sandals, white gloves and any or all kind of stockings. Please anything you can manage.

I still haven't heard from Martin. I hope to see him very soon. I just paid 625 francs for a bottle of brandy (that is $12.50 in our money). I thought it would be nice to have for Martin if he comes here. When I think of us hesitating when Scotch went up to $4.25, I get hysterical. One would pay almost any price for it now.

Rose, would you send a copy of the newer tunes with your letters? I would like to get one by the name of, *I'm Saving Myself for Bill*.

Love, MARGY

With the fighting over in North Africa, Martin's 2nd Amored Division secretly prepared for the invasion of Sicily.

Lt. Col. Martin J. Morin
41st Armored Inf. 2nd Armored Div.
Somewhere in North Africa
June 28, 1943

Dear Rose:

Your letter of May 19th with transcripts of five of Nell's letters was delivered this afternoon and, needless to say, I have been reveling in much pleasant reading.

I can think of nothing more to say that wouldn't be censored. The wild life, perhaps? Centipedes, spiders and scorpions are abundant. My Executive Officer and tent-mate says the other night he was awakened by some odd squeaky sounds. He flashed his light on a field mouse that ran up and down my mosquito bar.

I still get to the beach on occasion and am probably healthier than I have been since Turnverein days.

Love, MART

Margaret, still in North Africa, begged for mail from home and wrote of returning to the piano after being away from it for some time.

Margaret F. Morin
American Red Cross
Somewhere in North Africa
June 30, 1943

Dear Kids:

I haven't had any mail for an awfully long time. Have you all forgotten that I'm here? Rose, you asked who the man in the snapshot is. His name is Bill Giblin, Director of Civilian Relief here. He's very nice, a lot of fun and has a sense of humor that at times is so much like our Bill's it's amazing.

All goes well here. It keeps getting hotter and hotter. I feel slightly guilty about continuing this letter. There's a little sergeant sitting outside my office, drooling for conversation.

Janet sent *Black Magic* and *As Time Goes By*. I was very pleased to get them. Please call her and tell her so. We need music so badly.

Yesterday I found a piano. It's just for a week but I hope to get another later on. I've been asked to play in a musical on Sunday at the Opera House. I don't know if I'll have the nerve to go through with it, it's been almost a year since I played—the time has gone so quickly.

The little sergeant is getting to me, I've got to stop.

Best love to you all, MARGY

Martin participated in the invasion of Sicily on July 9. John arrived in England and was moving with his Bomb Group to their new base at Earls Colne, England.

Rose Mary Morin
New York City
July 14, 1943

Dear John:

You will probably enjoy the enclosed from Martin and Margy. I expect Mart's time is pretty well occupied these days. We scan the newspapers daily for fear of missing something that may concern him.

Mrs. Simon's sister Hilda keeps telling how much Mrs. Simon enjoyed your spending the day with her before you left and how handsome you were in your uniform. How about a snapshot since I missed seeing you in "mufti" when you visited after Thanksgiving.

A note from Jane today says she arrived home safely and found everything well. She said the bus was crowded but she managed.

Hope all is well, love, ROSE

On the 16th of July, John's 323rd Bomb Group became the first "Marauder Group" to go into action over France at medium altitude. Two other missions were briefed and scrapped before the group went on its second mission on July 25.

Rose Mary Morin
New York City
July 27, 1943

Dear John:

I thought you would be interested in Margy's two letters enclosed. The news of Mussolini's downfall has everyone excited. What may we expect next?

Nell has not written since June 22nd, which is a long time for her to go without a letter. We are wondering if the "burns" you mentioned on her hands incapacitated her. I guess she thinks I pay little or no attention to her requests. It must be discouraging when the time is so long between a request and the receipt of the article. A lot of the delay is because sometimes I have time to shop for several weeks after her request.

Much love, ROSE

P.S. I think Marg's "unsuccessful" trip means that she missed a meeting with Martin. He's probably riding donkey carts these days. R.

Martin had been riding much more than donkey carts in Sicily. Six days before this letter, his outfit had taken Palermo, the island's capital. In Italy on July 26, Mussolini was arrested and his Fascist government fell.

> Lt. Col. Martin J. Morin
> 41st Armored Inf. 2nd Armored Div.
> Somewhere in Sicily
> July 28, 1943
>
> Dear Rose:
> Long time no write. We have been making history though. It has been our privilege to participate in carrying the war closer to the heart of the octopus, and our pleasure to observe already one concrete and vital result, namely, the collapse of "that hyena" Mussolini. The battalion has been in action and has acquitted itself admirably. From D-Day the 10th, things have been continuously fast, furious and kaleidoscopic. At the moment, however, we are enjoying a comparative lull.
>   I feel curiously at home in this land of the Mafia or Black Hand. I guess my early association with the Raspanti's, the Diulus, the Pagannucis, the Tropeas and Sciulli's explains it.
>   This will never reach you before your birthday, but I have been thinking of you and wish you the greatest happiness.
>                                    Love, MART

On July 26, Allied bombers created a firestorm in Hamburg, Germany. Margaret wrote from a relatively peaceful North Africa.

> Margaret F. Morin
> American Red Cross
> Somewhere in North Africa
> July 29, 1943
>
> Dearest Kids:
> It's quite hot tonight, nothing, however like the ones we all have spent in Washington during the summer. We are very fortunate that the nights have been delightful.

Rose I do enjoy the copies of the other kids letters tremendously, as does my co-worker and roommate Molly. She started reading my mail one day when she was home sick, months ago, and now insists that I pass along every letter I get from you.

We are starting radio broadcasts next week. I'm very pleased about having the chance to work on them. The Special Service Officer who runs the station is very well known at home, and it should be an excellent experience.

All the kids are receiving packages. I'm going without stockings entirely now. The lisle is too hot and I will not wear those beautiful silk ones to work.

Please, all of you write to me.

Best love, MARGY

Nell has been transferred "somewhere in England" and compares the city to Pittsburgh, the family's long-abandoned hometown.

Mary Eleanor Morin
American Red Cross
Somewhere in England
July 30, 1943

Dearest Rose, Biz and All:
I didn't write anyone for two weeks because I was transferred amid much chaos and confusion.

Now I'm as far away from John as I can be and still be in England. My new hotel is enormous and located in a city that reminds me of a lot of Pittsburgh, walking out in the dim and smoggy air to the Cathedral in Oakland. The trolleys sound just like they did on Forbes Street. The two girls I'm with have inside rooms and are worried I won't sleep. They can't believe the noise is music to my ears.

My room is luxurious. Huge French windows open to a wonderful view of the city and river. The service is sensational and my conscience bothers me (very faintly) when I remember I'm supposed to sacrifice comfort for the war effort.

I haven't seen John in weeks but spoke to him on the phone. My long weekend comes up three days after your birthday, Rose, and I plan to be in town then and maybe he too can get leave.

The three of us had dinner with John Steinbeck, along with an English correspondent and an American infantry captain. It was all bright and scintillating, in spite of the bar running out of Scotch and gin. *The Grapes of Wrath Man* is nothing like I expected. We made hours of conversation over the coincidence that we both had lived on East 51st Street. His is the house with the bright red door between 1st and 2nd Avenues.

Tell our Bill to get cracking. They could use him over here.

Thanks again, Rose, for everything. Give my love to everyone.

Best to you and Biz, NELL

John's 383rd Bomb Group was briefed a total of 21 missions in August 1943, but only eight were flown. Targets were airfields, marshalling yards and special construction sites (widely believed to be in preparation for the V-1 "buzz" bomb, Germany's secret weapon).

Mary Eleanor Morin
American Red Cross
Somewhere in England
August 4, 1943

Dearest Rose:

I've struggled for the past week to get a cable off to you and here it is your birthday and I didn't succeed. So, Happy Birthday!

Dulcie Langman, the girl from Kenya that I worked with in New York, was up here last week. She's a Red Cross driver now and pops all over the country. We couldn't have had a better time. I gave her one of the pairs of mesh hose you sent and you can't believe how happy she was.

John called tonight. We had a terrible connection but I was able to hear that we may arrange a weekend together soon. He remembered your birthday too, even though I don't think he could do anything about it.

We met some young Navy officers last weekend. They gave Dulcie and me Nestlé bars and we helped them polish off a bottle of Four Roses. We were to have lunch on their ship, but missed out. It was such a pity. They had recent copies of *The New Yorker* and *Life* that we planned to pry away. We pray they'll show up again.

What do you hear from Mart? Tell everyone to write and give my love to everyone too.

Best love to you and Biz, NELL

Margaret was asked to play piano at the Opera House, causing her much trepidation.

Margaret F. Morin
American Red Cross
Somewhere in North Africa
August 4, 1943

Dearest Kids:
Here it is either Rose's or Patsy's birthday, I never can be sure which. In either case, I wish you a very, very happy birthday.

I've been double-crossed into playing at a recital Sunday night at the Opera House. Naturally, I'm terrified. I haven't practiced for so long. I'm to wear my black and blue dinner dress. The program is called, "Music by Candlelight." Perhaps it will be so dim the audience won't hear what's going on.

I haven't any word from Martin or from Nell or John.

Best love, MARGY

## Chapter 7

### New Neighbors

Across the walkway between our houses I noticed a girl about my age standing at her porch railing looking at me. She was in a powder-blue dress with a ruffled skirt. Light-brown hair touched her shoulders. I was startled because I'd never seen her before. I went in my house, thought for a second, and came back out as she was opening the screen door to her house. I said, "I'm George Morin, I live here."

She glanced my way and said, "I'm Margie Patterson, I just moved here," and disappeared as the screen door snapped shut behind her.

Then and there, I liked everything about Margie Patterson – the way she looked, the way she dressed, and the way she slid into her house before the screen door closed. I liked her so much I hardly ever spoke to her.

I also liked Margie Patterson's father's car parked in front of her house. It was gray Ford sedan with an "A" gas sticker and red pinstripes along its sides. FORD in wavy letters was in a small blue oval on top of the front grille.

It was one of only four or five cars parked along Pritchard Street. Every day I'd rub my finger along its red pinstripe and stand on the running board, pretending I was speeding down Pritchard Street waving to Tommy and Bobby and Frankie and Dickie.

Margie Patterson's father was in the war. She and her mother moved in with Margie's grandparents. I knew who her grandfather was because he was always hammering or sawing something inside their house, or out sweeping the front steps or carrying things to the curb to be picked up.

Just as we had done on Citadel Street, we bought all our groceries from the Kroger store on Chartiers Avenue. Anne, the store manager, seemed to be the only employee. My grandmother would telephone her with our shopping list and Anne would write it down on the back of a paper bag. By the time I walked down the hills to Kroger's, she had it ready for me. I had our family's ration stamp books, a handful of blue and red ration tokens and a little snap purse with bills and coins. Anne would take ration stamps, tokens and bills from the purse and give me back the ration books and change.

The bags of groceries were always heavy, but I managed to get them home. When my arms got sore, I'd stop and set the bags down on the sidewalk. Then, when the ache was gone, I'd pick them up and carry them until I had to rest again. Every time Anne handed them to me, she shook her head and said, "You need a wagon." One time she told me, if I had a wagon, she'd pay me to deliver groceries.

I started dreaming about getting a wagon. The next Christmas, it was all I asked for. When the big morning came, there it was with a red bow on its handle and filled with gifts wrapped in red and green for Nellie and me. It was beautiful, even though it was made entirely of wood. Even the wheels were wood. Everyone knew every chunk of metal was for tanks and planes – not boys' wagons.

There was no school for a week after Christmas and for the first time in my life, I was glad there was no snow. I took my wagon down to Kroger's ready to deliver groceries. Anne was almost as happy to see my wagon as I had been. Soon she had four large bags of groceries to be delivered to the big house on Kelvin Street at the bottom of Pritchard.

Pulling the wagon wasn't as easy as I thought it would be, but it was a lot easier than lugging those bags of groceries without it. I could hear the wheels rolling along behind me as trudged up Chartiers Avenue, turned right on Kelvin Street and crossed over the Belgian blocks at the foot of Pritchard Street.

In the middle of the street the wagon stopped with a crunch. The right front wheel had split in two. I was close enough to the big house on the corner to carry each bag up to the porch. The lady thanked me and gave me a dime.

I picked up the wagon front and pulled it on the rear wheels up the hill to my house. As I struggled to get it up our front steps, a voice over my shoulder said, "What happened here?"

Margie Patterson's grandfather came down the steps from their porch. "Look at that," he said. "Don't those people know any better than to try to make wheels out of wood? Why don't we see if we can fix this up." He picked up the wagon and asked me to follow him with the halves of the broken wheel.

It was warm in Margie Patterson's basement. Her grandfather had a workbench with saws and drills and tools I had never seen before. "You run along," he said. "I need some time to patch this wheel of yours up."

After dinner that night he knocked on our side door. The wagon had four wheels again. He had put the two broken pieces together with two metal straps screwed into the wood. I don't know what made me do it, but I started to cry.

"Now now," he said. "Let's just see if this does the trick before we get all worked up."

The next day I rode the wagon down the sidewalk almost to Kelvin Street when it crunched to a stop, leaving me sprawled on the pavement. The other front wheel had split in two and the screws in the straps on the repaired wheel had been wrenched from the wood. I looked at the pink scrape on my elbow and at the remains of the front wheels on the sidewalk. I left the wagon there and walked home, knowing that wagon would never deliver anything.

Then I remembered the tin cans in the cellar. I had to flatten them – they were going to be picked up tomorrow.

# Chapter 8

## Marauders at Work

John's Bomb Group continued a heavy schedule of missions over targets in France. The Group's B-26s had proven their worth with the accuracy of low-level bombing. Nell received a surprise call from a good friend from home.

> Mary Eleanor Morin
> American Red Cross
> Somewhere in England
> August 10, 1943
>
> Dearest Kids:
>
> This is one of those days that are perfect in every way. We had the best time in this new area on the Clubamobyle—as the natives call our conveyance. Tonight we had dinner with one Canadian and two English naval officers. I went to the local Roseland (the only dancy spot in this whirling metropolis) with the Canadian and one of the English Navy. In the Resident's lounge the page sounded that I was wanted on the phone. I rushed up to my room and practically fell to the floor when I heard John Dyer. He just arrived in London for two weeks leave. He said he would come here but it's such a jaunt I decided to go into London instead. It will be a run for the money. I'll have to leave after work Saturday, ride four or five hours on a grimy train and come

back Sunday night. However, it will be worth it to see John. I'll let our John know and maybe we can all get together.

Last night while we were assembling in the lobby with our Navy friends, a page gave me a small package that I ripped open and pulled out for all to see—a pair of pink panties. My friends burst into laughter. I decided I needed a double Scotch (that ended up being Irish whiskey) before dinner.

Well, this could go on forever and 7:30 will arrive surer than fate so I'd best pack off to bed.

Best love to you and Biz, NELL

P.S. My hands were burned through a series of grease splashes that looked much worse than they felt, but when I saw John he was probably impressed by my right thumb that I dipped into 450º fat and couldn't pull out quickly for fear the fork would catch the flipper. It's all better now and the boys have gotten over treating me as though I deserve the Purple Heart.

Love again, NELL

On this date, August 12, the 8th Army Air Force sent 93 B-26s to targets in France. Rose reported on a new musical, *Oklahoma!*, on Broadway.

Rose Mary Morin
New York City
August 12, 1943

Dear John:

Nell certainly comes and goes in and out of your life, but with it all she surely manages to have a good time.

On Tuesday we saw *Oklahoma!* an excellent musical comedy put on by the Theater Guild. The music, costumes, scenic effects, dance routines, etc., are very fine and there is an excellent cast but no outstanding stars. I liked it well enough to go again—in case anyone should ask me.

We've had no word from Martin, but I suppose he is much too busy. He wrote to Janet on the 2nd of last month and said not to worry if his mail were irregular that he would write when he could. Janet is trying to start Patrick in school in September. She has heard of a private Catholic school that may take him.

We haven't heard from our Bill since his last visit to town a couple of weeks ago. Hope everything is going all right with you and that you're not "going along for the ride" these days like you used to do.

Love, ROSE

Martin mourns the death of a favorite uncle and reports on Margy's latest performance as the Germans evacuate Sicily.

Lt. Col. Martin J. Morin
41st Armored Inf. 2nd Armored Div.
Unknown Location
August 16, 1943

Dear Rose:

The news of Uncle Johnny's death was a severe blow. He was a grand person in every way.

I was unable to see Margy before leaving Africa. I received heart-warming reports on her, however, from a fellow-officer who took a large detachment overland by way of her city. During a halt on the outskirts of town, Margy appeared on the scene. She amazed and delighted the men by riding down the column on a self-propelled artillery piece ladling out canteen cupfuls of ice cream. My informant says she was thoroughly charming and that her performance was the highlight of the entire trip. She's doing a swell job, Rose, I know.

I hope Bill gets over his yen for the airborne infantry. One must contend with just too damn many imponderables in that fledgling branch. Not a bit of local color in this area. Maybe next time.

Love to you both, MART

Margaret delivered another grand performance, this time with the piano rather than scoops of ice cream for the troops. In Sicily, the Allies reached Messina over treacherous mountainous terrain.

Margaret F. Morin
American Red Cross
Somewhere in North Africa
August 17, 1943

Dearest Kids:

I played in the recital. All day I had the most horrible case of nerves. I had only one week to practice—only three hours a day.

Anyway, it all went miraculously well. This Opera House arranged really lovely lighting. My black and blue dinner dress was a tremendous success—no one ever wears dinner clothes here. The music came out as well as I ever played. I had Molly and Marj and Bill and Don and all our close friends so worried that they were almost as nervous as I was, but once I got out on the stage and managed to smile, the rest came easily. The girl who sang had a lovely voice and a very important person gave a talk. I can't mention names, but it was very nice to be on the same program.

Bob Hope is doing a radio broadcast from here next week. I'm handling arrangements from this end. I go around counting chairs like a goon for fear that one will disappear and we won't have enough. If anything goes wrong, I may as well slash my wrists.

I must stop now, I've got to get home and change. My love to you and all and please write soon.

MARGY

John's Bomb Group continued to prepare for missions, although only one more had been flown in August.

Rose Mary Morin
New York City
August 18, 1943

Dear John:

We're so glad to have word from Martin that all is well with him. They have certainly been doing a good job.

Bill came down for the weekend. Marion has been in the country and he is taking over duties of two other officers. He's sure he will have enough to keep him busy for a while now. He is so afraid he won't get overseas.

Dot stopped at the apartment Monday to have dinner after a few days visit with Bess. She looks wonderful. George and Eleanor each had two weeks in camp and loved it. Jane wrote last week and said she had sent you a V-mail. She was wondering how long it would take to receive an answer. Nance said something about your "Madame Queen" remark getting Jane in Dutch with Mrs. Wilson. Jane was likely so proud of receiving your letter that she showed it to everyone without thinking. Everything here continues to be okay. Hope all is going well with you,

                                Love, ROSE


Nell's Clubmobile and crew moved on.

Mary Eleanor Morin
American Red Cross
Somewhere in England
August 23, 1943

Dearest Rose:

Your present came and I was so pleased with it. You don't know what joy a lighter is. I'm always fumbling about for a match and it's an awful bother. It's a smoothie lighter, Rose, and darn sweet of you.

At this new place we are living with a family on the outskirts of a large city. We have breakfast and supper here and usually lunch at camp or at a canteen. Because we have no transportation, we can't get to a movie or go out to dinner, so we won't spend any money except when we go in town for a day or weekend.

It's perfectly beautiful here. We came dreading the place for fear it would be dirty, ugly and distressed, but instead it is much cleaner than the last place. Outside the town there are lovely farms in all sizes and shapes and those white thatched roofed houses that I'm crazy about.

It's remarkable how we move from one place to another with no trouble adjusting—after being on the road since 7:30 this morning and decided to stop for a beer at a place we had never been before. The proprietress greeted us, led us to a small sitting room, served the beer and then produced a tray of chocolate covered cookies. We were absolutely dumfounded.

Please don't forget the 5 & 10¢ store lipsticks, Cashmere Bouquet, bright red, not orangey. Thanks again for everything.

I'll write again very soon, NELL

Meanwhile, for Margaret, North Africa is beginning to sound a lot like paradise . . .

Margaret F. Morin
American Red Cross
Somewhere in North Africa
August 30, 1943

Dearest Kids:

I'm now at a winter skiing resort and the most beautiful spot you can imagine. My French is flowing like glue. There's nothing to do but sleep and eat and climb mountains. Sunday night someone asked for butter, causing a lot of whispering at the kitchen door. Before I knew it, a pound of butter arrived. Needless to say, to a people used to severe rationing, "les Americaines" are more than welcome with their extra rations.

Last Thursday Bob Hope broadcasted from our Club. Did any of you hear it? It was a devil of a lot of work for me, but great fun. During the broadcast I was behind the stage listening to a shortwave pickup of the program from London. It seemed impossible that I could look over a rail and see the show and at the same time hear it from London.

Sunday we had lunch with Douglas Fairbanks, Jr. and Quentin Reynolds. Reynolds is a tremendous lump of a man, but always very amusing. Fairbanks isn't nearly as handsome as he photographs, but seems very nice—and doesn't try any funny business.

I haven't heard from anybody for so long. Rose, when you get the time, please let me know what Anne and Bob, Tom and Patsy and Bill and Marion are up to—as well as all the news of you and Biz.

Best love to you all, MARGY

P.S. I am writing this on the terrace of my French friends. They've asked me for dejeuner and have been working like beavers at it for hours. I brought up a bottle of white wine and they're now working on a sauce for the chicken made of wine, grapes and chestnuts. Le Chambord on Third Avenue was never like this. I wish Mary Moriarty were here—she'd snub that side of Third Avenue forever after.

# Chapter 9

## Blackout and Black Market

"Put out that cigarette!"

The air raid warden with his World War I helmet painted white looked up at us from the middle of the street.

It was a sticky, hot night and we were all sitting on the porch during the blackout drill. My mother, as usual, was smoking her Lucky Strikes, now in a white pack because "Lucky Strike green has gone to war."

"Don't you know the enemy can see a lit cigarette from ten thousand feet in the air?" the warden said.

The door to the house opened and shut behind me. I didn't even look. I knew Mother would take her cigarette inside rather than put it out.

"You could be fined for that," he shouted as he continued down the block.

Having a blackout drill was like having a family party. Somehow all day people knew there would be a blackout that night. Before dinner we closed the blackout curtains over all the widows. When Mother came home from work Grandmother had dinner ready to put on the table. After dinner Jane and Nellie helped wash the dishes. Instead of having to help dry them, I was given a quarter and a dime and sent down to Ralph's Drug Store at the bottom of Kelvin Street. I watched Ralph pack the container with half chocolate ice cream and half orange sherbet.

Then I trudged up the hill to our house just as it was getting dark and before the air raid sirens started. During the "air raid" we sat in the dark of our porch and ate our treat. Even though I wished ice cream wasn't rationed so that we had to buy half a container of sherbet with it, I grew to love the combination of orange sherbet and chocolate ice cream.

Before the war we had all the ice cream, all the sugar and all the butter we wanted. And my mother and her friends had all the cigarettes they could smoke. Now ice cream was rationed, and we often had no sugar, and hardly ever any butter. When a store got in butter or sugar, lines of customers with their rationing books formed like magic and the store quickly sold out.

Instead of butter, Grandmother bought oleomargarine that looked like a block of white lard. Each pound came with a big yellow pill that Grandmother put into a bowl with the oleo and started mixing it with a large spoon. It seemed she spent hours mixing that yellow pill, but no matter how long she mixed or what kind of mixing-method she devised, the result was always the same – a bowl of yellow lard streaked with white. I'd spread it on my bread and ate it only because she had worked so hard to make it.

One mild summer night Uncle Charles pulled up with his Dodge sedan and beeped his horn. Mother grabbed her purse and started out the door, but Nellie and I stopped her and begged her to take us. A ride in a car was a thrill we seldom had. Uncle Charles heard us and shouted up, "Bring 'em along, Dot. There'll be no trouble."

We ran and hopped in the backseat before Mother got down the steps. She and Uncle Charles talked as we gazed at the houses flash by that we had walked slowly past before.

It was a long ride. We drove down Chartiers Avenue past Langley High School, from where Jane graduated, and bumped along over the Belgian blocks and streetcar tracks through a dark tunnel and, after a sharp turn, beside the river on a long twisty road. In the distance I saw the steel mills' orange fire light up the sky and paint the river gold. Uncle Charles turned into another street that curved up another hill. Now he drove slowly past each house until he said, "Here it is Dot. You wait here." Mother handed him the folded dollar bills she had taken from her purse.

We sat in the car without talking. I didn't even wonder what was going on, because with grown-ups I never knew. When Uncle Charles came back he opened the car's trunk and put in two cardboard cartons.

Mother didn't say anything until the car was farther down the block. "Everything go okay?" she asked.

"Perfect. They're nice people," Uncle Charles said.

Mother turned and said. "Wait till you two see what we have for you."

When we got home Uncle Charles took one of the cartons out and handed it to me. I scrambled up the stairs over the porch and into the living room. Grandmother dropped her newspaper and got out of her chair, her face beaming. I handed her the carton and followed her into the kitchen, Mother and Nellie right behind me. Grandmother opened the carton and counted as she plopped each container on the table – one, two, three, four, five, six – pounds of butter. Real butter.

# Chapter 10

## No Letup

As Martin's 2nd Armored Division trained in England for the eventual invasion of France, John's 8th Army Air Force continued its relentless bombing of French military targets.

>Rose Mary Morin
>New York City
>September 2, 1943

Dear John:

I'm enclosing a letter from Martin and a copy of the prayer he composed. I think it is beautiful and all the more so because Martin was never religiously inclined. He told Janet he had developed a much healthier attitude about religion since going overseas.

    I guess things are very busy with you these days.

    Nance and Alvin have moved into larger quarters and Honey and her baby visited them. Bob was in Nebraska on maneuvers and was ordered back to Fort Benning to join a paratroop regiment.

    I haven't had any recent word from Jane but they were all well in her last letter.

                      Much love, ROSE

### MART'S PRAYER

(Somewhere in Sicily)
July 10, 1943

Lord God of Hosts, Our Heavenly Father, on this the threshold of our sternest trial, endow me with the talent in battle to discharge with honor my obligation to my men and to my country. For without Your divine guidance in this mortal storm any mere human is doomed to certain failure. Grant that I be calm and effective under fire. And if I must die, so be it; but let me die bravely as a soldier should. Bless my loved ones, Amen.

On Saturday, September 4, 144 B-26s were dispatched to four railway marshalling yards in France. Twenty-two B-26s were damaged and three crewmembers were reported wounded. The B-26 on which John was flying as an observer suffered engine failure and crash-landed in the English countryside. John splintered his arm in the crash and took pains to keep the details of his injury from the family.

Mary Eleanor Morin
American Red Cross-Clubmobile
Sunday, September 5, 1943

Dearest Rose:
Your last letter arrived on Saturday. That picture of Patsy and Paul is adorable.

Your head must be spinning with all the things I ask you to do. In the next war you can go away and I'll stay home and send things to you. That's the only way I can make up for all you've done.

I had a wonderful time while John Dwyer was here. We went to several restaurants, a marvelous show and a lousy, but fun, nightclub. I hated to see him go.

I'm going to a dance at our John's place. It should be grand.

If you can still get those little vials of Marie Chess Gardenia, send me a couple for a Christmas present for a woman who is mad about it. I wouldn't mind a bathtub or two of it for myself. Well, Rosebuddy, g'bye for now.

Love to all, NELL

The news from Italy was the big story of the week.

>Rose Mary Morin
>New York City
>September 9, 1943

>Dear John:
>
>The news of the Armistice in Italy yesterday caused great celebrating. The New York street cleaners had a job on their hands cleaning up the tons of paper and ticker tape. Biz had heard the news first through a friend in Wall Street where it came over the ticker before the newspapers were printed. By noon everyone was jovial.
>
>We are wondering where Martin is; there have been many reports about the landings in Italy.
>
>Amy and I saw *Kiss and Tell* Saturday night and Bob Hope was in the audience. Everyone made such a fuss over him.
>
>>Much love and good luck, ROSE

>Margaret F. Morin
>American Red Cross
>Somewhere in North Africa
>September 10, 1943

>Dear Rose:
>
>Wasn't news the other night exciting? It came just as we were working on a buffet supper for Red Cross chairman Norman Davis who is making an inspection trip here.
>
>I have received all the music you sent me. Thanks so much. I haven't received the black dress yet, nor the bathing suit. I'd also love to have the green suit and hat.
>
>I hate to bother you about money, but I'm behind in my accounts by $25. Could you send that much to me? There isn't any policy about raises yet, so nothing has been done about mine.
>
>>My love to you all, MARGY

Nell moved into a new line of work and John was sent off to school. Allies land at Salerno and Taranto, Italy.

>Mary Eleanor Morin
>American Red Cross
>September 10, 1943
>
>Dearest Rose:
>
>I'm on the threshold of another brave new world. I'm being transferred from Clubmobiles to clubs. The wire came in out of the blue this afternoon. I'm terribly pleased in spite of not knowing what or where the job will be.
>
>Our clubs here are very nice. However, I really hate to leave Clubmobile—slaphappy as it must seem to you, it is fun.
>
>Isn't the news about Italy wonderful? Why didn't I study Italian instead of China painting? *Allium Gallia est in tres partes*—wouldn't get me far. Maybe I should do as I did on my World's Fair application—say I understood Italian perfectly—but couldn't speak or write it.
>
>Meanwhile, thank you for the wonderful dinner dress! It's perfect, Rose! I like those flowers, though I think on me they'd ride better on the shoulder or neck. I had hoped it would arrive in time for John's dance, not believing that was remotely possible. Well, it arrived, but the dance fell through. John was sent off to school and will be gone for several weeks. That's always happening. It's sheer madness to make plans.
>
>                    Best Love to you all, NELL

# Chapter 11

## War Hits Home

One Saturday morning Frankie Newman and Dickie Roberts came up to my porch and rang the front doorbell. Jane answered and yelled upstairs for me to come down. Usually Frankie and Dickie would just stand on the sidewalk and yell for me to come down, so I knew this was different.

As soon as I opened the door Dickie said, "Donny Monahan's brother Jim got killed." Frankie said, "Yeah, he got killed."

Donny Monahan was older than we were so we didn't know him very well. But we all remembered when his brother Jim came home in his Army Air Corps uniform. He had wings on his chest and lieutenant bars on his shoulders. Everyone gawked at him. Jane knew him because he graduated from Langley High School in 1942, the same year she did.

Jane must have listened at the door, because she suddenly ran across the porch, down the steps and walked quickly toward Donny's house four or five houses down the hill on Pritchard from ours. She was crying. Then Grandmother came out on the porch, then Mother and Nellie. Frankie and Dickie repeated the news each time someone came out.

Later in the afternoon, Grandmother slid a macaroni and cheese casserole sideways into a brown paper bag and gave it to me. She told me to hold it at the bottom and take it to the Monahans. It was still warm.

Because their house was farther down the hill than ours, there were a lot more steps to walk up to their porch than to ours. By the time I got to the top my thighs ached from the steps and my hands burned from carrying the casserole. Just as I started to put the casserole dish down to ring the doorbell, the door opened. A lady said, "Oh, aren't you nice. Come in and put that on the table."

The table was crowded with many shapes and sizes of covered dishes and bowls. I told the lady my grandmother made it and she said, "Please thank your grandmother," she peeked under the lid, "for this lovely macaroni and cheese casserole."

I said, "I'm sorry Donny Monahan's brother got killed."

"Oh, thank you," she said, with a sudden sparkle in her eyes. "We're very sorry, too."

I turned and plunged down the steps.

Early Monday night people lined the sidewalk and steps leading to the Monahans. I was in my blue suit, with Nellie, Jane, Mother and Grandmother. Margie Patterson, her mother and grandfather were several steps ahead of us. Everyone waiting on the steps to go up was quiet, like in church.

Those coming down talked softly and sometimes, when their eyes met ours, slowly shook their heads.

I wondered what Donny's brother would look like in his casket. I hoped he would be in his uniform. When we got to the top of the porch steps, I could see the end of the casket in the living room with flowers all around it. When I got inside I saw that the casket was closed and covered with an American flag. On the center of the flag was a silver-framed, color photograph of Donny's brother Jim in his Army Air Corps uniform, like the one my father wore, except, Jim had a pair of gold wings above his campaign ribbons. Candles at each end of the casket flickered from the night air coming in the open door.

Mr. and Mrs. Monahan were across the living room at the entrance to the dining room. Both rooms were very crowded and very quiet. I could hear Mrs. Monahan say, "Thank you – bless you – you're so kind," as people filed past her and her family through the dining room to the side door and down the steps to the sidewalk. Mother, Grandmother and Jane stopped to whisper something to Mr. and Mrs. Monahan. I kept my eyes on the floor. Nellie pushed me to walk faster.

# Chapter 12

## War Around the Edges

On September 11, the Germans occupied Rome and the next day rescued Mussolini. North Africa continued to be peaceful, but hot.

> Margaret F. Morin
> American Red Cross
> Somewhere in North Africa
> September 13, 1943
>
> Dear Kids:
>
> We have had the hottest weather of the year these last four days. It's been stifling. The Chairman is still around and we must be very much in uniform. The fresh jacket I put on this morning is now dripping.
>
> I'm working on the Radio Quiz Program for tonight. We have one every week from the Club, which goes all over North Africa, but not to the States. Did you hear the Bob Hope program?
>
> Best love to you all, MARGY

John finally wrote to Rose, about everything but his accident.

Rose Mary Morin
New York City
September 17, 1943

Dear John:

It was nice hear from you about Nell's visit to Cardiff. Were you able to get together with her and John Dwyer?

Jane wrote to me about working in New York. Dot is agreeable and I would be all for it, but unfortunately we are giving up the large apartment and taking a three-room—bedroom, living room and kitchen—in the same building on the same floor. Carrying all that room for the two of us and using Nell's share to help seemed a waste of her money. Had Jane spoken sooner I'd have held on to the larger apartment. We can manage three in the new apartment by using the davenport, but that couldn't be a permanent arrangement.

I had thought that Dot wouldn't want Jane to come, but she feels there are more opportunities for Jane here than in Pittsburgh. We are moving October 1. Nell is going to be brokenhearted. You may have to bolster my side of the story to make her feel better about it.

A letter from Bill the other day brought news that he has been promoted to major. He didn't mention it. I learned of it from the return address.

I hope everything is going very well with you.

Much love, ROSE

On September 23, after being rescued by the Germans, Mussolini again established a Fascist government in Italy.

Rose Mary Morin
New York City
September 23, 1943

Dear John:

You and Nell certainly play hide and seek with each other. I know she must have been disappointed at missing the dance but now that she is assigned to club work, she will have her fill of dancing and be longing for the open road.

Patsy writes that Paul is crawling into everything. He pulls himself up, balances on one foot and grins at her. Then he races back and forth behind the bar, banging on the sides. He'll be a year old on October 1.

I haven't any word from Jane. I suppose the kids are back in school and that she is still at Boggs & Buhl. Her hope was to get a job here on her own and perhaps now thinks she should remain there until they can give her a good recommendation. Hope all is well with you.

Much love, ROSE

Nell wrote about her new life, cold living conditions and the lack of news from brother John.

Mary Eleanor Morin
American Red Cross
Somewhere in England
September 27, 1943

Dearest Rose and Biz:

Writing letters at the Club is hopeless. There are so many interruptions. I was so worried when I had no mail from you for about three weeks. Then all of a sudden your two letters came—the airmail with Mart's prayer—it's really beautiful—his letter and your V-mail of 9/9. Then came your package with the shoes, blue blouse and sweater, lipsticks and lanolin.

The money finally arrived. Everything is straightened out now and thank goodness I'm out of debt.

The club is the tiniest thing imaginable. But, we will have a terrific Service Men's Club eventually and this will become the Officer's Club. It had been a sporting goods store.

I may stay here or be sent to another club any minute. It's a great change from the gypsy caravan. But the struggle to have my hair, nails and uniform gleaming is getting to me. My blouses are ruined before the day's out. Since I'm at the club from 8:30 a.m. to 12 midnight, it's nearly impossible to wash and iron them.

My hotel is something. It was a castle! When I think of my childish dreams of living in as castle! Thank God they never came true. It's as cold as the devil and Lord knows when they'll put the heat on. However, it is only two minutes from the club, which is important since I can't ride a bike and it's not too far to walk in a blackout.

This afternoon, one of our volunteers had an officer and myself to lunch in a wonderful house in the country. She is an American who has lived here for 22 years. Most of the house is used as a hospital, but her rooms are extremely attractive. Her son, age 16, shot the pheasant we had for lunch and the officer brought sherry. I came home with catmint, sweet geranium, rosemary, lavender, yellow roses, apples and two eggs! Everyone wants to do good things for us. It's embarrassing—but awfully nice.

Did I tell you I have sinusitis? The doctor, an American from Lenox Hill hospital, told me that I probably had it for years. And I've been blaming all my aches and pains on my eyes. Otherwise, I'm fine, gaining weight again, but I'm too hungry to go on a diet. We have a chef at the club who makes me tea with toast or crumpets in between breakfast, dinner and supper.

I haven't heard from John in ages. I'll call and if he's back make a plan to meet him in town. From all accounts, he's fine.

Give my love to everyone, NELL

As she half expected, Nell received a new assignment and tells of news coverage about her work in Clubmobiles.

Mary Eleanor Morin
American Red Cross
September 30, 1943

Dearest Rose:
I feel badly about leaving this place but my new place will be just 30 minutes from town.

Because I'm going away, I was able to get out of the club for an hour and a half for dinner. One of the officers and two Red Cross men took me to the hotel where we live and indulged in double Scotches, a roast goose and a gay time.

I could kill you all for not having your ears glued to the radio. NBC gave a broadcast about Clubmobiles and featured a story about Gretchen, Kitty and me—even mentioning our names. They said we worked 36 hours straight, but we actually worked 47.

Clubmobile wasn't as glamorous as it might have seemed. But it was fun and I miss it a lot. However, that was one phase, this will be another. We will be very lucky if we get any farther overseas than we are. I'd love to go as our forces advance if they'd send me.

I met a 2nd Lt. here a few days ago from Pittsburgh, Ernie Holesworth. He's an awfully nice kid and he's dying to go to London. He asked me to show him the places, but as often as I've been there, I've yet to go sightseeing and probably know all the wrong places.

This is one of those nights. There's hardly a soul in the club. But the minute the pubs close we will be swamped.

Goodbye for now. Please write soon. Give my love to everyone.

Loads of Love, NELL

On October 1, the Allies entered Naples. John sent Rose a mention of his condition, but few specifics.

Rose Mary Morin
New York City
October 2, 1943

Dear John:

We were certainly glad to hear you missed whatever you are referring to in your letter of September 20th. I wish we could have the details. Now that it has happened is it necessary to keep it so secret? You remind me of Martin's counsel to Bill and Bill's to his men at the Point: It doesn't matter where you may be as long as you are filling a necessary job!

It's nice to hear you have met Bill McLaughlin. He is somewhat of a myth to me but having heard Margaret and Nell speak so much of him, I feel almost as though I know him.

Biz celebrated her birthday yesterday very quietly in our new surroundings. I suppose you have heard from Nell and know what she is now doing. She had not heard of your accident when she last wrote, but told of you missing the dance. I hope the bed rest and physiotherapy has done the trick.

Love, ROSE

P.S. I received the cable you mentioned in the your letter of the 20th. I hope that whatever happened to you wasn't the result of "just going along for the ride" as you used to do in the South last year. Bill was quite worried about it and said it wasn't such a safe practice. (And he's the one who would like to transfer to the airborne!)

In October, fog, rain and clouds seriously hampered the work of the 383rd Bomb Group. During the last three months of the year, only twenty-two missions were successfully flown.

Rose Mary Morin
New York City
October 6, 1943

Dear John:

Bill and Marion arrived unexpectedly at the apartment on Saturday evening. I had gone straight from the office to Glen Ridge to spend the weekend with the Froehlichs but Biz was at home waiting for Mary Lou Daschbach to show up for dinner. Marion's cook, Austin, had a third stroke and they have no hope for her recovering so they came in to see her.

Bill liked the new apartment very much. They went to dinner at Fred's L'Avion and then to the Ambassador for a drink and a dance. Biz says both Marion and Bill look great. On Monday he called to ask if the McKetricks would want any Army-Notre Dame tickets. They'll want four to be sure.

They had quite a religious rally out at Yankee Stadium with an attendance of over 70,000. Biz and Mary Lou went and entered all your names in their petitions placed on the altar during Benediction. So you should all get double value. Biz said the ceremony was very impressive. I'm sorry I missed it.

I hope everything is going smoothly with you now and that you are recovered after your accident. When you can, let us know what happened.

Much love and good luck, ROSE

Nell's career in the club operation keeps getting better as she is given a new assignment and a promotion to go with it. She also socializes with celebrities.

Mary Eleanor Morin
American Red Cross
October 7, 1943

Dearest Rose:

Everyone has been perfectly grand to me and given me the most wonderful welcome and every help in getting started. The club is pretty big and still growing. We are here from nine or so in the morning till about 12 at night. I like everything about it. When I came, Mr. Davis asked me to take over as Personal Service Director. I was pleased to death.

Late last night he came into my office and announced that I'd been promoted to assistant club director and showed me the supervisor's letter. Naturally, I was practically overcome. Please pray that I do as good a job as they expect, and I will make every effort to supplement your prayers. Everyone has been so grand.

The $25 you spoke of must be Margaret's raise. I guess they got us mixed up again. I doubt that this change for me will mean a raise. However, I won't turn it down. I was certainly overpaid on the donut wagon. Practically everyone I worked with got from $25 to $75 a month less.

When the bank account and time allows, will you buy two of the $18.75 bonds for me, payable to the National Catholic School of Social Service? I feel it's the least I can do to make up for the gratis course I stumbled through there.

I saw John Steinbeck in a restaurant the other night, but I was with a very conservative guy who didn't think I should go talk to him. I certainly will the next time.

It's the weirdest thing about the Bob Hope letter. I wrote a long one about meeting our John at the camp. It was mobbed for the show, and John insisted on slowing up the line at the Clubmobile by presenting his sister, Mary Eleanor, to everyone.

We saw the show together and later Dulcie and I stayed on at the officers' mess for dinner.

Bob Hope and Frances Langford talked to us for quite a while. He was, as Margaret says, as fun as he is on the screen. They left but John's C.O., who was a classmate of Bill's, Colonel Thatcher, had the rest of us to his place for drinks. We all had a wonderful time.

Well, I must close and get to work. Give my love to all at home.

Best love to you and Biz, NELL

John's 383rd Bomb Group was slated to be transferred from the 8th Army Air Corps to the 9th Army Air Corps as part of the preparation for the invasion of France. The mysterious "activities" Rose referred to may be related.

Rose Mary Morin
New York City
October 13, 1943

Dear John:
Your letter of the 27th came several days in advance of Nell's that is enclosed. She seems to be as much in the dark about your "activities" as we are.

Her new assignment sounds like a radical change from Clubmobile work. I do hope the hotel has heat—so many buildings over there are without it. I don't think she could have had sinusitis for so long without being aware of it. There seems to be something about that climate that brings it to the fore. She's not the type to let it get her down.

I hope I haven't given the wrong impression in my helping out on finances. Whatever requests I have filled from Nell and Margaret have been with their funds entrusted to my care. At times their requests have required considerable shopping, but I have been able to fill most of their needs. The funds, however, are all theirs.

Much love, ROSE

Martin's outfit will soon begin training for the invasion of France, but, for the time being, he seems more interested in French novels.

Lt. Col Martin J. Morin
41st Armored Inf, 2nd Armored Div
Somewhere in Sicily
October 13, 1943

Dear Rose:

It's been ages since I last wrote to you and I have no valid excuse for the long delay—Sicilian lethargy, I guess. It's inexplicable that I should be so remiss, since I enjoy your letters so much. Have patience.

The tide of war seems to have passed over us for the time being, and we are gently suspended in the backwash. The rains and winds have come at long last. Consequently, our camp periodically becomes a dilapidated quagmire. We have been varying the training routine by plunging into the nearby mountains. I have no idea how, when or where things will liven up again.

The French texts that I appropriated from you will, I fear, never be the same. They are bloated and stained from being submerged in the Mediterranean during landing operations. I still use them though. One day I hope to return them to you as curiosities. I visited a large Sicilian town not long ago in search of French novels. I finally located a shop where a large number were hidden away in an upstairs room. I doubt if I will ever be really proficient in the language.

Love to you and Biz, MART

Margaret celebrated her birthday and got ready to tackle her new assignments involving "white gloves and small speeches in Italian."

Margaret F. Morin
American Red Cross
October 22, 1943

Dearest Kids:

Rose, I received your card the day before Anne and Bob's on my birthday. It couldn't have been a more wonderful day. I got all sorts of lovely presents. Marjorie, Molly, and Bill Giblin and I had lunch together. In the afternoon Bill's chauffeur arrived with the most beautiful white roses I've ever seen.

That night he gave a dinner party for ten. We began with Scotch and finished with Courvoisier and Benedictine. I'm afraid the poor dear spent his heritage. I wish I could tell you who all were at the party, very fancy—including the American minister and several other "important people."

I was shocked to hear about John. Your earlier letters have just caught up. Congratulations to Billy on his promotion. The thought of the airborne still gives me chills. Incidentally, we are flying to our new assignments. At times, I can't believe that it's all happening.

Rose, my raise finally came through. It will be $50 a month. My title will be Special Representative—translated into Italian, whatever that is. I do hope this new work goes well. There are so many things about it that are completely beyond anything I've ever done. One thing I know there will be a lot of white gloves and making small speeches in Italian. Can you imagine it? I suppose I'll have to learn to drive a car, too—finally. Wish me luck.

>Best love to you all, MARGY

John's 323rd Bomb Group, reassigned to the 9th Army Air Corps, continues attacking targets in France.

Rose Mary Morin
New York City
October 28, 1943

Dear John:
We have had the nearest thing to the 1938 hurricane here this week and it is still raining. Four days has coats and shoes, to say nothing of hair, in rather shaggy condition. I guess that you have become used to cold, damp climates by now.

We were so glad to hear about Nell's promotion. It is quite a feather in her cap. I do hope she will be a success. I think it is about time she has a place she can stay for awhile—although driving around in Clubmobiles has given her a good look at the countryside.

Rumor has it that Margy is also in a different assignment. Nothing definite has come from her but her friend here in headquarters had a letter from one of the girls with Margaret who says the "three M's" have been assigned to Civilian Relief. We think that means Margy, Marj and Molly. It will doubtless take them into occupied territories and their work will not be as pleasant as it was in North Africa.

No word has come from Martin recently, but I take it that no news is good news. Anne writes that both the children had colds for two weeks. But all is well now. Robin is saying almost everything and Nunsey is sitting up and eating a varied diet. We haven't had any word from Patsy, but their weekend trips to the Hanson family in San Gabriel don't leave her much time to write.

Good luck and love, ROSE

Margaret, Marj and Molly visit Martin in Sicily and are invited to the Regimental Dance.

Lt. Col. Martin J. Morin,
41st Armored Inf. 2nd Armored Div.
Somewhere in Sicily
October 29, 1943

Dear Rose:

Big news! Margy is stopping over for a few days in a nearby city. She has a change of assignment. Her two roommates, Marj and Molly, are with her en route to the same area. However, it is not clear to me whether their new duties will permit their continuing to live together on the other end.

Margy looks fine, and she is enthusiastic about her new job. I saw her the other night, and spent the greater part of the next day with her. It's difficult to express how happy I have been being with her again. Much talk was in order and, naturally, a few drinks. I am taking her and her two friends to a Regimental Dance tonight, the second such affair that we have had since leaving the States. These affairs are rarely successful under overseas conditions, but I know, because of Margy, that I shall really enjoy this one.

Will give you all the details of her stay in my next.

Love, MART

Nell is swamped with work in her new job and gets sad news about a friend.

> Mary Eleanor Morin
> American Red Cross
> November 1, 1943

Dearest Rose and Biz:

You must think I've taken leave of my senses for letting so long a time elapse between letters. The truth is that this place is as busy as a beehive. I just get a notion that I'll get a letter off, when something turns up that I have to do—or interrupted by someone who wants to talk. I'm terrible. Please forgive me and I'll promise to do better.

Both blouses have arrived and I love them. You have no idea how needed they were. It's impossible to get anyone to do laundry. I get a few things done now and then, but it takes days for anything to dry in my room. There is no heat—no stove of any description, and the darn window won't stay closed. There is a dispute about whether the wing I'm in is 1200 or 1500 years old. I think it's more like 2000!

I had a terrible shock the other day. You remember the boy from my office in New York I talked so much about—Jim Gallagher? Well, he's been writing every now and then and I really thought he would get over eventually. I had a letter, two weeks ago saying he thought he was on his way. That was sometime in August. I came into the club for the mail and found the letter I had written to him with "Accidentally Killed" written over the address. I couldn't believe my eyes. I can't remember feeling so badly about anything. He was such a grand kid. I'm going to get a Mass card and send it to his mother.

What do you hear from Mart? I keep wondering where everyone is and what they are up to. Did Bill do anything about the airborne business? Why don't he and Marion write? Incidentally, I think of Marion every time I see an English person's handwriting. She writes just like they do.

Give my love to everyone and write real soon.

> Lots of love, NELL

# Chapter 13

## The Bradleys

Tommy and Bobby Bradley's father was a policeman who had been in World War I. At lunchtime he and his partner would pull up to Tommy and Bobby's house in their police car. While his partner waited in the car and listened to the police radio Mr. Bradley stomped through his house for the bags of sandwiches Mrs. Bradley had made for them. He wore large black shoes with thick soles and heels and when he walked the porch creaked and the house shuddered.

The police radio crackled every now and then, but we couldn't understand what it was saying. One time the radio crackled while the two cops were eating their sandwiches in their car. They dropped the sandwiches, put on their hats and screeched away with siren screaming.

We ran down the hill and watched as they disappeared around the corner, listening until the siren faded out in the distance. Our lives didn't get much more exciting than that.

Whether cooking food or scrubbing floors, Mrs. Bradley stopped humming to herself to sing out to each kid as we clamored into her kitchen: "Helloo Georgie, Helloo Dickie, you too Frankie." On her feet she could scoot around the house like a bee in a flower garden, but pulling herself up off the floor took some holding on and a few grunts.

The Bradley kitchen was the neighborhood headquarters. If Frankie and Dickie weren't in their yards or on their porches, I'd go over to the Bradleys, sure someone would be there and there'd be something to do.

Tommy and Bobby had profiles of American, British and enemy aircraft tacked on the kitchen wall. I'd stare at the chart trying to sear into my brain the differences between an American B-24 and a German Do-217; and the look of British Spitfire compared with that of a Japanese Zero.

They also put up charts showing the ranks in the Army and Navy, from General to Private, from Admiral to Seaman Recruit. It was information every boy had to know if he wanted to hold his own in our many the arguments about such things.

The Bradleys' large backyard was bare, shaded with high trees, but the side yard next to the house was grassy, open to the sky. On nice days we'd lie on the soft grass and look up at the airplanes flying to the Pittsburgh airport in the distance. Sometimes the planes were Army B-17 Flying Fortresses or B-24 Liberators. We never knew why they were flying over Pittsburgh, but we were excited when we saw them.

They had four engines and were painted a dull brown with a white star and stripe on the wings. One bright, clear day a bomber came over lower and louder than usual. The propellers on two of its four engines weren't moving. Tommy jumped up and screamed, "It's gonna crash, it's gonna crash."

Mrs. Bradley bolted out of the house, screen door slamming behind her, to watch the plane fly low and loud over the houses and into the distance. After it disappeared beyond the trees and the noise faded away, she went back in the house and we laid back down on the grass – disappointed – to watch the sky again.

Each summer, Mrs. Bradley rounded up the kids in the neighborhood to help raise money for organizations so they could send packages to the boys overseas. First we'd sell poppies for the American Legion. Poppies were little red-cloth flowers with green wires that could twist around buttons or go into lapels to show you gave to help the soldiers and marines.

A few weeks or a month later it was forget-me-nots for the Veterans of Foreign Wars, so sailors would also get packages. They were like the poppies only blue. I thought selling forget-me-nots was more fun than selling poppies because Mrs. Bradley taught us a song to sing: "Bell bottom trousers coat of navy blue, buy a forget-me-not to help the Navy through."

When she handed out the flowers she gave each kid a tall cardboard "money cup" with a slotted cover. On the day we handed out forget-me-nots, a big box of Donohue's candy was in the middle of the living room coffee table. Whoever came back with the most money would win the candy. It was the biggest box of candy I ever saw. I went out and sang my heart out to win it.

We started early in the morning and swarmed around the streetcar stop on Chartiers Avenue. Then we ran across the street to the 5-and-10 then to the garage on Mutual Street and to Aunt Ruth's movie house and finally to Grandfather's firehouse.

On the way back up to the Bradleys, I stopped in front of the Sheraden Tavern on Chartiers Avenue. When Mother and Aunt Ruth wanted to "have a little fun" on a Saturday night, Nellie and I would go with them through the side door. We played the jukebox and I sipped the foam from Mother's beer glass. We both ate as many peanuts and pretzels as we wanted.

I stood outside wondering if it was okay for me to go in the front door. Then a bunch of men came out and I started singing "Bell Bottom Trousers," and one man said, "Get a load of this."

They all stopped and I belted out my song again. When I finished the men clapped and dropped coins in my cup. One said, "Kid, sing like that, you might win the war all by yourself."

All I wanted to win was the candy, so I pushed my cup at them again and sang, "Bell bottom trousers coat of . . ." They just laughed and walked away.

I didn't win the candy. Tommy and Bobby's big sister Luball did. She was Nellie's friend and everyone liked her because when a group of kids were at the Bradleys on a day that was too rainy or snowy to go out, she'd tell us scary stories about dark nights and evil people out to harm scruffy young boys and pretty little girls.

On Easter morning Tommy and Bobby found a whole box of baby peeps next to their Easter baskets. All the kids who came over were allowed to chase the peeps around the kitchen. When they caught one they could pet it a little and then put it back into the box. When the weather got warmer, Tommy and Bobby put the peeps in the coop they helped Mr. Bradley build in the backyard.

For the rest of the spring and into the summer every time Frankie, Dickie and I went over to Tommy and Bobby's we'd look into the coop to see how the peeps were doing. Every time we looked they were bigger than the last time. Before we knew it the chicks had grown white feathers and were walking around the backyard.

One Saturday, sometime later, after school started and it was beginning to get cold, we were all over at the Bradleys and Tommy got out the hatchet he used to split wood, and announced they were going to have chicken for dinner Sunday night. Bobby got a hold of one of the chickens and held its neck on the tree trunk and Tommy whacked the chicken's head off. When Bobby let go, the chicken stood up and walked around the yard in circles with thin squirts of blood popping up where its head should've been. Then it slowed and fell over on its side – and lay there with its feet twitching.

Everybody laughed, but it wasn't very funny. Mrs. Bradley said raising chickens for food was something she decided to do for the war effort.

# Chapter 14

## New Assignments

The family was scattered across Europe but still managed to stay in touch. Margaret told of her new assignment in Sicily and the good time she was having with brother Mart.

>Margaret F. Morin
>Special Representative, War Relief
>American Red Cross
>November 4, 1943

Dear Kids:

I just received Rose's letter of the 20th, Biz's birthday card and Anne's (or rather Robin and Nunsey's) birthday card. I also received Rose's and Biz's gloves and earrings. Thanks so much. They are lovely and exactly what I need.

    I've been here now for a week. It's quite different than I expected, very interesting country, but not comparable to Algiers. I keep thinking that Nell with her background should be doing this work.

    It is peculiar that Nell should go into club work and I'm doing civilian social services that she's trained for. However, I like it very much so far.

I've spent all my free time with Martin. He's very well and we've had a lot of fun. It surely has been good to catch up with him finally. His regiment had a party in what was a beautiful palace. It still is magnificent, but has been used by some of their officers since the occupation.

Biz it was swell hearing from you. Mart got the shock of his life when he got your letter. You should try writing more often.

Best love to you both—all family and friends included.

MARGY

Still puzzled over John's subtle references to his "accident," Rose nevertheless reports the news, including her invitation to the Army football game against archrival Notre Dame.

Rose Mary Morin
New York City
November 4, 1943

Dear John:

I'm so glad you keep us advised of Nell's visits. She moves so often it must be hectic. I hope her new position will result in a more permanent arrangement.

Your letter was most subtle. I agree that you were most fortunate. Someone must have been carrying a few St. Christophers and rabbit's feet. And I am glad to know you are finding your new work interesting.

Bill phoned last night and invited Biz and me to go to the Notre Dame-Army game Saturday. Marion is in Newport and won't be down for it. There is a chance we will have dinner afterwards with the McKetricks and Bill will stay here at the apartment for the weekend. I'm sure you will enjoy the enclosed encouraging word about Martin. He is bound to become proficient in French.

I surely hope you will have no further mishaps.

Love, ROSE

Mart reported to Rose that Margaret and her Red Cross colleagues visited Sicily in time for the regiment's Halloween Party.

Lt. Col. Martin J. Morin
41st Armored Inf. 2nd Armored Div.
Somewhere in Sicily
November 6, 1943

Dear Rose:

To amplify the recent flash on Margy's visit: The most singular thing was how well she looked. She is blooming, alert, immaculate. Her stay bracketed a regimental party and two or three less formal get-togethers at a small officers' club. Margy, Molly and Marj attended the regimental affair; and Margy always, Marj sometimes and the others seemed to have a good time. Margy wore her black dinner-dress once, and looked very chic indeed. The prelude to the Regimental party—a Halloween dance—was most appropriate, in that it was eerie, even cadaverous, to the nth degree. The dance took place in one of the many bona fide palaces that dot the island. Everyone agreed that the function was far-and-away the best since our departure from the States.

One afternoon we visited the shrine of a saint on a cliff high above the sea. Last Sunday morning we attended Mass together at a mammoth, ancient cathedral. A curious thing about Catholicism here is that, in the main, only women seem to take it seriously. The proportion of women to men at church is about 20 to 1.

Margy made vast strides in her French while serving in Africa. Her new duties will require a working proficiency in Italian. Even this prospect fails to daunt her—she is plunging into it.

I gave her a War Department phrase book and an Italian-English dictionary for what they might be worth. I was struck by the intelligence and articulateness of Margy, her roommates, and Bill Giblin. They were very interesting and "quick-on-the-draw" at all times. They "capped" me several times in the evening, which perhaps is no spectacular accomplishment.

If you transcribe this, Rose, please send Janet a copy, as I have a phobia against writing the same letter twice.

Love, MART

On this date Britain bombed Berlin with a large air armada.

Rose Mary Morin
New York City
November 18, 1943

Dear John:

I know you will enjoy the news of the enclosed letters. I was about to write Margaret and tell her to be sure to ferret out Martin when his letter came saying they had already met. Wouldn't it be grand if she remained in the same vicinity for the holidays?

A letter from Nance said Bill Mente was finishing his course tomorrow, and then going to Washington via Columbus, Pittsburgh, and New York. A letter from Alvin today says Nance is on her way and will be in Washington for Thanksgiving, in New York early in December, and then to Honey's in North Carolina for Christmas. That leaves Alvin alone over the holidays.

Bill and Marion are expected to arrive this afternoon to see *Oklahoma!* and spend a day shopping. I tried all over town to get them hotel reservations and finally located one in the Duane at 37th and Madison. I had called 16 other hotels with no luck.

Biz is laid up with an infected knee from falling up a curb. She had gone a day without washing it. To add insult to injury, one of her teeth acted up and had to come out. The doctor thought that removing the infected tooth would hasten the healing of the knee. She has the worst luck.

Much love from all, ROSE

Margaret announced she had arrived at her "final" destination without revealing where it was.

Margaret F. Morin
Special Representative, War Relief
American Red Cross
November 19, 1943

Dearest Kids:

I have arrived at my final destination. I would have written sooner, except it has been hectic getting settled. The third day I was here I had dysentery. It made me so mad that I went through 8 months in North Africa without a sign of it, and then, bang! I was laid up for three days. The bug is now finally demolished.

It's lovely here. Nicer even than North Africa. I didn't like Sicily one bit, except for seeing Martin and the work he was doing. I'm assigned here to make a survey of food and medical supplies for the institutions in the Province. It's very interesting, and the people think that we are going to fulfill every request that they make, so until the fatal day arrives, we are wonderful.

Yesterday I received a lot of mail. A letter from Billy, a letter from the LaGuardias, Mary Moriarty and a Christmas card from Rita and Minor Jamison. Thanks so much for *The New Yorker*, Rose.

Molly and I are living together in a very nice apartment. It has a foyer, dining room, two bedrooms, a bath and a kitchen. It's nicely furnished and the building is very modern, with an elevator and a wonderful view.

Marion's farm sounds marvelous. I feel as though I know every piece of stock on the place. Please keep on writing. I'm anxious to know the details of everything. Rose, Mary Moriarty implied that you were worried about making the move. I think it was the only sensible thing to do. I'm so glad that you find the new place comfortable.

Best love to you all, MARGY

John received his Christmas presents early and had success addressing some officers.

Rose Mary Morin
New York City
November 24, 1943

Dear John:

Your letter of the 11th and your cable have arrived—the letter on Saturday, the cable yesterday. I hope everything arrived in good order. Don't even think of sending packages from over there, although we do appreciate your efforts during your visit to Belfast.

The merchandise on display for Christmas is far below par and I imagine you found the same situation there if not worse. It is too bad the packages arrived so far in advance of the holidays, but better early than never or too late. At least it is a break for those receiving edibles, as the two to three month interval allowed by the P.O. department was a rather long time for any tasty morsel to remain so.

I am so glad you were such a success in addressing the officers. Martin and Margaret's letters will explain Margy's activities. Strange isn't it that as she was thinking that Nell should really be doing her job—Nell was having a dream about Margy being under her! Looks like a little mental telepathy.

Biz's knee is improving, but she is home again with a stomach upset, probably the result of anxiety over the knee, the sulfa, abscessed tooth, etc., all at once.

Happy Thanksgiving!

Love, ROSE

Martin wrote to Rose about promotions, "priceless" photos and the trouble with French "prepositions used before infinitives."

Lt. Col. Martin J. Morin
41st Armored Inf. 2nd Armored Div.
Somewhere in Sicily
November 25, 1943

Dear Rose:

Biz's letter of October 13th has been received and greatly appreciated. I was very happy to hear that she likes her job. It was nice to hear of Nat and Jim. Be sure that they are given my regards at the first opportunity. I wish Jim were with me so that we could evaluate the imponderable together, as we used to at Schofield Barracks over a bottle of Okoulehau.

Please tell Mr. McKetrick not to "sweat out" my promotion so. Promotion is all out of kilter. My classmates vary from majors to brigadier generals. My Regimental Commander is a West Pointer with nine years more service and ability than I have. He is doing a splendid job. Rank, really, is a trifling incidental. It is among the least of my concerns. As Alexander Pope put it over 200 years ago:

"Honour and shame from no condition rise; Act well your part, there all the honour lies."

During my recent visit with Margy she showed me a snapshot of Patsy and young Paul at the beach. He was laughing uproariously. It was priceless! I wonder if you could get me a copy of it.

Also, Rose, I am having difficulty with the French prepositions. Would you mind looking in at Brentano's and picking up a book that might enlighten me? I'm sure you know what I mean: mainly the preposition used before infinitives, and after verbs, before pronouns and things. Thanks ever so much!

Love, MART

Mart arrived in England amid a "staggering" number of Christmas presents. His premonition about the Army-Notre Dame game came true. Notre Dame won 26 to 0.

Lt. Col. Martin J. Morin
41st Armored Inf. 2nd Armored Div.
Somewhere in England
December 7, 1943

Dear Rose:

Since arriving on this "tight little isle" I have received three letters from you covering the period October 28 to November 18.

The trip up was quite an odyssey, long and leisurely, quite pleasant, too. We felt immune to the Doenitz menace, as most of the passengers were completely baffled as to our whereabouts.

England seems to be a very nice place (though I haven't had a chance to wander yet), and I am living in comparative luxury—electricity, a clean bed, a bathtub and a fireplace. Regarding the fireplace, 99% of the heat goes right up the chimney. Still, the psychological effect is wonderful.

I have received, and blush to say, already opened, a staggering number of Christmas parcels. In former years, I was distinctly a bush leaguer. Perhaps this war business has its points after all. If I survive, I may put in for the army of occupation for several years over the holidays. Thank Biz for me for her stunning, leather edition of *Vanity Fair*. I had never read it and, having started it, am completely captivated. The one exception to the premature opening spree is your box of cookies from Schrafft's. I know they will be delicious at the proper moment. Thanks eversomuch! Your generosity and thoughtfulness have certainly insured the pleasure of my 1943 Christmas.

I haven't contacted Nell yet. As luck would have it, though, her post is only and hour or so drive from here. I plan to get away to see her within the next two or three days. By some mystifying means, she seems to have learned my exact location, because the other day a male Red Cross emissary contacted an officer friend of mine and told him to pass on to me her whereabouts. Further, this mysterious agent told my friend to tell me not to try to get in touch with Nell over the weekend as she planned to visit John at that time.

Was sorry to hear about Biz's recent bad run of luck—the fall and abscessed tooth. Hope she's 100% again.

That Army-Notre Dame game must have been a marathon. I had a premonition that Army would "blow" that day. Tried to dissuade a recent graduate from betting on them, unavailing.

Merry Christmas, you two!

Love, MART

Margaret F. Morin
Special Representative, War Relief
American Red Cross
December 8, 1943

Dearest Kids:

I received your Nov. 5th and 10th letters yesterday. Was thrilled to hear from you. Can't understand why you haven't heard from me for so long. I haven't written too often but certainly once a week. I suppose you know that I've transferred to War Relief. I like it very much. My chief struggle now is checking on food and medicine distribution. Received a letter from Nell yesterday. It was the first one since she sent me the music. Nell's new job sounds swell.

We had a wonderful Thanksgiving. A friend of Molly brought a turkey and cranberry sauce. We were going to a cocktail party and dinner, so we had the turkey for picking at in the apartment. Sorry to hear Lenoir went and bought a piano. She'd have taken good care of mine.

My love and Merry Christmas to you all, the McKetricks, LaGuardias, Moriartys and others. Will write soon again,

Love, MARGY

Nell regretted not heeding Marion's advice to take hot water bottle. She dreamed of heated stones in bed. John had been transferred to Northern Ireland with the usual secrecy about job and location.

> Mary Eleanor Morin
> American Red Cross
> Somewhere in England
> December 8, 1943

Dearest Rose and Biz:

The Army game sounded marvelous. You must have had a lot of fun. Tell that Bill to write. I haven't heard from him in ages and I've never heard from Marion. I miss her letters. She always managed to get a lot of news in hers—full of what Austin and everyone was up to.

I'm sorry about Mr. Meyer. He was a nice man. We're lost now. No one else will be so nice to us. I was no place near that dance hall catastrophe. It's queer that you should have thought that I was, because one of our porters imagined that I might have been there too and was very relieved when I appeared the next day.

What is Anne's address? Is her house nice? Tell me all about it. That snapshot of Nunsey is adorable with the hair bow on her three "top hits." I don't think there's a chance they will take Bob Brown but Anne will worry anyway till it's all over.

I thought I described the inn in my letter to you in Oct. It is the coldest so-and-so place in the world. I'll probably perish. It takes two hours after I get in bed until I begin to feel warm. By that time, I'm too tired to care. I certainly regret not taking Marion's advice about a hot water bottle. You can't get them here. They have stone ones though, that are grand. I used one at Dulcie's one night. 'Course I couldn't get to sleep all night, wondering where the best place to put it would be. I woke up with it in my hand and dreaming I was asking someone to heat it up again.

We are going to have a Father, Mama and Baby Santa Claus—gives you the creeps doesn't it? The girl in charge is getting a G.I. from Pittsburgh to be the baby! That's what she knows about Pittsburgh bad boys!

I must tell you about my leave. I went to Belfast, flew both ways. The weather was very good. I stayed in a big old hotel that has gone modern with a red and chromium front and horrible red leather and chromium chairs in the lobby. But it was comfortable. I had breakfast in bed and two eggs each morning.

John was in most of the time and I'm afraid I wore him to a nub by talking his ears off. We went to two big parties and saw *Margin for Error* played by the theater group there. We rode home in a carriage with two horses and two men on the driver's seat.

I enjoyed the trip thoroughly and was very lucky to be able to fly. John looks very well. I think he doesn't mind the transfer so much, but I don't blame him for feeling bad because his first group was very nice.

Well, Rose, I'd better close and get out in the canteen. Write soon and tell everyone else to do the same.

Love to you, NELL

P.S. John is not in Belfast but miles from there. M.E.

# Chapter 15

## General MacArthur

"Girls on the left, boys on the right. Tallest in the back," Mrs. Bradley sang as she crisscrossed the stage. Several other ladies in housedresses and aprons stood back from the stage and eyed us to make sure we lined up obediently. The American Legion's Christmas pageant was coming up and we were going to be in it – at least that's what Mrs. Bradley told us.

After all the kids were more or less lined up, the ladies got down off the stage and stood back. Then they asked us to line up in the front, then go back to the back, then turn around and walk to the front. Then walk to the side. There were kids from all over and I hardly knew anyone.

Frankie and Dickie were laughing and pushing each other. Tommy and Bobby shuffled along like they couldn't wait till this was over. I acted like I didn't care, but was really curious about what was happening.

Finally a lady next to Mrs. Bradley said, "Thank you, children, come down now and have your refreshments."

Everyone tumbled off the stage and raced to the long table that held pitchers of lemonade and plates of cookies. The girls waited their turn to get their refreshment at one end of the table; at the other end the boys pushed and shoved to get theirs.

After a while a lady came over and said, "Now, children, I'll call your name and announce which American hero you'll represent in the pageant."

"Donnie Kirkman, you'll be George Washington and Peggy Robbins, you'll be Martha Washington."

She went on and on, with names of some American heroes I knew, and many I didn't. I was bored and hardly paid attention as she went through Abraham Lincoln all the way up to President Roosevelt. But when she said, "George Morin, you'll be General MacArthur," I felt an electric shock in my head.

Tommy Bradley, next to me, stood at attention and saluted, "Yes, sir, General." Then Bobby and Dickie and Frankie also snapped to attention and saluted. I puffed out my chest, folded my arms, and – trying not to laugh – said, "At ease, men."

The girl who would be Mrs. MacArthur had black hair, blue eyes and a very pretty face. But we were both too shy for words.

When the big day arrived, my family and friends treated me like I really was General MacArthur. I went to the American Legion Hall early with the Bradleys to change into my general uniform. The ladies tied my necktie, helped me on with my jacket and straightened out the rows ribbons on my chest.

Then a lady came over with a powder puff in one hand and a tube of lipstick in the other.

"Let's get some makeup on you, General," she said.

"No," I said. "Boys don't wear lipstick."

"But you need it because of the bright lights."

"No lipstick," I said, fending off the red tube heading for my lips.

"But you have to have it."

"No no no," I said, squiggling and squirming away.

She chased me around the stage, but finally gave up, settling for a few dabs of powder.

When the curtain went up all the seats in the hall were filled. From where I waited in the wings, I could see my mother, grandmother and sisters.

The music started and the American heroes with their wives were introduced and marched two-by-two to the front of the stage.

"President and Mrs. George Washington . . ." the announcer said over the music.

When each couple reached the front of the stage they turned left or right and stood at the side.

Me and Mrs. MacArthur were the last couple. When the announcer introduced us, people clapped louder for us than they had for the others.

Later, in the Christmas part of the pageant, I was out of my uniform and in the audience. The boys in red lipstick looked pretty funny – just like girls look in red lipstick. I was glad I hadn't let that lady do that to me.

# Chapter 16

## Hope for the New Year

Rose reported about Jane and Nellie in Pittsburgh and offered the hope that the whole Morin family will be together again soon.

> Rose Mary Morin
> New York City
> December 9, 1943

Dear John:

A letter from Jane says that Eleanor is pictured in the *Bulletin Index* as a model for children's clothes. She is sending us a copy and will send you one also.

Jane also says she is working 12-13 hours daily and is crazy about her work. She hasn't heard from you in a month. Nance came in after visiting Pittsburgh and said Jane would like to get a full semester of day school to help in her work. The few courses she can get at night don't fill the bill. I wish I could help her, but never seem to get ahead.

Our Bill telephoned this morning. He hopes to get a day next week for some shopping and to see Nance before she leaves for Christmas in the

South with Honey. Marion is in Virginia, but will return to West Point on the 20th so they will have Christmas there.

I hope your Christmas will be as Merry as possible under the circumstances and maybe the New Year will bring us all together again.

Love, ROSE

Rose Mary Morin
New York City
December 14, 1943

Dear John:

Your Christmas Card V-mail came yesterday. You must have a very clever "artist" in your midst. The characters in the drawing remind me of some Martin used to depict in his cartooning days.

Nance's business is keeping her here and she is beginning to become jittery. She wants to be with Honey over Christmas and had planned to be down there before the heavy holiday travel period.

She had a letter from Sybil yesterday reporting on Bill Mente's course at the Ordinance Ground School. He received a "superior" mark and was first in a class of 16. He was commended by his Commanding Officer and recommended as an "instructor."

Our Bill came in unexpectedly for the weekend. He found out on Saturday that he could get the afternoon off and drove in with some officers on business. We had dinner at the apartment and spent the evening talking. He left Sunday after church to drive back. He was wearing his new uniform with insignia embroidered into the material instead of pinned on. Sure as shooting, he will be ordered elsewhere but seems to think the investment is worth any change should he get into something more active—and away from a desk.

Love, ROSE

Margaret reported on living conditions and what she missed most about not being home for Christmas.

Margaret F. Morin
Special Representative, War Relief
American Red Cross
December 14, 1943

Dearest Kids:

I came home from work early so I have some time to kill before dinner. We are trying to get furniture to make the place more comfortable. Molly's bedroom is very comfortable, but mine is impossible. After three hours on the bed you're numb. The living room is filled with dining room furniture.

The weather has been lovely here in the last few weeks. I've never seen such magnificent views as there are here. Whether it's sunning or raining the cloud formations are unbelievable. This city is so different from the other. It's much larger and mostly very old. However, the modern buildings are really something—every imaginable gadget and indirect lighting all over the place. We are making plans for Christmas. Molly and I and Bill Giblin are having drinks in the afternoon. We haven't got any further.

There are lovely Christmas trees in the city. I saw a beauty for two dollars yesterday. I keep thinking of how difficult it was for you to find a nice one last year.

Fredric March was here last week, but I didn't see his show. I ran into him with Mike Cullen, that friend of John's from the William Penn in Pittsburgh.

There is a correspondent here by the name of Morin. His nickname is "Pat." Most people think we're brother and sister. He's very nice but admits only to French background, so there's no blood kin.

My love to you all. Will be thinking of you on Christmas. One thing I'm sure of, there will be no sausage, scrambled eggs and biscuits this year. I'll miss unwrapping the presents and "saving the paper for next year."

Will write soon again, MARGY

Mart showed up at Nell's club and caused a "flurry of excitement." After the new year, Nell, Mart and John plan to go to London.

# HOPE FOR THE NEW YEAR

Mary Eleanor Morin
American Red Cross Clubs
December 16, 1943

Dearest Rose and Biz:

Honestly, I feel like a snake for not writing earlier but things here have been hectic—or have you heard that song before?

First of all, I've seen Martin. He came into the club last Friday and threw everyone into a flurry of excitement. We all went out and had a few drinks to celebrate. The manager cooked a lunch that was the best I've had in months and months. Everyone is crazy about Martin and that is something, as this club is 100% G.I. He'll be here for Christmas Eve and Day. Soon after New Years we plan to go to town—John, Mart and me—get a suite or a couple rooms for the weekend and see London as it should be seen. It will involve a lot of traveling and planning, but it should be fun and worth the effort.

A friend of mine has a contact at Claridges and she thinks we may be able to get a suite. John called the night before last. He was on an assignment and had the evening to himself. He had two reservations at Manetta's and wanted me to have dinner with him. I mustered up the courage to refuse. Manetta's has super food and we have "sausage" here. But my work has piled up to the point I'm sure I couldn't make it.

Bill McLaughlin called last night. He seemed very well and was pleased to hear about Margy and Martin. I asked him to try to leave at the same time Mart, John and I do so we can all be together. He's on General Staff now and may not be able to spare the time.

Did I tell you that Mart had about 10 days with Margy on the way here? They evidently had a grand time and she's got an interesting job. What is there about her that tends to black chiffon nighties and dressing gowns? Her birthday party must have been sensational. This Bill Giblin sounds very interesting. Mart says he's an awfully nice guy.

Tomorrow I'm supposed to have a new uniform fitted and John wants me to have dinner with him. Meantime, I don't have a clean blouse, my hair hasn't been done in three weeks and my nails look like mice have been chewing on them.

Best love to you and Biz and hope you will go to Anne and Bob's for Christmas. I know you will all have a grand time.

Love again, NELL

Rose Mary Morin
New York City
December 21, 1943

Dear John:

Nance left for Washington today and will leave there for Southern Pines tomorrow. The legal matter for which she has been here the past three weeks was postponed until late January.

Last night she wanted to say good-bye to "cousin" Mary Sullivan, so I went up to the Bronx with her, on the promise we would stay but a short time. Well, Jack wasn't home when we arrived—being out searching for a Christmas turkey—and Cousin Mary insisted that we wait for him. Finally, when he wasn't home by midnight we had to come home.

Now that Christmas is over (when you receive this) I hope your packages were in reasonably good condition when you finally opened them, and that you had a nice day.

Love, ROSE

Margaret wrote that Christmas is quite different where she was and that the "powers-that-be" changed her title so as not to offend "important" visitors.

Margaret F. Morin
Special Representative, War Relief
American Red Cross
December 23, 1943

Dearest Kids:

Here it is the day before Christmas Eve and the most un-Christmas day I've ever known. It's very strange not to see the usual Christmas crowds and hear the Salvation Army bells, etc. Last Sunday we had lunch at a little restaurant near the water and didn't even wear coats. We've had some beautiful weather these last few weeks, and when the sun shines here, it's really magnificent.

Rose, I received the Christmas cards the day before yesterday. It couldn't have been timed better. I plan to distribute them throughout the offices. It will be a very nice touch of home. I love the selection. Betty Brown sent me a pair of hand-stitched fabric gloves. The box of paté, kippers, nuts and chocolates that Aunt Maizie and Uncle Dan sent will not be touched until Christmas Eve, when we hope to get hold of some good Champagne.

This afternoon I'm going to take time off and get a small tree. They have lovely ones here. I've never seen holly as lovely. I've got to get some for our place and Bill's apartment, where we are having an "at home" Christmas afternoon. That is if a deal for some liquor goes through.

My title has been changed to Field Representative, because headquarters decided that if Mrs. Roosevelt or someone should decide to come over as a Special Representative there's should be no other title as distinguished.

Rose, you asked how the language was coming. It's not. I just don't have time to sit down to daily lessons. I'm getting so that I can understand some of it, which is a little helpful.

I've got an appointment in a few minutes and must line up the questions that I hope to get answered.

Merry Christmas again. I hope you can go to Washington and be with the kids there.

Best love to you all, MARGY

Nell reported on her Christmas with John and Mart.

Mary Eleanor Morin
American Red Cross
December 27, 1943
"Boxing Day"

Dearest Kids:

I'm glad you were all together Thanksgiving. I'm dying to hear if you got to Anne & Bob's for Christmas. Their house sounds very nice.

I didn't mean to worry you by telling you about the sinusitis. Everyone has it. It's just one of those things.

You must have my letters now about visiting John. We had a very good time. Dulcie and I had dinner with John and Major Fitzgerald at Claridges. It was super. I can't understand how they manage, but the chef there really is a wizard. Next day John and his friend met me at the tailor's and approved the progress on the material you sent. It should be ready in a few weeks. We all met Dulcie at the restaurant in the American Embassy for lunch and then went to the movies.

Major Fitzgerald, a French gal, John and I had dinner at Manetta's. We went back to the Park Lane for a nightcap and ran into Bill McL., so we all went to the Embassy Club and had a good time. John is a marvelous dancer. I had never danced with him before! I left town at dawn.

Mart showed up for Christmas Eve, day and Sunday morning. I enjoyed having him so much. He's looking very well in spite of a cold and a tooth extraction without benefit of Novocain. Martin, John and I plan a weekend in town in January.

The club was jammed. We did our best to decorate and it looked pretty nice. Everyone exchanged presents. I received earrings made of thre'penny bits.

John Dwyer sent me two pairs of hose, a bottle of Yardley's Lavender and an E. Arden Lipstick. I was so surprised and pleased.

That brings me to your wonderful presents. I'm keeping the food for when we go to town and have a cocktail party. Thank you for everything, Rose. Your boxes with blue and black dresses and shoes. Everything fits beautifully. I must confess, I cheated and opened all my presents with the exception of one from Aunt Mazie before Christmas. I opened that Christmas morning (over Mart's Scotch). It's a lovely twin-sweater set in white, that is needed, useful and really very pretty.

I must close now and take a look in the canteens. Everyone is more or less subdued today. It's crowded, but terribly still. Too much Christmas no doubt.

Best love to you all, NELL

P.S. Thanks for the letters from Margy, John and Mart. Margy's job sounds grand. I envy her. N.

Rose wrapped the year up with details of her Christmas visit to Anne's new home near Washington.

Rose Mary Morin
New York City
December 31, 1943

Dear John:

We had a wonderful time at Anne's. Her new home is very attractive and you would think she had selected the furniture for it herself. We had such fun with the children, both are adorable and so well behaved.

I had quite a time walking Nunsey around during most of her waking hours. We got a kick out of Robin's reaction to the Christmas tree. He discovered it behind the closed door of the sun porch. He saw it through the curtain and exclaimed, "What's this?"

His toys included a truck, a dog on wheels, picture books, several suits, a darling Tyrolean outfit, crayons and a rocking horse. He sat rocking the horse with the ease of someone riding in a Rolls Royce. Eleanor had wonderful "cuddly" dolls and animals. She has just two lower teeth but the ones on top seem ready to come through. She is very cute and smiles and laughs all the time.

We attended midnight Mass after trimming the tree. The Browns had come over to help. Mr. Brown prepared delicious hot buttered rum. Christmas afternoon we went over to see their new home on the banks of the Potomac above Chain Bridge on the Virginia side.

We had to leave Sunday afternoon and take the 3:45 train. A sleet storm turned the roads into a sheet of ice. Anne and I struggled for an hour trying to get to Mass, but never made it. On the way to the train we passed any number of accidents.

The train was quite delightful, not overcrowded and with dining service as in "old times."

Dot and Jane sent us a lovely liqueur set—decanter and glasses of amethyst glass. Did you hear that Marge Foster had died and that Mrs. Wilson is very ill?

I hope you, Nell and Mart will be able to get together for a trip into town.

Happy New Year & love, ROSE

*1944*

# Chapter 17

## Getting Ready

January's bad weather limited John's Bomb Group to eight missions for the month. While Martin was called to Washington his "Hell on Wheels" division was transferred to England to prepare for the invasion of Europe.

Rose's report that Cousin Alvin "Pat" Mente's 7th Amored Division was involved in the fighting at St. Vith was incorrect. His division did not arrive in Europe until three days after this letter was written.

> Rose Mary Morin
> New York City
> January 4, 1944
>
> Dear John:
> I have heard from Janet that Martin's address in Washington is 1712 Seventeenth St. N.W. Apt. 22, Washington 9. D.C. He has a room in someone's apartment. He has been out to Anne's for dinner but left at 11:30, as he had to be up at five in the morning.
> Patsy wrote about all the things she and the children received for Christmas. The Hansons were most generous with gifts and Patsy felt ashamed that she was enjoying the holiday so much even though Tom was away.

We had a very quiet New Year's Eve. I had to get to early Mass and to work on Monday morning. Biz had a cold that kept her in bed. We were almost asleep shortly after midnight when Anne's call came through.

Jane writes that they had a grand Christmas and said that they are the only members of the Morin and the Wilson family now in Pittsburgh, since Dot's sister Ruth and her family moved to Florida. I don't know why you don't write the children oftener. They would get such a kick out of hearing from you.

We are anxiously awaiting word that Pat came through the recent heavy fighting safely. His outfit has been identified with the early defenders at St. Vith.

Hope all goes well with you, Love, ROSE

Margy had money worries after her move from North Africa and thought she might move again soon.

Margaret F. Morin
Field Representative, War Relief
American Red Cross
January 5, 1944

Dearest Kids:
I'm rushing this letter off in the midst of a madhouse. Thank you all for your wonderful gifts.

They helped make a wonderful Christmas. The holidays have been very gay. Although nothing could make up for not being home. Rose, I received the black dress and it's practically worn out I love it so. All in all it was a very, very merry!

Rose, there's a chance that I will be moving on very soon. It's in the planning stage and I don't know how it will turn out. It's most exciting and say a prayer that it does go through. If it does I'll need money badly. The move from North Africa and getting settled here and the holidays have taken a terrific toll on my $200 advance.

Could you beg, borrow or steal $200 against my account and send it to me *as fast as possible*. I hate to press like this, but the fact is that things are liable to happen very, very fast. I've got to rush off now. Thanks a million to all. Please forgive my haste.

Love, MARGY

Martin returned to England from Washington before Christmas and spent the holiday with Nell. A reunion of Mart, Nell and John was in the works.

Lt. Col. Martin J. Morin
41st Armored Inf. 2nd Armored Div.
Somewhere in England
January 5, 1944

Dear Rose:

Your second Christmas box containing the soap, peanuts, and candy was delivered about three days before Christmas. After the first package, it was totally unexpected. How nice of you, Rose! It made my holiday just that much more memorable. Thanks ever so much.

I joined Nell on Christmas Eve, and stayed with her until the 26th. The club was doing a peak business so she was on the job. They have special parties for orphans on Christmas Eve that we enjoyed no less than the kids. On Christmas night over five hundred dinners were served. Nell is indefatigable. In addition to her club activity she managed to lead me a merry whirl. We had our Christmas dinner together at the hotel and listened to the broadcast of the King's traditional message. On both nights there were long jolly sessions in the hotel tap room. For wartime overseas, the Christmas of 1943 was a huge success.

Everything is arranged for Nell, John and I to meet in London over the weekend of the 14-15.

Love to you and Biz, MART

Rose reported on the family's holidays in New York. The festivities made it difficult for her to attend her daily 7:00 a.m. Mass.

Rose Mary Morin
New York City
January 5, 1944

Dear John:

Janet wrote that Martin expects to have leave some weekend this month. I hope you will get the same time for your reunion. It should be fun.

    We had a quiet New Year's Eve. It was hard though to make seven o'clock Mass and be at work by 8:30. I caught up on the sleep however Saturday night at Amy's. Margaret's letter sounds as though she is in the "thick of things." I do hope her packages caught up with her and on time for Christmas. They were sent from the same sources as yours, Nell's and Mart's so she should have something soon.

Love, ROSE

On the Eastern front, Russian troops entered Poland.

Mary Eleanor Morin
American Red Cross Clubs
January 6, 1944

Dearest Rose:

It beats me why you don't receive any mail from me. It would come back quickly if censored and none has. So it must be lost en route. Christmas and New Year's left us all haggard shadows of our former selves. It was busier than you'd ever imagine.

    I'm saving the box of goodies you sent for John, Mart and my weekend to London. I've held so many people spellbound with tales of them I think it will be fun to show them off—not the "goodies" but the kids.

    I have a new assignment! An officer's club is badly needed in this town. The poor souls come around here like waifs and strays. So a house was found near town and I am to be the director. I'm terribly pleased about it. We hoped to get it open by the first of next month.

    My leave in Belfast was fun. John and I had lunch and dinner at the hotel where I stayed practically every day, and the last night we went to a party at the officer's club in town. It was terrific. John, some of his friends and I had a drink and dinner before hand and then had a good, noisy, time. I hated to leave.

I'll let you know about our weekend in London. We (John, Mart and I) have reservations at Claridges. I enjoyed Mart being here so much and everyone—British and American—liked him a lot. I'm constantly being asked when he's coming back.

Well, wish me luck and pray that the officer's club will work.

Had a letter from Margy. She seemed very happy and satisfied with her job.

Best love to all, NELL

Margaret F. Morin
Field Representative, War Relief
American Red Cross
January 13, 1944

Dearest Kids:

I have a few moments before the day starts so will rush off a note. It's a beautiful day, just like spring. We had cold wet weather for the last few weeks. Without central heating and with tile floors and no hot water, it's as cold as I've ever known. I'll have to be reminded to bathe when I get home, it happens so seldom here.

Rose, I hope you got the letter about the $200. I surely will need it if I move. Everybody's getting itchy. I'm keeping my fingers crossed.

Patsy and Tom's box of bath oil for my birthday came just the other day. It was grand getting it. I don't know when I'll get to writing individual thank you notes, but please believe—all of you, that it's only because the days are too short, not lack of appreciation.

It's hard to believe that in a few more weeks I'll have been away a year. The time has flown.

Best love to you all, MARGY

In Italy, the Allies attacked Monte Cassino. In Germany, three airplane factories were bombed and 64 U.S. aircraft were lost.

Rose Mary Morin
New York City
January 13, 1944

Dear John:

Your weekend with Nell in December must have been fun. I guess you and Martin are on the verge of meeting.

I always figure no news is good news, but with all of you doing things that are much more interesting than what I am doing, we are anxious to have the latest word. Things here seem quite dull in comparison.

I take it you didn't like *Stage Door Canteen*. I didn't see the picture, but liked several of the musical numbers from it. However, almost everyone who has seen it didn't think much of it.

Patsy wrote about her Christmas with Tom's family. They had an enjoyable Christmas, but the rest of the week sounded hectic with Tom's brother, a doctor, collapsing with a hemorrhaging ulcer, a fire in the office and a sister taking sick.

Patsy said they spent a very quiet New Year's Eve, thankful to be alive after all that happened during the week.

Much love, ROSE

On January 15, the U.S. Fifth Army broke the winter line in Italy. On the 20th, Allied forces made an unsuccessful attempt to seize Cassino, Italy.

Rose Mary Morin
New York City
January 20, 1944

Dear John:

Your long letter describing your gifts and the picture showing them was most appreciated. Mr. MacLennon, Nell's Field Director for the first three months of her Clubmobile work, was at the apartment the other evening. He was sent home because of ulcers and is on a speaking tour for the Red Cross.

When Bill was in last week he told us that he was to go to General Staff school and was to leave for Fort Leavenworth today. He appreciated the advantage of being at the Point, but didn't think it a good assignment for someone who wants to take an active part in the war. Of course, people will make remarks about those in "easy" jobs, even though the jobs are assigned, not chosen.

A letter from Nell to Biz said she had been sick in bed for two days with a cold, but was getting up to start her new job as acting director of a new officer's club. I hope you found out how she liked it in your reunion last week. MacLennon certainly raved about her accomplishments and personality.

Love, ROSE

On January 22, United States and British forces landed in Anzio, Italy.

Mary Eleanor Morin
American Red Cross Clubs
January 25, 1944

Dearest Kids:

Did I tell you about our séance in London? We had a marvelous time. The weather even cooperated by providing a real "pea souper" to lend local color. We had rooms at Claridges and had dinner each night at Manetta's. Dulcie and Bunnie (her husband—Lt. Longman) were with us one night and Bunnie took Mart and John to Wellington Barracks on Sunday for drinks and lunch.

I trapped John and Mart into going to a cheesy little photo place on Oxford St. and have a picture taken. You'd have died at the posing. We wouldn't have been surprised if they'd clamped our necks to hold us still. I'm sending some to you to give to people. I gave Mart and John each two to send their families. I hope Margy will be with us next time.

Disappointment Dept: No officer's club. We had everything all set up, staff hired, furniture requisitioned, etc., when headquarters disapproved it. We are opening a sort of day room (for officers) where the greatest asset will be a place to sit during the day and have donuts and coffee—so I'm back in the fat again.

Let me know how everyone is at home. I haven't had a letter from you or anyone in a week or so.

Best of love to you all, NELL

Rose Mary Morin
New York City
January 29, 1944

Dear John:

I am late in getting your letter off this week and as a result have a copy of Margaret's that arrived yesterday.

After I had written to you last week Bill called and asked us to have dinner with him before he took the evening train for St. Louis and Fort Leavenworth. He and Marion had shipped their furniture to Newport then came to town Thursday evening, stayed at the Ritz, did a few nightclubs and spent Friday shopping. Marion left for Newport on the five o'clock Friday and Bill left on the 7:30. He seemed quite excited and hopes that on the completion of the course, April 1, he will be assigned overseas. He will return to West Point for a short time to await assignment.

There have been several newspapers stories in the past week about Col. John McCormack, Military Commentator of the Allied Forces at Headquarters in North Africa, and he turns out to be the "Little Mac" to whom Margaret has referred to in her letters. One clipping described him as having, "a ceiling barely above five feet in clear weather," so he is well named.

Much love, ROSE

Martin was back in England with his 2nd Armored Division working diligently on his French while preparing for the invasion of Normandy.

Lt. Col. Martin J. Morin
41st Armored Inf. 2nd Armored Div.
Somewhere in England
February 8, 1944

Dear Rose:

The French grammar and the book of idioms have arrived, and along with them a pound of Schrafft's chocolates and Clark bars. Thanks ever so much.

So far as I can determine, the grammar contains everything under the sun, and the book of idioms is of extraordinary interest because of its practical and comprehensive selection and its alphabetic arrangement. I have now assembled enough French text and reading matter to keep me occupied for years to come. I sometimes wonder if I am capable of assimilating it. This much is certain: there is no easy way. A French officer who was an interpreter with the division told me that his knowledge of English represented seven years' study. The claims of the ad writers of the various "methods"—*Berlitz, Hugo, Linguaphone*, etc., are preposterous.

I haven't heard from John since our London visit. Nell has written a couple of letters and last night I talked to her on the telephone. She seems to be even busier than usual. She thinks Margy might put in an appearance this weekend. She is going to London just in case.

My life here does not admit of much to report. Except for the two fly-by-night visits with Nell and the four days' leave, I have not left the area. My existence has settled into an official routine, albeit a rather active one. It is pleasant enough, because of the favorable contrast with our extended field service in Africa and Sicily. The electricity, cot, bathing facilities and private hearth have lost none of their earlier charm. I feel fine, notwithstanding a siege of colds and some extensive dental work.

I finished *Vanity Fair* last week. I enjoyed it immensely. Thank Biz again for having sent it to me.

Love to you both, MART

Mary Eleanor Morin
American Red Cross Clubs
February 10, 1944

Dearest Rose and Biz:

It's been a long time since I've written and I'm sorry, but there just isn't time to sit down and concentrate on writing.

I haven't heard from you in at least three weeks. However, I did get a very cute valentine today from—what's the name of that place in Jersey, across the river—Hoboken!

I'm going to see Bill Giblin and some other friends of Margy this weekend. That Giblin guy is a smoothie! We had a very pleasant visit together last Saturday and he told me all about Margy and the other kids.

The first officer's club I told you about was disapproved in mid-stream. I was disconsolate but we've got another scheme working now. It won't be the same as the other as it is right in the heart of the city, but it will be nice—if it works out as planned. I live in alternate joy and horror at the prospects of it. Find the patron saint of officers' clubs, Rosebuddy, and give him the business. This must succeed! After a year in the E.T.O. I should have something to show for me trouble.

Ach! That reminds me. My shots are overdue. I'll have to steel myself one day next week and march to a dispensary for them. I wonder if the contents of that dread needle couldn't be spilled into a glass of "mild and bitter" and have the same effect?

I'm sending you these pictures to dispense. These are copies of the first set and slightly more blurry. I sent Mart and John copies for their families.

Best love and write soon, NELL

In Italy, the Germans counterattacked the Allies at Anzio while John's Bomb Group prepared for the "Big Week" of massive attacks against the German aircraft industry.

Rose Mary Morin
New York City
February 17, 1944

Dear John:

Enclosed is a copy of Nell's account of your reunion in London. I guess she had heard from John Boland when you last saw her. I'm beginning to wonder where they are finding room for everyone over there. Janet sent us the play-by-play of the five days in London she received from Martin. It was most interesting—from the sumptuous quarters at Claridges to the well-known fog and even a party being canned by an air raid, though no bombs fell.

Anne wrote last week that Bob has received his classification: 2-A until July. She thinks he will try for a commission in the Navy. Anne also wrote that a former co-worker of Margy's in Italy had been to Washington and reported that Margaret is well and happy and doing an excellent job.

We are all sorry about Nell's officers' club plans falling through, but I'm sure she will do as good a job in the "day room."

Hope everything in your part of the world is doing well.

Love and luck, ROSE

Mary Eleanor Morin
American Red Cross Clubs
February 21, 1944

Dearest Rose, Biz and all:
I've had a V-mail and two letters from you in a week's time. I've done very much better on receiving than I have in sending. There are always so many interruptions.

Margaret, Bill Giblin, Butch and I had lunch together at Claridges on Saturday. Margaret alighted all done up in a beautiful gray uniform. She couldn't look better and naturally was full of exciting stories. She and Molly have a smooth flat—a la Swedish moderne. Best of all, there's a bed I can climb into. I've had a fiendish time getting a place to stay and have recently been to Claridges but it's too expensive—though it is wonderfully cozy after the rigors of the 16th Century.

My club should open March 1 or the following week and then I'll be tied down until it gets running smoothly. We've been held up so long that I'm straining at the leash. This one has definite possibilities. Keep your fingers crossed.

Rose, I'm down to one Red Cross pin. Ask Janet Shair if she can get some. You can't get them here and still we must wear one on our cap and collar.

Margy, Bill and I went to a nice quiet restaurant near her place and had a delicious dinner.

After we went back to the flat and had brandy that Bill had been saving. Margy and I talked ourselves silly but there is still a lot to be gone over. I want her to come down to see my place before she gets too busy. Everyone is anxious to meet her and I'd like her to see the club.

Well, I must close now. It's pretty late. This has been written over a period of hours, as you can gather.

Best love to you both, NELL

In late winter and spring of 1944 Allied efforts focused on creating the impression that the forthcoming invasion of France would be directly across the English Channel and not to the south on the beaches of Normandy. Amid these preparations Margy arrived in England in the lap of luxury. A reunion of the four siblings was now almost definite.

Margaret F. Morin
Field Representative, War Relief
American Red Cross
February 23, 1944

Dearest Kids:

I arrived last Saturday. Came down from the center on the night train—private room, bed, hot water and tea on waking. Went to Claridges where Nell was staying for the weekend, had a Scotch in the room. I can't tell you how strange it all seemed. I couldn't close my mouth. Molly arrived the day or so before. We have a lovely apartment—heat, hot water, and the first since we left home. It has two bedrooms, sitting room, dining room, bath and kitchen. There's an extra room where Nell can stay when she comes in.

We got our new uniforms and they turned out very well. The color is a light gray and has caused quite a stir here. In fact the day Molly arrived plans were made to issue us new ones. However, they've run out of cloth for the coats. In the meantime, we are being very conspicuous as "those two from Italy."

I love this place. It reminds me of Washington on a larger scale. The weather has been fine, much warmer than Italy. It's going to take me forever to find my way around. The temptation to pick up a cab is terrific. We are going to see *Something in the Air* tonight. I can't get used to theatres and civilization again.

Rose, the money came the day I got my orders to get ready to leave. The timing was perfect. I could only bring 55 pounds with me. My footlocker with all my summer clothes and uniforms is being shipped as well as my bedroll with everything else I own. Pray that it arrives okay. A friend of Bill's had everything in his stolen.

Nell looks wonderful. She keeps saying that she has gained weight, but I don't think so.

Will write soon again, in the meantime, take care and let me hear from you soon.

MARGY

John's Bomb Group made sixteen raids on special construction targets in February even though bad weather persisted. The Group lost three airplanes and crews during the month, but destroyed seven enemy planes.

Rose Mary Morin
New York City
February 23, 1944

Dear John:

Enclosed is a letter from Martin. Last night we received word from Red Cross headquarters in Washington that Margaret had arrived safely in London. No doubt by now she and Nell have been in communication and by the time you receive this you will have heard from her. She had me cut out a paragraph in the last letter I sent you in which it mentioned her expectation of being in England. She wanted to surprise all of you, but some of her advance guard let the cat out of the bag to Nell.

We have been anxious to hear of Margaret's safety. It is a year almost to the day since we heard of her arrival in North Africa. She has certainly been on a Cook's tour!

We've had no word from you in some time. I hope everything is going well.

Much love, ROSE

Royal and U.S. Air Forces attacked the Schweinfurt ball-bearing factory during the week.

Lt. Col. Martin J. Morin
41st Armored Inf. 2nd Armored Div.
Somewhere in England
February 24, 1944

Dear Rose:

Your letters with the enclosures and clippings continue to arrive with clocklike regularity. Every time I receive one I vow that I will step up my correspondence with you, but somehow something always intervenes.

Margy is definitely here. I talked with her for about two minutes on the phone the day before yesterday. As luck would have it, I was not at my headquarters when she called, and by the time I was located and rushed back, her long distance time had almost expired. Just hearing her voice again, however, was quite a thrill. Nell had visited her over the weekend, and was waiting at the station to welcome her when she arrived.

It seems that she will be doing war relief work out of a London office. She is already installed with Molly R. in a well-appointed apartment. Marj B. is expected to join them in the near future. Isn't it amazing how that trio has managed to stick together? According to Nell, Margy looks fine.

Plans for a four-way reunion are in the making. The period tentatively selected is the 13th-16th of March. Immediately after Nell flashed the good news I wrote John outlining the plan. Nell is to stay with Margy at the flat, and John and I will put up at a nearby hotel.

Your mention of spotting "Little Mac's" picture in the paper is most interesting. Did I tell you that he was the one who sent me the long-traveling bottle of Scotch? It completed a full circuit and never caught up with me, but his fiancée gave me a duplicate when I met her with Margy in Palermo. Incidentally, the fiancée is not Marj B. but a Miss Wiley, considerably older, but most charming.

A letter from Patsy recently had picture of young Paul taken within the past month. What a fine youngster he is! Your word that Bill had been selected for the Command and General Staff school was music to my ears. I must write him and insist on his stopping over in Columbus on his way back East.

Love to you and Biz, MART

P.S. The London fog that Alfred Lunt refers to in his letter in Ward Morehouse's column is undoubtedly the very one that John and I stumbled about in. The papers credited it with being the worst in four years. It was great fun, but once is enough, especially when one's opportunities for seeing London are as limited as mine.

Love, M

Margaret F. Morin
Field Representative, War Relief
American Red Cross
February 28, 1944

Dear Kids:

It's a beautiful day here today, like Washington in the fall. We had a quiet night last night. I'm still not quite awake. Nell was in Saturday and returned yesterday morning. The flat is becoming more like our own.

We even have a radio now. I cooked dinner there last night. We had loin lamb chops, soup, baked potatoes, cheese, cake and coffee. I was surprised that I could still handle a stove.

Did I tell you that Molly and I are being issued new blue uniforms? The gray ones were a good investment. We can wear the topcoats with civilian clothes and the uniforms on off days for a change. Marjorie is on her way. We expect her almost any day now. She's coming by boat. Tiley has not been released from the other theater yet. It may be a while before she can come up.

Did I tell you we went to see *Strike a New Note* the other night? The comedian, Sid Fields, is marvelous. He's a cross between Ray Bolger, Abbott & Costello, Bob Hope and every other good comedian you can think of. He carries the whole show. Bill White, the *LIFE* correspondent, is taking Molly and me to lunch with Fields on Wednesday. Bill says he isn't at all funny off the stage, but we shall see.

I'm waiting for a call from Nell. She may have to come up tomorrow to select curtains for her new club. It's to open next week. Martin, John and Nell plan to be in town the 12, 13 and 14 of March.

Best love to you all, MARGY

Rose Mary Morin
New York City
March 4, 1944

Dear John:

It is certainly nice to know you are all within phoning distance and can see each other now and then. It is also nice that Margaret's location will permit Nell to spend her day off in London without having to spend so much for a hotel.

By the time you receive this you will have been together for the second "reunion." How I envy all of you. Things here can be very dull here with so many of you away.

I saw *Tomorrow the World* last night, starring Ralph Bellamy and Shirley Booth. It was very good. A Nazi youngster is brought to live with his American relatives after the death of parents. While the boy led them a merry chase for a while, they finally subdued him with kindness and persuasion.

Nell sent a copy of the group picture and it is wonderful. You seem to be thinner. Nell is certainly a glamour girl. Now we will be looking for one including Margaret.

Take care of yourself, Love, ROSE

P.S. Pat Mente has been transferred from Fort Knox to Headquarters of the 7th Armored at Fort Benning. If it is a field assignment I don't think he will mind. He has been dreading another spell of teaching.

R.


Mart hoped the four-way reunion would come off and encouraged brother Bill to visit wife Janet and the kids in Columbus, Ohio.

Lt. Col. Martin J. Morin
41st Armored Inf. 2nd Armored Div.
Somewhere in England
March 6, 1944

Dear Rose:

Just received your letter recording Aunt Tat's visit to New York. Janet has idolized Aunt Tat since earliest childhood. She has been knitting and sending me superior woolen socks for the past four or five years.

It looks as if Nell, Margy, John and I will be getting together a week from now. It is not so easy to maintain communication as one might suppose. I talked to Nell by phone within the past week but the connection was so poor that we couldn't put much across. I've got my three-day leave, though, and Nell can get away. Margy is supposed to have reserved accommodations for John and me at a hotel near her flat. I hope everything meshes, as it is very unlikely that such an opportunity will develop again this side of Tokyo.

I have written to Bill urging him to visit Columbus on his way back East. Janet and the kids would be overjoyed to have him. Patrick might insist on being taken to the zoo, or sled riding, or something, but Bill could cope with that with the greatest of ease.

The deeper I get into the French books you sent me, the more I appreciate the skill of your selection. The grammar covers the points that I was interested in, and the text on idioms has opened a vast new vista. Unfortunately, what I have learned is 99% theoretical. What I need now is much conversation.

Everything is going well with me, Rose. How is with you and Biz?

Take care of yourselves, Love, MART

John's Bomb Group took advantage of the improved weather and sent many missions against enemy targets.

Mary Eleanor Morin
American Red Cross Clubs
March 10 & 17, 1944

Dearest Kids:

Don't mind if you notice signs of butter or jam all over this. I'm sitting on the floor with the little electric stove on a low suitcase rack in front of me with a tray of tea at my knee and writing on a book I purchased in Belfast. This isn't going to be a long letter because the position is so darned uncomfortable.

The past few weeks have been busy—between the excitement of Margaret's being here and starting the club. We have the ground and first floors of a large department store. The upstairs opened last Friday night. The ground floor is still being fixed up.

Friday, March 17th

(Happy St. Patrick's Day! You can see that I was slightly interrupted. Here we go again—with any luck.) The club should be very attractive when it's complete. The ministry promised us that all work will be done by April 8th so we will open Easter Sunday with a reception in the afternoon and a dance that night. We can only make sandwiches, salads, canned soup and scrambled powdered eggs. We have no rooms for sleeping, but we have ferreted out families who will put the officers up overnight and let them have a bath and breakfast.

We try to get them in the hotels first, but only manage a few a week, as they are all so darned crowded and understaffed. I'm lucky in having an excellent manager, receptionist, cashier, porter and four good souls who clean, prepare food and do everything in general.

We have three days, Tuesday, Thursday and Sunday when the officers can bring "lady" guests. They can bring Allied officers at any time. It always strikes me funny when I say that. Can you imagine anyone showing up with a swastika on his sleeve?

John, Marty and I knocked ourselves out on my AWOL day by seeing two marvelous shows in succession: *While the Sun Shines* and *Sweeter and Lower*. It was all good fun and I hope to do it again. Marty and I plan to take a day or so off together and see the horse races near Salisbury.

Well, I must sign off and go home and dress for tonight's onslaught.

Lots of love, bye again, NELL

---

The U.S. Army Air Force began a large-scale offensive over northern France in preparation for D-Day.

Rose Mary Morin
New York City
March 10, 1944

Dear John:
Since you have seen Margaret it seems unnecessary to send the enclosed copy of her latest letter, but in the excitement of your reunion you may not hear some of the things she has told us. Even though she is the last to arrive

in Great Britain she seems to get all kinds of special service on her mail—her letter arrived within 5 days of the day she wrote it.

I had a note from Dot last week saying that Eleanor remains at the head of her class. They all have had colds but are better now. Jane is putting on a fashion show and getting a big kick out of it.

Biz and I went down to St. Vincent's to see Mrs. McKetrick Tuesday evening. She said she got a bigger kick out the picture of you, Mart and Nell than anything else she had seen while in the hospital. Mr. McKetrick said you look five years younger in the picture than when he saw you in Pittsburgh.

We shall be anxious for word of the reunion next week.

Much love from all, ROSE

P.S. Mart's birthday is April 9.

Margaret, John and Martin were in London and Nell was due to arrive soon.

Margaret F. Morin
Field Representative, War Relief
American Red Cross
March 13, 1944

Dearest Kids:

I'm sorry that it's been so long since I wrote. We aren't too busy in the office yet and have taken advantage of the free time to see something of the city. I love the place. We've had wonderful weather—unheard of for this time of the year. I've seen three good shows and we're seeing *There Shall Be No Night* on Saturday. Last Saturday Molly and I went to the country home of a family friend for tea. It was a lovely spot.

John and Martin got in for lunch today. Nell gets in this evening.

John has been transferred to the same place as Bill McL. for a while at least. Bill McL. is coming in tomorrow night. He's been very busy, John tells me.

Our apartment is a constant source of joy to both of us. Molly has a butcher bewitched and he gives her the choice cuts. We can manage one dinner a week at home. Bill G. gave us his ration book, which helps, except that he eats with us most of the time. I'm struggling to get some liquor for our get-together tomorrow, but it's terribly difficult here. In North Africa and Italy no one expected good drinks and lapped up anything they could get hold of.

I hope Uncle Dan is better. Please give them my love.

Best love to all, MARGY

Rose Mary Morin
New York City
March 16, 1944

Dear John:

We are wondering if the recent ban on travel in your part of the world interfered with the plans to meet with Mart, Nell and Margy. I hope not as they had counted on all of you being together.

Patsy wrote after her trip to San Gabriel they had a fire in Tom's brother's house but put it out before the firemen arrived. Patsy was glad that young Paul was away from the noise and smoke.

We shall be anxious to hear about the reunion and that none of you were in the parts of town so badly hit the other day.

Best of luck and love, ROSE

Rose Mary Morin
New York City
March 21, 1944
V-MAIL

Dear John:

We had a special airmail from Nance on Sunday saying that Honey had a 7-pound baby girl on Friday evening, St. Patrick's Day. They are both doing nicely. Until Honey is home from the hospital, Nance has Honey's little boy, Allen, with her and Alvin at Fort Benning.

Sunday morning was quite cold, but beautiful. I planned to go to New Jersey to have dinner with friends but at about 7:30 a neighbor dropped in and said there was already a heavy snowfall. It came down hard and fast and looked more like a winter blizzard than the evening before the first day of spring. It took me a full hour longer to get home. The snow continued yesterday but the sun is quite warm today and melting it.

Biz met with an accident on Friday night—she does have the worst luck. She was in a car with her dinner escort and as he attempted to turn his car out of a parking space he moved too quickly and struck the curb. Biz was thrown off balance against the dashboard. She had several scratches on her lower left jaw, a bite inside her cheek and considerable swelling on the right side of her face. But applying ice on Saturday and Sunday brought down the swelling and relieved the soreness. She has since been as active as usual—both socially and in the office—so her luck was better than usual.

Much love, ROSE

## Margaret had settled in London.

Margaret F. Morin
Field Representative, War Relief
American Red Cross
March 29, 1944

Dearest Kids:

I received your letter of Feb. 18, forwarded from Italy. We are moving into another flat on Saturday. We found a place with two sitting rooms, three bedrooms, one bath and kitchen. It's delightfully furnished and almost half as expensive as the other apartment. It is on a square with the trees and bushes now coming out. I can't wait to get moved into it.

John is in this area. He's been reassigned and thinks he'll like it very much. This week he is at a training school. I saw him Sunday and he's taking Bill and me to see *Lisbon Story* Friday night. Bill McLaughlin has been promoted again. He's coming in for dinner Monday. He surely looked wonderful when I saw him a few weeks ago. Nell is coming in tonight until Thursday morning.

Marj finally arrived. Went to a party at the Savoy Monday that the correspondents who were in Africa gave sort of a reunion. Molly, Helen

Kirkpatrick (also a correspondent who wrote the story on all of us) and I were the only girls among 23 men. It was great fun.

There's a page in Quentin Reynolds new book about Molly. I wish you would send it to us. She's always bragging about it, but doesn't know what it actually says.

Must get set for my French lesson. I'm taking them every day—one hour of conversation.

Three of our men who came up from Italy are taking a flat with two grand pianos in the sitting room and one in two of the three bedrooms. It's about three minutes from the office so I expect to be able to use them.

Love to all, MARGY

The news of the family reunion had hit the newspapers.

Rose Mary Morin
New York City
March 29, 1944

Dear John:

Uncle Bill sent several of the enclosed clippings from the *Pittsburgh Press* with the question, "Who's your new publicity agent?" It's very similar and more in detail than the clipping that was in the Columbus, Ohio, paper which Janet's mother sent us. Incidentally, Nell sent one of the photographs of the four of you and it is very good of you and Nell, but both Margaret and Martin look like someone drew a circle around each of their left eyes and that they are suppressing a hearty laugh, or afraid that the "birdie" will jump out of the camera at them. Nell's account of your visit makes us most envious.

Biz and I have been making a mission given by two Fathers of the Precious Blood. So far it has been very interesting. One of the priests is a dead ringer for Charles Laughton, even in his speech, and the other one is from Waukegan and says he grew up with Jack Benny. He has a wonderful sense of humor, but at the same time tries to be a "tough guy."

Bill sent a message that he is graduating this weekend from Fort Leavenworth and sends love to all.

Happy Easter, good luck & love, ROSE

Martin reported on the second foursome reunion.

> Lt. Col. Martin J. Morin
> 41st Armored Inf. 2nd Armored Div.
> Somewhere in England
> March 30, 1944
>
> Dear Rose:
>
> Have been back from the second London assembly for a fortnight, but this is the first real opportunity I have had to write about it. It was only for three days this time. They were delightful. John and I stayed at the Cadagan in Chelsea, within easy walking distance of Margy and Molly's flat. It was not as flashy an establishment as Claridges but it served our purpose better. Nell, Margy, John, Bill Giblin and I had dinner there the first night and returned to the apartment afterwards. The apartment is a dream, roomy, comfortable, modernistic. The second night after a cocktail party at Margy's, the same group augmented by Molly, Bill McLaughlin, and a high-ranking general's naval aide dined and danced at Manetta's. The third day John, Nell and I went in for some concentrated theater, seeing the matinee performance of *While the Sun Shines* (an excellent comedy), and immediately afterwards attending the evening performance of a popular English revue, *Sweeter and Lower* (good, but not up to *Strike a New Note*). We had dinner with Margy, Bill and John Boland in a well-known Soho restaurant. Margy kept working on a reduced schedule throughout the "séance" as Nell calls our get-togethers. We all had lunch and did a lot of wandering around London at odd moments all three days.
>
> Though nothing was needed to add to the excitement, the Germans contributed air raids the second and third nights. You have no doubt received a copy of the picture we had taken. Isn't it a howl?
>
> Margy seems to have a most interesting job. John is back on the "tight little isle," and in line for a new and, I think, better assignment. All three of them are in the best of health and spirits. I had met both Molly and Bill Giblin in Palermo, and my opinion of them hasn't changed: they're tops.

We had a whirl at Manetta's. The two family reunions couldn't have been more successful.

From what you mentioned of Pat's latest assignment, I wouldn't be surprised to meet him in these parts soon. Everyone seems to be headed East or West.

Things are going very will with me, Rose. My teeth are going to pot, but that, I guess, is a minor consideration in the world as it goes today. I made my Easter duty a couple of Sundays ago.

You and Biz take care of yourselves.

Love to you both, MART

John's Bomb Group attacked the railroad marshalling yards in France after which it was taken off combat operations for a weeklong refresher course.

Rose Mary Morin
New York City
April 6, 1944

Dear John:

Well, here it is Holy Thursday already, but a rather cold one. We had quite a lot of snow yesterday. It is still on the streets and a glance into Central Park on the way down by bus this morning showed that the trees there are all snowy. I suppose those who have an Easter outfit will either be uncomfortable or put off wearing it.

Incidentally, when speaking to Anne the other evening she said that Bob had applied for a commission in the Navy and has passed the physical. Now if they can find a vacancy for one with his qualifications he'll probably be joining our other brother-in-law in that branch of the service. Anne and Bob are both very hopeful about it. Patsy and Tom are spending the holiday with the Hansons in San Gabriel. Tom still doesn't know if he will be going to sea or transferred to Los Angeles.

All best wishes for Easter and love, ROSE

On April 12, more than 2,000 American aircraft engaged in an air battle over Germany.

# GETTING READY

Mary Eleanor Morin
American Red Cross Clubs
April 13 to 21, 1944

Dear Rose, Biz and All:

Your Easter card came today. Thank you very much for keeping up your weekly effort. I've thought of you often but life for the past six weeks has been a gold fish existence.

The most upsetting transfer of the past 14 months has taken place! We had the official opening of the club Easter Sunday. It was perfect. We worked frantically to make the date. I might have known our pleasure would be short lived. The zone supervisor came in and announced he had another job for me! He suggested that I take a week's leave and then start a wandering tour from club to club doing any sort of job from staff assistant to acting club director. It may be a day, week or couple of months in any club as needed.

I would have preferred staying where I was. I had so many plans for the place and still have a lot to do to get it really going. However, ours is not to reason why . . .

The next day he sent word that I was to start leave immediately and report to work next Wednesday. I've been frantic ever since: finishing up, packing, collecting clothes and getting away.

Lord only knows what I'll do with the leave. The kids had company so I couldn't stay with them and, as usual, I'm broke until payday.

John Boland came over to see me off last night. We had dinner. I took him to see the club and then called on a few pubs before he left me at the hotel. He looks very well, has lost tons of weight.

That was the craziest newspaper account I've ever read! We were all having a whirl at Manetta's. I heard the signal, but didn't think anyone else did. We were having a grand time. Shrieks of laughter, slightly pixilated, are the truest part of it.

Well, I had better take advantage of having an "early night" as they say. Also it's damned uncomfortable writing in bed. Give my love to all the kids—especially to you and Biz.

Write soon, NELL

P.S. How is Bill doing? I can hardly wait to hear where he's going. Sure wish he would come here. Mart will be pleased that he saw the family. M.E.

Thursday (4/20)

Well, I've reached one of my spots. The most attractive officers' club. It's a big house, rugs and some of the furniture were left and the balance filled in generously with good utility stuff, fireplaces in every room and millions of enormous windows. God only knows what I'm supposed to be doing. The director is an aloof dame who's evidently waiting for the zone supervisor to clarify my presence.

The town couldn't be more attractive. It is the nicest I've seen. I'm staying with the American staff at the men's club. The most comfortable bed, large room, steam heat and a fireplace. I wouldn't mind staying here but I'm afraid that won't be my lot. I believe I'm headed for a Do'nut dugout!

Best love, NELL

4/21/44
Rose:

As you can figure out, this has been written over a period of time and not much concentration involved. I still don't know what I'm going to do. I'm pinch-hitting here. I think the director is going on leave so I may stay on.

Morty came out here for a day and a half and was a great help in the club. He looks very well and gave an interesting account of his time in Hawaii. I don't know when I'll see him again. I'll probably just float around here doing odds and ends. That's a damned silly promotion, still, it could be worse. I come to the officer's club about 11 or 12 noon and then stay until 12 or 12:30 at night.

I have cleaning and laundry all over England and hope I'll get it all together some day.

Write soon, Best love, NELL

# GETTING READY

Rose Mary Morin
New York City
April 14, 1944

Dear John:

Biz had a grand visit with Anne, Bob and the children last weekend in Arlington. She said the weather was wonderful (80°) and that they had a good time. Bill was there, having taken two weeks leave after graduation from C&GS before returning to West Point. He hopes to get away from there soon. He was enjoying his visit in Washington seeing a lot of old friends.

Bill stopped in Columbus, Ohio, on the way east and spent three days at Martin's. Janet wrote that he followed Mart's instructions to show her a good time and took her out all three evenings. During the day Molly and Patrick kept him pretty busy. Molly wouldn't let him out of her sight and insisted on holding him by both ears so he couldn't pull away while she kissed him. He apparently took her out several times and said everyone on the street stopped to look at her she is such a beauty.

Margaret writes that you are now in her area. Not having given us a new address, I am hoping this will eventually catch up with you. She also said Bill McL. had been promoted again—does that make him a colonel?

I have been reading Quentin Reynolds' book *The Curtain Rises* which Margaret asked me to send her. He mentions so many people that she has mentioned in different letters and several pages before the one he devotes to Molly F. he mentions Gerry Hayes who went to Notre Dame with the McSorleys, etc. Let us know about your new work.

Best of luck and love, ROSE

Martin reported about Bill's visit to Mart's family in Columbus, Ohio.

Lt. Col. Martin J. Morin
41st Armored Inf. 2nd Armored Div.
Somewhere in England
April 17, 1944

Dear Rose:

The most interesting development of late took place, not over here, but in Ohio. Bill visited Janet and the kids. I only hope he enjoyed the stay as much as Janet's letters indicate she and the kids did. I wrote to him while he was at Leavenworth urging him to stop over, but I didn't know what his final decision would be. He was with them for a few days and they hated to see him leave. He took Janet dancing and went out with David and Charlotte. Molly was wild about him—grabbed him by the ears and kissed him, crawled into bed with him and invited him to take a bath with her. Finally Bill said, "Look Molly, how about coming around about April 2, 1960."

He's something! When you see him Rose, tell him he's got a real following in Columbus and that I am most grateful.

Thanks for your Easter-Birthday card. I can hardly believe that I'm actually pushing 40.

The newspaper clipping about the London reunion came as a surprise. Margy told us that a friend of hers, a reporter for the *Chicago Tribune*, had wormed some vital statistics out of her. I scarcely believed that the item would be published, however. The "rockets red glare, the bombs bursting in air" touch must have put it across.

I managed to make a day at the races not long ago. Even though I didn't pick a winner, I got a great kick out of it. Many features of the English setup are quite different from ours. The horses run in a clockwise direction, in addition to the tote there are bookies galore, the tracks are turf and undulate—and there is no public address system.

Spring is upon us, and very lovely it is after the dreary winter. One newspaper observed that the only Easter Parade was the streaming of bombers and fighters across the Channel.

Forgive me for not writing more often. I think of you and Biz continually.

Love, MART

# GETTING READY

On April 18, the Allies launched a 30-hour air offensive over France and Germany.

> Margaret F. Morin
> Field Representative, War Relief
> American Red Cross
> April 19, 1944

Dearest Kids:

I won't be able to write much. Our French teacher is here, full of energy. This one has a glint in her eye, we'll probably learn something.

Racing has started at a few tracks. We have been dying to see some of it, but the system here is most peculiar. You have to be a mental genius to figure out where and when they are running. We are going to a place in the country that Marj knows for this weekend. I'm looking forward to it. Nell's leave was pushed up a week, which disrupted her plans, but I spoke to her on the phone last night it sounded like she had a very gay weekend.

I hate even to think of it, but it seems that the Red Cross did nothing at all about my bedding-roll, which contained all my civilian clothes, spring uniforms, silk blouses, soap, lipsticks, dinner clothes, good underwear, etc., which I couldn't bring on the plane with me from Africa. Therefore, "We have no trace of it." It will take years to amass all that stuff again. The shoe problem is becoming acute. My good uniform shoes that I had never worn were also left behind, as well as my civilian ones. Horrors, I get ill when I think of it.

Did I tell you of Tiley being killed in a plane crash in Italy? Naturally none of us can get over it. We were expecting her here any day. "Little Mac" who is in Cairo must be desolate.

Please write soon.

      Love to you all, MARGY

Rose Mary Morin
New York City
April 20, 1944

Dear John:

A change of address card arrived from Pat Mente the other day so I guess he is on his merry way. I haven't heard from Nance since we received his card and Honey didn't mention that Pat was expecting to leave in her letter last week. Nance had an idea Pat would be going when he finished his tour of teaching, but then when they went to Fort Benning, I doubt she expected he'd be off so soon. I'm sure Honey and the babies will help prevent her worrying too much.

Margaret said you are now in their area but since no one has given us a change of address I'm continuing to write to the old one.

Nell hasn't written since the 17th of March. I expect it is because she has little free time with her club and spends her off days at Margy's. It is nice they can be together so much.

When your training is over and you have a chance to write, let us know how you like your new assignment.

Good luck on the new job and love, ROSE

Margaret F. Morin
Field Representative, War Relief
American Red Cross
April 25, 1944

Dear Rose:

Your letter of the 8th just arrived. It has been so long since I've had any mail that I dropped everything to read it.

You can't possibly imagine such a beautiful country. The flowers, bushes, blossoms, hedges, trees, etc. all make a setting positively magnificent. We are planning to go to a spot near the races next weekend in the hope we'll see Martin.

Rose, I received the black I. Miller shoes. You can't know how thrilled I was. I've attempted to break them in at the office a few hours at a time. That's about all I can take at this point.

Haven't seen John for a few weeks. He's been sent away from here for a time. Nell is on a roving assignment. I'm pretty sure Bill Giblin has decided to take her with us when we go. I have been keeping my fingers crossed.

We all got a kick out of your picture in the mob scene at St. Patrick's. That "old hat and older fur coat" surely looks good to me. What is Biz up to? Why doesn't she write?

We got a letter from George Slaff, a great friend of ours in Italy, who went to Tiley's funeral. It was terribly sad. She is buried in the Army graveyard at Bari, which is on the east coast. He was thoughtful enough to get a wreath of flowers before the funeral and signed them "To Tiley—from Bill, Margaret, Molly and Marjorie."

Take care all of you.

Best love and please write soon again, MARGY

Rose Mary Morin
New York City
April 25, 1944

Dear John:

No news from you in ages. Margaret and Martin have kept us up to date on recent events. Honey wrote the other day that they baptized her baby, Anne Patricia, on Easter Monday at St. Anthony's in Southern Pines. She was to have been christened at the post chapel but there was a Scarlet Fever quarantine.

Pat spoke to them on the telephone Easter and they had a letter from him during the week.

Patsy writes that Tom expects to remain ashore until after the baby comes in July. She describes the new house as "crummy" but she considers herself lucky to have found anything. Friends live several doors away and will be company for Patsy in Tom's absence.

Much love and best of luck, ROSE

Margaret F. Morin
Field Representative, War Relief
American Red Cross
April 27, 1944

Dear Kids:

Enclosed is a set of pictures that were taken on the terrace of Bills' apartment—I should say—penthouse on Christmas morning. The girl with her arm in a sling fell down the stairs at the Municipio.

We are planning another weekend in the country. If the weather holds it should be lovely. Today is Thursday and it is very clear. It's almost too much to expect that this will continue.

I'm in the midst of a limited diet. I've gained five or six pounds. You can see in the pictures that I wasn't "maigre" in Italy and if this continues I'll be back to the Mercy Hurst level—so no bread, potatoes or puddings till I lose ten pounds.

I feel that I'm making some headway with French, although my speaking is halting and completely without a proper accent. However, I read the French newspaper every morning and listen to the French news broadcast as often as possible. I'll just have to brazen out the speaking when the time comes.

I received your Easter card, also Anne and Aunt Mazie's. Thanks all of you.

Best love and write soon, MARGY

May 1944 was classified bridge bombing month because the B-26 Marauders concentrated on river crossings in an effort to seal off Western France from the rest of Europe prior to the D-Day invasion.

Mary Eleanor Morin
American Red Cross Clubs
May 2, 1944

Dearest Rose:

John Dwyer was in to see me Sunday. He is thrilled to be here and looks very well—all sunburned from training. His hair seems very much grayer.

He planned to come over this weekend but I just found out that I'm leaving tomorrow. I may get a day or so off but at the moment the thought of the difficulties involved in travel accommodations throws me—so I don't know where I'll be or what I'll do.

*Next day*

Just had my orders and have today off. Now what to do with it? I had everything packed two weeks ago, but have since dipped into everything so the performance starts all over again. Because of the possibility of going into Marg's work they don't think it is wise for me to be popping around as a relief—so they decided to give me a "Donut Dugout" until the time comes. In that way it will be simpler to relieve me. It's a day club for all ranks of our forces and their "male" guests of other forces. We just give out donuts, coffee and cakes. It is located in a small town not far from one I was stationed in last fall in my first club assignment. They ship the "horrible things" (donuts) from a central kitchen and we only make them when we run out or the supply doesn't show up. Please God, that won't happen often as I'll be on my own and will probably drown in a pan of boiling grease.

I'll write as soon as I get settled in my little Dugout. Best love to all. Be good and take care of yourselves.

Love again, NELL

P.S. You often end your letters with "be good and have fun." That's damned incongruous. M.E.

Martin's division prepared for their role in the coming invasion of France.

Lt. Col. Martin J. Morin
41st Armored Inf. 2nd Armored Div.
Somewhere in England
May 3, 1944

Dear Rose:

I have done more reading during the past week and a half since I don't know when. It started with *How Green Was My Valley* being thrust upon me with a resolve to skim through it just to be polite. Surprisingly, it proved to be most interesting. Mrs. Westwater, my favorite mother-in-law, sent along *A Bell for Adano*, which I happened to be most curious to read because of the Sicilian setting and the reputedly thinly disguised "General Marvin."

I enjoyed it immensely, in spite of the General being most maliciously and unfairly drawn. *Adano* lived for me, it might have been any one of a score of towns I became familiar with last summer.

Incidentally, Mrs. Westwater circumvented the postal regulations by cutting the book in half and mailing it as two parcels. She's wonderful. Before this reading spree, except for Biz's *Vanity Fair*, most of my reading has been devoted to studying French. I have not advanced very far, but it has proved to be, strangely, a pleasant hobby.

Nary a word from John since the March reunion, but both Nell and Margy assured me that he is fine and getting on handsomely. We don't write to each other because the four of us know we can get in touch quickly in case anything urgent arises.

I was amazed by your revelation that Bill had actually won a prize for painting. It's the first I had ever heard of it. I felt certain that he was just joking. I shall have to write Janet and retract my remarks on how gullible she was to believe him.

Last Saturday I managed to get to the races again. Did much better with my bets—almost broke even. Basically, though, it's the spectacle that attracts me. It was a lovely day, a beautiful setting, an interesting crowd—and the horses were superb.

I feel fine, Rose, and things are going along very well.

       Love to you and Biz, MART

P.S. The mail service is apparently improving in both directions. Your last letter arrived in exactly one week.

Rose Mary Morin
New York City
May 3, 1944

Dear John:

I hope this mail is finally catching up with you since we don't have your change of address. Letters from Nell and Margaret arrived Monday and gave us the latest news.

I hope Nell's fly by night existence isn't getting her down. I'm sorry they snatched her out of her club before she had a chance to officiate after the time and effort she spent getting it organized.

The roving assignment sounds rather hectic but they must think she is qualified to do any of the jobs available. At any rate it is giving her a good look at the countryside.

Anne telephoned Thursday that Nunsey had walked for the first time that day. Anne and Bob are thinking of coming up to New York for a purchasing agents convention. It is sometime at the end of this month and they will be here about four days. She thinks she can get a nurse to take over the children.

Bob hasn't heard any more about his commission, but they told him it would be about three months. If he hears anything they'll probably cancel the trip because he feels he shouldn't take the time off if he is going to leave.

Lots of luck and much love, ROSE

Margy described her living conditions.

Margaret F. Morin
Field Representative, War Relief
American Red Cross
May 4, 1944

Dear Kids:

As you can see we are running low on stationery in the office. Paper is very difficult to come by here. Molly had to pay 2 and 6 that is about 50 cents for a roll of toilet tissue.

Oh well, it's war. I talked with Martin this morning after several days of trying to get through to him. He sounded almost monosyllabic, which might have been his official voice. I hope I didn't disturb him at a busy time. He's very well and sends love to everybody.

I'm keeping an eye out for Pat Mente.

Rose, my allotment was to have been changed as of the first of April, but so far there has been no increase in my checks. I'm still getting the $50 a month. Do I have one hundred dollars in the account? If so, would you send it to me in a money order? Things are very expensive here.

The weather has been positively beautiful. The flowers are magnificent. Things are going nicely, except for our landlady who is an old hen. The maid complained to her that we were destroying all her furniture. It isn't true. We have broken two glasses and one plate, there's a hole from a cigarette in the rug, which is really serious, and we broke a plate that the old goat says she had sent from France. Amazingly enough, "Made in England" is plainly written on the back.

Please write soon.

My love to everybody, MARGY

Margaret F. Morin
Field Representative, War Relief
American Red Cross
May 8, 1944

Dear Kids:

I've just come from the most lovely weekend with Bill McLaughlin at a small inn about three miles from his field. The weather turned lovely after a very dull Saturday morning. He looks very well and seems to have the situation well in control.

Rose, since everybody seems to have given up hope of having any of my belongings turn up, I desperately need clothes. The only things I have with me are practically worn out. I need—don't faint—white silk blouses, nightgowns, white doeskin gloves, lipsticks, and a black wool suit.

I get ill when I think of my green suit, and striped suit, untrimmed black coat, blue and black dinner dress, my black nightgown, etc., etc., etc., but there's not a damn thing to do about it all. I'm putting in a claim, which will not cover half of the things that are there, but I'll let you know how it comes out and have the check sent to you.

Fortunately the boys brought my trunk from Italy, which has my summer civilian clothes and cotton uniforms.

I can hear you screaming when you read this, and can quite understand how you must feel. It's impossible to get any clothes here. My spring uniforms are gone too. I'll have to get them from Washington.

Nell called Saturday. She had a letter from Pat Mente and spoke to Martin. John is around somewhere, but hasn't been in for a while. Bill McL. spoke with him and he is well.

Love to you all, MARGY

Rose Mary Morin
New York City
May 9, 1944

Dear John:

From the number of the letter it looks as though you have been gone a year, and it has doubtless been a busy one for you.

Kash Gallagher wrote last week that Alice is in Brisbane. For a long time she had nothing to do but play in the sun of one of the beach resorts but she was recently assigned to a Red Cross unit at a Navy hospital. Doubtless she is happy in having something to do. Jim Gallagher recently got a commission in the Navy which leaves just one of their boys out—Vince who is working at an oil field in the Midwest.

Are you back with your former unit or with a new group? You never have told us about your change of assignment.

Anne and Bob were not able to get a nurse to stay with the children while they came to New York so I offered to go down and stay with them. Anne is afraid it would be deadly for me to be alone with the children, but I don't think I'd mind it. I know enough people in Washington who would come out to visit.

Anne doesn't want me to use my leave if there is a chance of my going out to see Patsy later on, but I think a visit to California in the near future is out of the question.

They haven't yet heard about Bob's commission but are hoping it will come through soon.

Best of luck, much love, ROSE

U.S. Army Air Forces began a campaign of raids against German airfields.

Mary Eleanor Morin
American Red Cross Clubs
May 10, 1944

Dearest Rose:
I think Mary Moriarty's mother will take her leaving pretty badly. With both Mort and Mary being away—it will be hard for her—but she'll get over it—and I can hear her telling "the girls" all about it.

It will be the best thing in the world for Mary. She should try for field director with a medical unit. She might be lucky and be assigned to an outfit that has doctors from New York and make contacts for hospital work when it's all over.

Pat Mente blew in yesterday. He couldn't look better. He hasn't adjusted to the cold yet and was bundled up to the ears. I didn't think it was cold at all, but they had been traveling quite a distance in a jeep. That will freeze your ears off. I hope to see more of him but it isn't likely unless he's moved nearer.

He was going to try to see Mart. I don't think he'll manage to see John, as he is very far away.

You've probably had my letter about being moved. I had been in a grand officer's club for a couple weeks then came here. It's a tiny Donut Dugout in a very picturesque town, not too far from my first club. I live in a spotless hotel with a room with a double bed. The sun comes in the morning and the bath is across the hall. The food is good, too, better than any hotel I've been to in the provinces. And they have white linen napkins! I have an English girl with me and four regular staff. The rest depends on volunteers.

Dulcie is in a Dugout not many miles away—but transportation is difficult. I haven't seen her in ages.

If Mart isn't busy, I may go over to see him Friday.

How's Billy? Is he still at West Point? Tell him to write. I haven't heard from him in ages and ages.

John Dwyer came down for the weekend. He had been on a bike all morning. Claims he climbed a mountain or something. He brought me two pairs of lovely hose and some Coty's Eau de Cologne, not to mention a bottle of rum that we polished off.

Well, I'd better finish and close up. We've been terribly slack today. I don't think we've had a hundred people in all day but tomorrow will probably be a humdinger.

Goodbye now, best of love, NELL

Rose received a note from a surprising source.

THE GEORGE HOTEL (established 1506)
Reading, England
May 12, 1944

Dear Miss Morin:
You will wonder who on earth is writing to you—but Nell stayed here a long time and have now gone to Cheltelham so I promised her a few weeks ago I would write you a letter. I met two of your brothers also and they all seemed

so happy to meet each other. We miss your sister here. She always seemed to be—unruffled—(if you do not know what that means) well, never cross or snappy and every morning a cheery greeting. The day she left she looked so nice in a light blue summer costume and her hair all pretty and wavy as usual.

I see a lot of your boys around. They seem to fall into the new life very well

Last Sunday I went to London. We are only about 30 miles away and visited the *Prisoner of War Exhibition* at St. James Place. You see exactly how the boys live in the huts and the wonderful work they have done is just marvelous—paintings—drawings—knitting—crochet and wood carving, also some wonderful models mostly made out of the Red Cross parcels packing. I feel sorry for them. They must long for home. I spoke to one who returned and he said never a row or a cross word was heard.

This is a nice town and in the summer the river Thames offers many attractions. You must miss your brothers and sisters badly. Your other sister stayed here, but I was ill so I missed her.

Well, goodbye, greetings to you from England.

                Sincerely yours, EDITH RANT

P.S. Also brothers John and Martin and sister Margy visited here.

---

A record of 5,000 Allied bombers raided twelve railway targets and 9 airfields in northern France and Belgium.

    Margaret F. Morin
    Field Representative, War Relief
    American Red Cross
    May 17, 1944

Dear Rose:

I am going to the country Friday—out to the inn by Bill McLaughlin's for a week's leave. This weather has me down, although until this past week there was nothing to complain about. I hope it warms up. The place has wonderful food, the best since I left home, and a good bar, even though the beds aren't too comfortable.

Had dinner and saw a show with John Dwyer, Monday. He had been down to Nell's the weekend before. He looks fine.

Nell saw Pat Mente the other day. She also saw Martin. I have a picture of Tiley and me taken on the terrace of the club in Algiers, which I will send you.

I wrote Mary Sottle in Washington and asked her to send me two spring uniforms. If you get the bill you'll know what it's for. Could you find a hat—beanie type—in either white or powder blue? Pretty please? The enclosed is a publicity picture when I arrive from Naples.

Love, MARGY

On May 18, Monte Cassino fell to Polish troops. Two German armies were defeated and 20,000 prisoners taken. The Benedictine Monastery was demolished.

Mary Eleanor Morin
American Red Cross Clubs
May 17, 1944

Dear Rose and All:

I'm afraid I'll gain tons in this job. It seems to me that all I do is eat. We have lunch at a little place near the club where the meal mostly consists of chips, buttered toast and some kind of spongy cakes. I eat dinner at the hotel and have soup, more potatoes and cheese for dessert. We have meat or fish, too. Tonight we had white fish, very brown and crispy on top, with a cheese and cream sauce. It was delicious. Last night—ox tail. I'm always by myself for dinner and seem to put away more food. It's all I can do to stagger back up the hill to the club.

The worst thing of all, our cook has magic with the donuts. She mixes the batter out of the same stuff we used in Clubmobile but fries them in deep fat in a fish and chips gadget and the result is much more tempting than the machine jobs—so I've taken to eating two or three a day. I must go on a diet tomorrow!

All the candy has come intact, but Rose, I don't think you should send it, because you can't get much at home. We get two bars a week at the PX and seven packs of cigarettes. One bar is English and I always give that to the maids. The other is American and I devour that on my way back from the PX It is all very strange, I can't remember being so fond of candy at home.

I've given up trying to figure out the reasoning behind my assignments. One thing is sure, I've only argued with them once over one and learned my lesson. I got my way and it turned out to be a mess. Since then I'll grumble, but do as they say.

I thought it would be very lonely here. I'm the only American girl in town and I'm in the club from 10 a.m. until 11 or so at night. When I get back to the hotel I just have time for a beer and retire to my room. Everyone feels sorry for me and all the people in the hotel are grand. They buy me drinks and make a great fuss.

I enjoyed my day off last week very much. I set out in the morning in a bus and then was picked up some kids with a jeep and went to see Mart. He got away and we went to a "nearby" town, saw its beautiful cathedral, had dinner and went back to his place. We sat up and drank the bourbon Pat Mente brought him. Pat gave me one too and I meant to take it, but rushed off without it. I'll save it until next time I go.

You should see the "pin-up" Mart has in his room! A little Chinese, done by Patrick at the age of 3 or something. Mart has carried it all around with him. It's getting pretty dog-eared at this point.

Pat Mente came through town one day last week. He looks marvelous We had lunch and then had to dash. I hope I'll get to see him again.

The Red Cross sent a box of pins, so now I'm fixed plus the ones Edith sent. Lord knows, how they vanish but they do. I'll try to hang on to these.

Well, Rose, I'd better end this. Be good and be sure to keep up your weekly letters. I enjoy them more than I can say.

                      Best love, thanks for everything, NELL

Rose finally heard from John.

Rose Mary Morin
New York City
May 17, 1944

Dear John:
Your nice letter came this morning—the first in I don't know how long. You certainly sound busy. Are you going out on some flights or did I misinterpret your expression about "avid reprise"?

A letter from Patsy last week says they moved April 16th. I knew they were planning to move but never thought it would be so soon. They were able to sell their house at a profit ($1,200). Tom is still stationed in San Diego, but has had several temporary assignments in Los Angeles for a week at a time. Other weeks he makes the trip from San Diego to L.A. by train.

Dot wrote the other day. Jane has been promoted to fill the vacancy of the production manager who quit at Boggs & Buhl. It means a nice raise and a lot of responsibility.

Georgie makes his First Holy Communion Sunday the 28th. At this point he thinks he will be a priest or a teaching brother! Eleanor continues to lead her class. George and Eleanor are going to camp in July for two weeks and Jane plans to come to New York for her week's vacation. She will be here with us and it will probably be at the time Biz is on her vacation at the shore so there will be a bed without having to resort to the sofa, as she did last year.

> Best of luck and much love, ROSE

# Chapter 18

## Eyes Front, No Talking

Even though it was almost June, it was cold waiting in the churchyard that Sunday morning. We were lined up in two rows, boys in white suits with short pants and red carnations next to girls in white dresses with lacy veils and bouquets of red roses. I put my Sunday Missal under my arm and shoved my fists into the warmth of my pants pockets – until I heard the rattle of Sister Agnes Vincent's rosary beads behind me.

I looked up to see a finger pointing at me through the black sleeve of her habit. The finger said, "No hands in pockets." I retrieved my hands as Sister weaved through the rows of first communicants, a black crow among white doves.

Our mothers, fathers, brothers, sisters, aunts and uncles drifted into Holy Innocents Church – some looking back to wave or blow kisses.

As the tallest boy, I was at the end of the line next to the tallest girl. We started to move, slowly, no shuffling, eyes straight ahead and NO talking. Four altar boys and Father Keefer fell in behind us as we passed through the vestibule. The altar boys wore white surplices over black cassocks and carried candles with waving flames and a golden incense censer rocking on a chain. Father Keefer wore a bright green chasuble over a pure white alb with a black, three-corner hat with a puffy ball on the top.

The only sounds were soft notes of the organ, squeaks from the censer chain and coughs from the faithful. Then the organ held a high note and the choir erased all earthly sound with, "Sanguis Domini, Domini nostri Jesu Christi . . ."

The boys filed into the two front pews on the right, and the girls the ones on the left. Our knees endured the wooden kneelers until Sister gave us the signal to rise as Father Keefer began Mass.

Later, when Father genuflected at the altar and moved toward the pulpit, Sister gave us the signal to sit – hands crossed, feet together. He read the Epistle and the Gospel and then delivered his sermon.

"You are now soldiers in the Army of Christ," he said. "The world has never needed that Army more than it does now. Your mission is to pray for the priests and nuns and boys and girls and all the people in Europe, China and the Philippines – to keep them safe from the evil of Hirohito, Hitler and Mussolini."

I vowed to pray every day – and to keep studying the profiles of Japanese and German airplanes so I could spot them if they tried to sneak in and bomb us.

The Mass continued. Now the altar boy rang the bells three times and we knew what was coming. We rose and walked slowly, quietly, hands together, the tips of our fingers level with, but not touching, our noses and knelt along the altar rail.

Father Keefer came down to the rail with a large gold chalice filled with the sacred hosts. The altar boy at his side held a wide gold disk under the chins as Father placed a communion wafer – now, we believed, transformed into the body and blood of Christ – on our waiting tongues.

When Father came to me, I closed my eyes and opened my mouth and laid out my tongue. When I felt the wafer on it, I closed my mouth, got up, genuflected, and returned to my pew to pray for my mother, sisters, grandmother and that we beat the Japanese and Germans.

# Chapter 19

## In the Calm

Allied forces defeated the Germans at Monte Cassino in Italy while American and British forces in England secretly prepared for the invasion of France. John and Martin were undoubtedly involved in those preparations – but no one would know it from Martin's letter.

> Lt. Col. Martin J. Morin
> 41st Armored Inf. 2nd Armored Div.
> Somewhere in England
> May 19, 1944
>
> Dear Rose:
> Since I last wrote Nell and Pat have visited me here. As the camp is not one of the garden spots of England this qualifies as a most noteworthy event. Last Friday, Nell put up for the night at the local Red Cross Service Club. We had arranged the rendezvous by phone. The colonel's jeep was made available for the occasion. We drove to a history-steeped town to see the sights and have dinner. On our return, I sneaked her into my room and we talked and talked and talked. I had never realized until after the aforementioned dinner that she was on the English civilian ration, which is very sketchy indeed.

It has not affected her healthy look, however, nor has her present assignment in a veritable forgotten village (she is the sole American resident) undermined her morale. Her buoyant slant is magnificent. As you probably know, she is curator of a "Donut Dugout" recently established for the edification of the troops stationed in that Arcadian area. She has the true "Shangri-La" touch, and I am sure that the enterprise will flourish, as long as she presides.

Even so, we all hope that she will get a quick transfer to the Civilian Relief Section. I drove her back the next morning and visited the Dugout and her hotel.

If she ever writes her memoir, she will be peculiarly qualified to include a chapter on Rural England. She is living at another "Hotel George"—the place is lousy with them. Though not so antique, the hostelry is much cleaner and more attractive in many ways than the one at which she lodged when I visited her at Christmas.

Pat Mente dropped by about ten days ago, and then came through again yesterday and spent the evening with me. I was bowled over when he appeared at my C.P. notwithstanding your saying he would soon be headed in this direction. I hadn't seen him for 2 1/2 years. There's a "soupcon" of premature grayness, otherwise he is as young looking as ever.

He has a very responsible job and is getting it organized like a master. His only lament was that on passing through New York en route he was impounded and couldn't contact you.

He brought me up to date on Nance and Honey, the Louisville scene, and life in the Australian bush. I look forward to another visit early next week.

I'm enclosing for Uncle Dan's benefit an account of the second of the Annual Horse Racing Classics. It is gratifying to know that he is interested. Of the millions of race-goers in the world it has always struck me as strange that practically none will admit to the charm of the sport. The clipping is from the August "Times."

Tell Uncle Dan that they're running at Windsor, Newmarket, Pontrefact and Salisbury—but on a rather unique schedule, about twice every three weeks at each place. The hush-hush policy prohibits my revealing the track I have patronized.

Warmest regards to Aunt Mazie. I'm in the pink, Rose.

Love to you and Biz, MART

Rose Mary Morin
New York City
May 24, 1944

Dear John:

We had a nice note from Pat Mente last week. He said you and Margaret were not located where he could reach you but he had seen Mart and Nell. From all accounts he is finding the weather there cold. He wrote to Nance for a dark green woolen shirt, which they were unable to get in the south as all the Post Exchanges had stored their winter stock for the summer. I found one here for him. From the length of time it has been taking for packages to reach Nell and Margaret, he will be used to the climate by the time it arrives.

I am going down to Anne's this weekend to stay through Wednesday of next week with the children while Anne and Bob come up to New York. Bob gets off work Saturday at noon so I'm trying to get away from here Friday evening so Anne can give me a few instructions before they leave. They will be here until Wednesday afternoon and I'll be back Thursday. A friend of Biz is having them to lunch Sunday and the McKetricks are having them out to dinner one evening. Seeing the nightlife and attending a few of Bob's convention functions should keep them busy.

Hope everything is well with you.

Best of luck and love, ROSE

On this date the Germans retreated from Anzio – and Margaret scored a ride in an ambulance.

Margaret F. Morin
Field Representative, War Relief
American Red Cross
May 25, 1944

Dear Kids:

I went off for a week's leave last Friday—to the inn near Bill McLaughlin's field. I wasn't feeling too peppy and was looking forward to a week of plain and fancy sitting. Bill was very surprised when I called him. He came over each night and we had some fun.

The place still had quite a good cellar—some really fine port and Cognac. I had noticed little bumps forming behind my ears Friday morning and by Sunday they were beginning to be most disagreeable. Sunday night Bill said he'd send a car for me to come see one of their doctors. When I got out of bed after eating a hearty breakfast I happened to look in the mirror and of all things—measles—all over me.

Fortunately, R.A.F. friends of Bill are still staying at the inn and they called Bill who sent a doctor and an ambulance. They turned out to be the German variety, thank Heaven, so since the first few days I've been comparatively comfortable. Where or how I got them, I'll never know. What kills me is spending all that time in Naples running in and out of typhus hospitals and then coming here, living the soft life and contracting measles.

The doctor says I could leave at the end of the week.

I'm going to try to write some extra letters while I'm here. They've given me a thorough going over and can find not one thing the matter except these darned bumps.

My love to all, MARGY

Nell reported that Martin surprised her with a visit and a container of strawberries. He was the first person she had seen wearing the "blue and silver pin." She may have meant, the blue, silver and red pin: the Silver Star.

Mary Eleanor Morin
American Red Cross Clubs
May 28, 1944

Dearest Rose:

I'll take advantage of it being too hot to go to sleep and write. Marty appeared unexpectedly Sunday. It was great to see him. He brought me strawberries. You really can't imagine what a treat they were. I've developed a holy respect for fruit of all kinds. He stayed for dinner that turned out to be very good. We "managed" a few gins and had an extremely pleasant time.

A girl that I came over with, Edna Oxford, is attached to his crowd. She came in unexpectedly Saturday and said I could stay with her any time I came to see Mart. He's the first person I've seen wearing the blue and silver pin. It looks very smart. As usual, everyone at the hotel has taken to him and nothing is too much to ask when he's around.

We are going to have two dances a week. I've been promised a G.I. band (all four pieces)—they have a trumpeter, but no trumpet—and their pianist might have to find something else to do, because our piano hasn't come yet.

All I have to do now is make a poster and tickets—and pray the recreation room will hold at least 50 couples. (I also have to find some girls). There is nothing for the men to do in town: two movie houses with pictures as old as God and pubs crowded but with nothing to drink—so dances with donuts and coffee really help.

I think my mice affair is squelched—I'll know better in the morning. I told some of the boys about the problem so one nice little Alabaman flattened two milk tins and offered to come and nail them over the holes.

I was afraid the management might take a poor view of that, but I brought the tins home anyway. Tonight when I came back to wash, the maid asked what they were for. She'd come in to set her evening trap. I explained and she took to the idea marvelously. When I got back tonight she'd taken away the trap and had the tin nailed down. I think if I were a mouse I might climb under the part near the pipes, but maybe I overestimate the power of a vermino.

Well, Rose, I must close—it's stuffier than anything with the blackouts closed. Give my love to all the family—and write soon.

Love to you and Biz, NELL

On June 1, the first coded message announcing the approaching D-Day invasion was broadcast to the French Resistance.

Margaret F. Morin
Field Representative, War Relief
American Red Cross
June 2, 1944

Dear Kids:

Rose, I got your letter today telling of all the things you have sent me. I can't say how grateful I am for all your struggles. Pat Mente is coming into town tomorrow with two other officers. I'm waiting for a call from him now.

I'm getting a raise beginning the first of June. I've lost money up to now by coming here. The raise was recommended in Italy and all the others down there got it, except me. My salary will be $250 a month. You should be getting the additional amount soon. I think the best thing to do with it is to buy a $37.50 War Bond each month. Would you arrange this for me?

Enjoyed Pat Moore's letter. A great beau of mine, one Relman Morin, is in New Delhi now. I'm going to write Pat to get in touch with him. Relman's nickname is Pat so along with other things they should have a lot in common.

Will write soon again. Hope you enjoyed Washington.

Love, MARGY

P.S. We all got a kick out of the clippings about LaGuardia. I've lost weight since that picture I sent was taken—*Dieu merci!*

In the days leading up to D-Day, John's intelligence section guarded the briefing details 24 hours a day.

Rose Mary Morin
New York City
June 2, 1944

Dear John:

I arrived from Anne's yesterday morning at six, none the worse for wear. I had a grand time with Robin and Nunsey and they were as good as gold. The weather was perfect. It gave us a lot of time out of doors. Nunsey wants to walk all the time and she doesn't care to be held. She falls down but never whimpers, just picks herself up and goes on again. Except for her eyes, I think she looks a lot like our Patsy. Robin looks exactly like that baby picture of Anne, except his head is shaped like Bob's.

Anne and Bob had a good time here. They had dinner at the New York Athletic Club with the McKetricks then a friend of Biz had them for dinner at his penthouse. Saturday evening at the Plaza they ran into a girl who had gone to Mercy Hurst with Anne and whom she had not seen since graduation. They went to the Stork Club. The girl is in the Red Cross in Alabama and was on leave to see her beau, a Navy officer, who was in town for a few days.

Anne's only complaint was that they had such a good time she got no rest before going back to her household duties.

Hope all is well, much love, ROSE

On June 6, John's Bomb Group sent fifty-four B-26 Marauders in the pre-morning darkness to attack enemy coastal batteries a few minutes before American and British assault troops dashed onto the Normandy beaches. No planes were lost.

Mary Eleanor Morin
American Red Cross Clubs
June 6, 1944

Dearest Rose, Biz and All:

Two letters arrived yesterday. I was glad to hear from you, as I'd had no mail for ages. If I'm lucky in getting a ride I'm going over to see Mart this Friday, my day off. I have a bottle of Scotch to take with me. One of the men has been scouting for days to get it for me.

The dance last night was a great success. We put a nice looking crowd of girls together and it was all good fun. All the men had to dance with Elaine and myself in spite of our efforts at providing girls. By the end of the evening I was worn to a nub and have been yawning in people's faces all day today.

Lord knows what will happen Thursday. We still haven't an orchestra and the men have been after me for tickets all day. It sure is marvelous to be young!

I've never seen the dancing that went on. Jitterbugging is mild by contrast—and me strictly of the old slow-glide school!

June 12, 1944

No matter how I plan I never seem to finish a letter in less than two weeks. Spoke to our John on the phone tonight. I'd love to see him and hope it can be arranged. My plans to see Mart failed because we were busy at the club and I couldn't get away.

Saturday was the opening of Salute the Soldier week in this little town. The hotel where I live had a reception for all the town and county notables and invited me. It really was a good party. The local Lady Member of Parliament greeted me enthusiastically about how smartly dressed the Red Cross and our women's forces are—and there I was in a uniform that has had coffee spilled all over it at one time or another.

    I don't know what news you all get at home. Probably the same as we do in *Stars and Stripes*. It sounds good and I hope it really is. Lord knows when, if ever, I'll be moved.

Best love to you, Biz and all, NELL

# Chapter 20

## D-Day on Pritchard Street

It was a bright blue-sky summer morning and I was sitting on the glider on the front porch. Mother had gone to work and Nellie and I were enjoying the first days of summer vacation. Suddenly the screen door burst open and Jane announced, "It started. The invasion. Started."

I didn't know what she was talking about, but it sounded like I should have.

"Oh, I bet Father. And Uncle Martin," she went on, blurting sentence fragments. "Come in, listen, on the radio."

Grandmother was sitting and looking at the radio as a voice from behind the orange light was saying, *"A landing was made this morning on the coast of France by troops of the Allied expeditionary force."*

Grandmother got up from her chair, shook her head and said, "Well, God bless them and keep them, is all I can say."

She returned to her kitchen and I took her place in front of the orange light. The announcer said, *"That was General Dwight David Eisenhower, Supreme Commander of the Allied Forces, announcing that the invasion of France has begun."*

Jane said that the invasion is how we would win the war and that she is absolutely certain Father and Uncle Martin are involved in it.

Later that morning, Frankie and Dickie came up to our porch and we listened to the radio. Grandmother came out with a pitcher of lemonade and a plate of oatmeal cookies.

We drained the pitcher and stuffed the surviving cookies into our pockets and invaded the woods below Dickie's house.

Our invasion ended when it was time for our afternoon radio programs. I went home to listen to my favorites, *Jack Armstrong* and *Tennessee Jed*. Then, as always, the grown-ups took over the radio to listen to *Gabriel Heatter and the News*. I lived for the day when Gabriel Heatter would come on the radio and announce, "This is my last news broadcast, the war is over."

I reasoned that when the war was over, there'd be no more news to report and I'd have the radio to myself.

That night, after Mother came home from work, Jane called Aunt Rose long-distance to ask if she knew if Father and Uncle Martin were involved. Aunt Rose told Jane that she believed John and Uncle Martin were in on the planning, but didn't know if either one was in the invasion force.

# Chapter 21

## In My Mind and Prayers

John's Bomb Group continued to attack road junctions, bridges and marshalling yards to separate the invasion area from the rest of France.

> Rose Mary Morin
> New York City
> June 7, 1944
>
> Dear John:
> Well, the news of the invasion was a great shock when I first heard of it on my way to work yesterday, and all of you were in my mind and prayers all day and still are. You must be very happy to be on hand for such a wonderful undertaking. Of course, everyone here is proud and envious of those members of the family who are taking part. Martin having been in Sicily was doubtless among the early arrivals—I do hope he came through safely. You can be sure there was a shortage of newspapers yesterday as everyone wanted to read every bit of news and all workable radios were turning out the news broadcast all night long.
>
> I went over to see Mrs. Bolger and Mrs. Morrison about 8:30 so I missed the subsequent broadcasts, as their radio was out of order. I brought pictures of the two reunions as well as some of Patsy and Paul and Anne's children.

They were unanimous in saying the children are all Morins! I agree that Robin and Nunsey look more like us than the Browns, but I think Paul favors the Hansons so far.

I don't know if you are in a spot to come in contact with any of the officers from the 359th Fighter Group, but a good friend of the Froehlich family (where I visit almost every weekend) has that address, Major Robert Wallace. I met him a few times at parties in Glen Ridge. Maybe you'll run into him some day.

Biz is looking forward to her first visit to their seaside cottage this weekend. The other girls went last week but she couldn't make it.

Best of luck and much love, ROSE

On the night of June 13, the German secret weapon, the V-1 "buzz bomb," was used for the first time. Before the war was over more than nine thousand "buzz bombs" would be launched against England.

Rose Mary Morin
New York City
June 14, 1944

Dear John:

The enclosed copies received since the news of the invasion are both interesting and reassuring even though they were written beforehand. I suppose we won't be having any mail for a while now.

I had a long letter from Jane the other day, the first in months. They have had no word from you since March and with news of the invasion were worried. I think you should write her from time to time even if there may be a delay in her replies due to your change of address.

She made an "A" in her course at Pitt and is thrilled that one of her assignments will be published in the Pitt theme book. She is planning to come to New York next month for her vacation.

Too bad about Margaret's measles. If you went into town the weekend you mentioned in your last letter it is just as well she was away, as she may have passed the germ on to you. Enclosed is the weekly announcement from St. Ignatius Loyola mentioning the anniversary Mass for Mother and giving the Archbishop's prayer for D-Day.

Much love, ROSE

Margaret F. Morin
Field Representative, War Relief
American Red Cross
June 16, 1944

Dear Kids:

I just got your June 3rd letter. The black suit arrived the other day and I think it is very smart.

John has been in town for the past two days. He is looking very well. We've seen two good shows and the last night Ruth Wehle joined us for one of them. Then we went dancing at Manetta's. It turned out to be a very late night—or I should say early morning—sixish! Ruth asked me to stay and help console the boys with some Schenley's bourbon. She's now with Office of War Information as a program manager, much the same work she did with CBS.

Thanks for the pictures. Today I look so messy it seems impossible that I ever had that clean fresh look. I got a card from Anne and Biz from Copacabana. Anne's writing looked a little the worse for wear. George Allen is here as Personal Representative of Norman Davis. He's one of the most amusing men I've ever met. We were all out together the night before last.

I got official notification of my raise—$250 a month beginning the first of June. You got the letter about buying the $37.50 bond a month didn't you? Bill has persuaded me that they are the best investment there is.

I'm off to lunch now. Please all write.

Best love to you all, MARGY

On June 18, a buzz bomb struck the chapel across from Buckingham Palace during Sunday morning services. One hundred and nineteen British soldiers and civilians were killed.

Mary Eleanor Morin
American Red Cross Clubs
June 18, 1944

Dearest Kids:

I feel so pleased with myself and the world in general that I'm bound to come to any minute and discover that something horrible has happened. For the first time in the six weeks that I've had the Donut Dugout, I not only got the weekly report to come out right, but have it in the mail a day ahead of time! To add to that I moved from my little dovecote up in the eaves to a, comparatively speaking, luxurious room. It has French windows with both morning and afternoon sun and a featherbed with a blue silk quilt, pretty chintz curtains and mahogany furniture.

It's all very nice but so comfortable that they'll have more pains than usual getting me up and out in the morning.

Our cleaning woman at the club left Thursday to take a quick trip to Wales. That was bad enough, but Friday her daughter came in to say her Mum had "a severe chill" and wouldn't be in for a week and could she please collect her money. Since then the floors have been getting filthier and filthier. Today the cook threatened to walk out because she couldn't cook on a dirty floor!

Looks like Elaine and I are going to have to make with the brushes and buckets tomorrow. You know my leanings in that direction. Elaine always appears with well-brushed blonde curls, nail polish, two or three bright red roses pinned on the lapel of her uniform and good-looking hose and shoes—in spite of five years of war. So you can bet that it will be a dirtier Monday than usual.

Thursday night they had a very good dance at the hotel. It was my night off and I'd hoped I could get to town but as usual things popped all day and well into the evening, so a very nice sergeant (who was a bookie prewar) and I went to the dance.

Must go now, love to all, NELL

---

The U.S. Army Air Force introduced night bombing by using "Pathfinder" aircraft to drop flares ahead of the bomber force. The tactic made around-the-clock attacks on the enemy possible.

Margaret F. Morin
Field Representative, War Relief
American Red Cross
June 19, 1944

Dear Kids:

I received your letter with the pictures of Anne's kids Saturday. They are wonderful. I was so pleased with Robin's curly hair. All the kids remarked on them and said how much they looked like the Morins.

I suppose you've heard the news about the activity. It isn't nearly as shocking as the papers would have you believe, so don't worry. We are moving to another apartment in a week or so. It's in the same building as Bill Giblin's—he can hold our hands once things get hot.

I had a letter from Washington saying my bedroll turned up in Cairo, Feb. 24th. If you haven't ordered the spring uniforms, or if you can cancel the orders, it would be better. If not, I'm sure that I can sell them here. I am very anxious to have it arrive and it should be here the end of this week. I will let you know when it arrives, and whether there's anything left in it. Three people I know received their luggage empty.

I wore the new suit over the weekend. Everybody liked it. I fixed the black chenille hat so that I think it looks quite smart. Bill G. doesn't. He says I should wear only large hats or none. Please write soon.

Best love to all, MARGY

---

Martin's "Hell on Wheels" 2nd Armored Division landed in Normandy on D-Day plus 6. By June 17, over half a million Allied troops had landed.

Rose Mary Morin
New York City
June 21, 1944

Dear John:

Biz's weekend at her seashore retreat was quite a success and she enjoyed it a lot. They had quite a time on Friday evening getting something to eat on arrival and had to be satisfied with a sandwich but she didn't mind.

They had two beautiful days at the beach and she is all set to go again this weekend. It seems they take turns being cook, shopper and redder-upper and Biz drew the job of cook last week. She wanted to get it over with and it won't come again for five weeks.

We have received all the enclosed mail since Invasion Day—but nothing written since June 7th. I got quite a kick out of the letter from Nell's English friend that arrived last weekend. I guess she doesn't know Nell had moved again by then.

Much love and good luck, ROSE

Mary Eleanor Morin
American Red Cross Clubs
June 25, 1944

Dearest Rose, Biz and All:

It doesn't seem possible that it's June again. The time surely whizzes past. You should see the wonderful roses we have.

I went up to town on my day off this week. Margy and Bill Giblin took me to lunch at the famous officers' mess. It is enormous and the most efficiently run place you can imagine.

Then we saw that crazy Danny Kaye picture, and can't remember when I've enjoyed anything so much. We had dinner at a very good French restaurant in Soho. I ran into many of the kids I'd worked with in Clubmobile and haven't seen since.

Pat Mente was over last night. He looks marvelous and was in wonderful spirits. He had to leave early to get back but thought he might come again next week. I'm sorry to say I haven't taken any glamorous or exciting part in all the goings on to date, but I'd certainly love to be involved.

You shouldn't continue that subscription to *The New Yorker*. I've only received two or three copies. Martin has received all of his. He gave them up and sent a lot to the officers' club I had worked at. They were greatly appreciated, chiefly by me.

Best of love to you, Biz and all.

Love again, NELL

Lt. Col. Martin J. Morin
41st Armored Inf. 2nd Armored Div.
Somewhere in France
June 28, 1944

Dear Rose:

Invasion or no, your letters continue to arrive with beautiful regularity. I have been very remiss in writing to you for the past month, but doubtless you can easily surmise the reason why. We have been on the move over the period, and taking one's pen in hand has been out of the question. That makes your performance all the finer, Rose. Thanks ever so much.

Because so many things happened of late, it's rather maddening not to be able, because of censorship, to give you any of the details.

It's good to be in France again. I've always felt that the European phase of the war could not end until this operation took place. This is the blow that will break the back of German resistance.

For the time being, we are bivouacked on a farm comprising about twenty acres of apple orchard and pastureland. It is a beautiful spot. The owner is so unobtrusive that, although we literally surround his house, I haven't had a chance to subject him to my French. He sent me three eggs at breakfast time yesterday, and I have some ration cigarettes and matches with which I will reciprocate when I see him.

I'm fine, Rose, and hope that you and Biz are too.

Love, MART

Rose Mary Morin
New York City
June 29, 1944

Dear John:

Honey Mente arrived last evening for a short visit in New York. Bob is out at Mitchell Field on some jumping problem today and then is taking leave. Since they have not been away together for 2 1/2 years he obtained some leave to see something of the big city. We arranged reservations for them at a hotel.

Bob loves to hunt and fish so is going to Maine for about four days. He wanted Honey to go along but she thought it would keep her away from the children for too long. He likes to be alone so will probably love being off in the woods with no people around.

Jane's vacation starts July 23 and she plans to arrive here to see if there are any opportunities for work in New York. Boggs & Buhl doesn't pay much and there would be much better chance of advancement here. If she should make a change, she could share our apartment. Hope everything is going OK.

Much love, ROSE

Margaret asked Rose to not believe all that was written in the papers about the war: "Ten to one they're exaggerating."

> Margaret F. Morin
> Field Representative, War Relief
> American Red Cross
> June 30, 1944
>
> Dear Kids:
>
> Yesterday I had a letter from Anne and one from you, Rose. I suppose by now you have received my letter saying that my bedroll has been found in Cairo. I haven't actually received it, and will believe that it's found when I do. I hope that there is something left in it, so many people have received their luggage practically empty.
>
> It would be wonderful if you could go out to Patsy's. If you are short of money, and there is any balance in my account, for Heaven's sake, help yourself. I feel that you're a much better investment than the War Bonds and I'd hate to think of your or Biz eating your hearts out for something when there's money available.
>
> The money for my raise will probably not come for a while, but when it does it will be retroactive to June 1. I've asked you to buy me a $37.50 War Bond with it, but start that only when the extra money begins coming in. I'm quite serious about you using any funds I might have if you decide to go to Patsy's.
>
> I hope my not having written for a time hasn't caused any anxiety. I don't know what the papers or radios are saying, but ten to one they are exaggerating.
>
> Six of us are going away this weekend. I haven't been out of the city since I came back from the hospital. We moved again to the same building as Bill Giblin. It's a very small apartment and since we've been spoiled by so much luxury, it's going to take getting used to.
>
> Nell was in last week. She's as untiring as ever. God knows where she gets the vitality.

Pat Mente sent me two cartons of cigarettes last week. It surely was a windfall as I can't manage on seven packs a week that we're allowed in the PX.

I must close. I'm the only one here this morning for the "advanced" French class and Mme. Viron insists that we'll converse, "perhaps about politics." This is going to be good!

Best love to you both, MARGY

Mary Eleanor Morin
American Red Cross Clubs
July 3, 1944

Dearest Rose:

My friends who are transferring to Clubmobiles keep saying I should go with them, but I'm sure that would be impossible. Anyhow when I go I want to go with Margaret's crowd or the medical unit. The latter is hopeless at this late date. I was offered it at Christmas and I'm sorry now I didn't take it because I'm afraid that I will be lost in the shuffle when Margaret's crowd takes off.

I enjoyed Mart's letter and his impression of my place. I wish headquarters thought as much of my efforts. I didn't know Margaret was ill or in the hospital. If she had let me know I could have gone and seen her very easily.

My teeth situation has been eliminated temporarily. I went to a nearby unit and had two mammoth cavities filled. It was *really* fun going to the dentist this time. One of the sergeants from the base picked me up this morning and deposited me in the dispensary. He introduced me to a Doctor Gallop. After a bit of conversation I learned the doctor had gone to school with Tom Hanson's brother Paul. Afterward the dentist took me to the officers' mess. A very nice Texan sat across from me. I was remarking on the coincidence of meeting a friend of the brother of my brother-in-law and it developed that the Texan knew Tom Hanson in Dallas. Then a lieutenant who had taken me to a dance Saturday night appeared and said there was an officer on the base who was in Martin's outfit and had met Margaret in Sicily. He's sending him to see me.

We're planning a small private 4th of July party if our agent doesn't cross us up on the gin.

Be good and write soon.

Best love to you all, NELL

Rain prevented bomber missions from flying for the first 17 days of July. The English described the weather as the worst in 50 years.

Rose Mary Morin
New York City
July 5, 1944

Dear John:

Honey and Bob stayed in New York until Sunday when Bob left for a fishing trip in Maine. Honey came up to the apartment to remain overnight to take the early train Monday for a stop over in Washington before her return to Southern Pines.

We called Anne Sunday night to tell her Honey's plans and she told us of an accident she had Friday. At the grocery store she put a bottle of beer in the carriage in front of Nunsey and it exploded in her hand. By some miracle the glass scattered in Anne's direction instead of the baby's. She has a cut on her finger and left arm. The sound scared Nunsey but she was unharmed. She didn't like that store in the first place so won't go back.

A letter from Pat Mente describes Martin's mental attitude as excellent before he took off across the channel. Pat has been awarded a citation as a member of MacArthur's General Headquarters in the South West Pacific Area, cited for outstanding performance of duty in the Papuan campaign from July 1942 to January 1943.

He doubts his next citation will come so easily. Now that the rest of his outfit has arrived he is no longer acting company executive officer but back at his old job.

Biz went to the beach Monday afternoon and came back this morning. She said it was wonderful over the Fourth. We who stayed in town were drenched by a sudden downpour.

Love, ROSE

Mary Eleanor Morin
American Red Cross Clubs
July 10, 1944

Dearest Rose, Biz and all:

Your letter of June 22nd arrived today with one from McLennon and one from a friend in France. McLennon is working in N.Y. for Carter Hotels Corp. at the Dixie. He said behavior problems arising from the war kept them on their toes. I can't wait to tell him that as far back as 1933 Jim O'Donnell had to put a dressing bureau in front of his door to save himself from female patrons in that spooky establishment.

I don't think you've had all my letters. I sent a lot of pictures taken at this club and the previous two. I hate to have you send any more things until things are more settled. It's such a risk and the problem of carrying things around isn't easy.

I wrote Bill but haven't heard from him. I'm still waiting for my transfer but expect to continue to do so for some time. It's nerve wracking. Hope I'll be hearing from you soon. Give my best to all at home.

Best love, NELL

British and Canadian forces captured Caen while American divisions surged toward St. Lô.

Rose Mary Morin
New York City
July 11, 1944

Dear John:

I was speaking to Anne on the telephone Friday evening. She called to say that William Basil Mente, Jr. had arrived that day and weighted 7 1/4 pounds. Sybil is going to call him "Basil," something Bill would never stand for in his own case but since she was to have full say in the naming of the baby if it were a boy, I think she will have her way. Honey had planned to leave Washington after the Fourth but Sybil went to the hospital the next day and Honey waited to greet the new member of the family.

Jane is arriving on the 23rd. She has given up the idea of looking for something in New York since they have made her editor of the store magazine!

I'm not sure if she is staying for one or two weeks but if she has two weeks we may even be able to visit Biz at her seashore retreat. I trust everything is going well with you.

Good luck and much love, ROSE

P.S. Nell's birthday is on the 28th in case you are close enough to get in touch with her. Janet had a letter from Mart, written June 15th from France, where they were bivouacked on a beautiful farm, with everything to his liking.

On July 18, American forces reached St. Lô and Martin shared the letter he wrote to his wife, Janet, with Rose and the others.

Lt. Col. Martin J. Morin
41st Armored Inf. 2nd Armored Div.
Somewhere in France
July 17, 1944

Dear Janet:

Right now the Command Post is set up in an abandoned farmhouse. The front lines are just over a rise on the forward slope. From time to time a lot of enemy shelling comes over. We have suffered casualties—they are unavoidable, but are carrying out our mission.

The house was hit the other day. Some slate and the ridge pale were torn off the roof. No one was hurt. The owner came back to collect some clothes for his *cinq enfants*. He is very philosophical about the whole business. One has to be. He gave us permission to tap his private stock, a huge hogshead of *Calvados*, compared to which New Jersey applejack seems as innocent as barley water. We have taken him up to the extent of an occasional small nightcap.

Six very tame rabbits—white, gray and brown—and a couple of cows wander about the premises. A friendly white collie trots in to the office when the shelling picks up. A bed of artichokes and a plot of pansies border our camouflaged latrine. It is a strange affair, war.

The rations are excellent. Ten-in-one they are called—most of the stuff is precooked, but delicious nonetheless. There is a cereal to which one has to add water and stir. It has shredded wheat, Post Toasties, puffed rice and such beat a mile. In addition, we rate an extra coffee ration and oranges every other day. I have been eating like a wolf.

I'm enclosing a clipping from the Columbus paper that has a picture of me with Winston Churchill. It bowled me over. One of our best lieutenants, Ray Earhardt, a Columbus lad, gave it to me.

If you are really enthusiastic about it send Pat to St. Joseph's by all means. Encourage his musical bent and have him take a bit of French, if at all possible. I have been too busy to get postcards for the kids. They must be a couple of wonders from what you say. Tell them I love them dearly.

MART

British troops advanced inland from Caen, France. Jane arrived in New York on vacation.

Rose Mary Morin
New York City
July 18, 1944

Dear John:

Your letter came after I had written to you last week. Many thanks for the check. I know Jane will want to see some shows and although it is not easy these days to get tickets we should be should be able to arrange that she sees a couple. She may also like to go to one or two of the nice eating places.

She will probably be in and out of town like she was last year spending some time with Anne Darr. I think Jack Darr is in the Navy. After I see her Sunday, I'll know more about her plans and will let you know.

Your letter and Nell's arrived on the 12th and then Mart's came a day later. His former colonel (when they organized the 41st) was killed with other officers in a plane crash on Saturday: Maj. Gen. Paul Newgarden who was commander of the 10th Armored. Martin was very fond of him.

I am sending clippings on the tragedy to Janet so she can forward them to Martin at a later date. The general was on his way to a troop review in celebration of the 2nd anniversary of his command. His wife insisted that the review go on as planned and she and the widow of Col. Lawrence who was killed in the same crash attended the review as planned.

Nell certainly seems in a stew about her transfer. I do hope she won't be lost in the shuffle. Tell her that she is doing a good job wherever she is. Also tell her John Dwyer is finding it difficult to shower in his helmet.

Much love and best of luck, ROSE

Nell has been assigned to Red Cross War Relief, the same kind of work as Margaret. On July 20, Hitler survived an assassination attempt.

Margaret F. Morin
Field Representative, War Relief
American Red Cross
July 19, 1944

Dearest Kids:

I'm ashamed for not writing more often lately, but we have been opening new offices for the training program. Every time I have a minute to write all my things are in the wrong places.

Nell's in town. She is officially assigned to our department now. I'm glad it's finally decided.

I have received three packages in the last week. I can't thank you enough for them all. The gowns and blouses are perfect. The beanies are just the thing—they fit well and thanks so much for the pins.

Don't worry about the spring uniforms, I can surely get rid of them here. Incidentally my bedroll has not yet arrived. I'm not counting on it until I see it. I do need shoes badly. It takes three weeks to get heels changed, and I only have the I. Miller numbers and one pair of uniform shoes.

I enjoyed the picture you sent of Anne, Bob and Biz. Nell got the picture from the Stork Club today. It's much better.

John and Pat Mente are in town today. The three of them (including Nell) have a very merry look.

Hold onto your hats. Things have been quite exciting lately. Don't let the reports frighten you. The old saying—"If you have your name on one"—is all that one can hope—that is, not having your name on one. We are all well. Pat spoke with Martin last week and he was fine too.

Happy Birthday Rose and Patsy if this is held up.

Best love to you all, MARGY

On the eve of the American breakout at St. Lô, Martin's visitor suggested the war in Europe may soon be over.

Lt. Col. Martin J. Morin
41st Armored Inf. 2nd Armored Div.
Somewhere in France
July 23, 1944

Dear Rose:

Now it can be told—we arrived on D-Day plus 6. The intervening seven odd weeks have flown by. There have not been any dull moments, although, about half the time we haven't been as actively involved as I had expected. Things will pick up, no doubt.

This has been interrupted by a visit by Morty Simon. He is on a brigade staff. His duties carry him from one end of the zone to the other. He and four men are trouble-shooters in connection with the same specialty he was pursuing in England. I tried to draw him out on how he became an expert in such a complicated field. He was extremely modest in his responses, but I gather that it all started during his hitch in Hawaii.

He was grinning and laughing and looked very fit. He is big and solid, but for some inexplicable reason I had imagined that he'd be gigantic, which of course he isn't at all. As you know, he had seen both Nell and Margy in England, but not John. Morty predicted that the war would be over in Europe quite soon.

He also commented that you were an astounding person by keeping in touch with each of us and keeping all of us in touch with each other. Another way of saying, "Keeping the Morin family together."

Your service, Rose, is invaluable and all of us appreciate how wearing it must be on you. My only regret is that I can't remotely keep up with you. It seems that I manage to get off about one letter to you for every three or four received. This twinge of conscience, however, is outweighed by the pleasure I derive from your letters.

You haven't visited Janet and the kids for going on two years now, if I remember correctly. They would be delighted to have you anytime, you know.

I have had letters from both Nell and John recently. They seem to be carrying on quite well. Nell gave me a pair of swell fleece-lined gloves the last time I saw her, and I have worn them with much comfort many times since.

Yesterday I saw my first American Red Cross Clubmobile in these parts. It was barreling down a road toward the Front. Everyone shouted and waved. The girls looked heavenly.

Happy Birthday, Rose. I hope the war will end so that I may see you before your next one.

Love to you and Biz, MART

## Nell arrived in London to train for her new assignment in War Relief.

Mary Eleanor Morin
American Red Cross
Civilian War Relief
July 23, 1944

Dearest Rose, Biz and all:
This is going to be brief and to the point as this is the only sheet of paper I can find.

I joined the kids last Monday. We have been in a training course since. I'm living in a hotel that is very comfortable but on the expensive side, which brings me to the point of the joke. I'm going to cable for money so I can take care of all my expenses and not get all jammed up in the event of sudden transfer—and also to have some money to spend as it's been a long time since I've been around here and somewhat free to enjoy the place, see some shows, etc.

I don't know how much of a balance I have but whatever it is—unless it doesn't warrant the expense of cabling it, please send it as quickly as possible.

John and Pat were in this week and we had a lot of fun. Pat Mente had some friends with him and a few bottles of Irish whiskey. They just stayed the day but John stayed over two and a half days. He had a room in the hotel where I'm living—in fact the next room.

I'll write more in a few days. Rose, did the war correspondent call you? He took your name and office number and said he would. I don't even know his name and you'll see why if he explains the circumstances of our meeting.

Very best love, NELL

On July the 25, U.S. forces broke out of St. Lô with the support of 1,500 heavy U.S. bombers.

Rose Mary Morin
New York City
July 26, 1944

Dear John:

Well, Jane arrived Sunday morning at 6:30 but had to wait three hours to get her bag and arrived at the apartment about ten. She looks grand and reports all's well at home. Nellie and George have both returned from camp and Nellie had gained four pounds that Jane says she needed. Jane spent most of Sunday afternoon in bed getting some shuteye because she sat up on the trip over.

Monday evening Jane and I went to see *Searching Wind* in which Cornelia Otis Skinner, Dennis King and Barbara O'Neill are stars. It was very good but I would have preferred a good funny musical. Jane, however, wanted to see it. Bess got her a ticket to see *Oklahoma!* at the matinee tomorrow and she is very excited about it.

I hope we can get in another musical before she goes home but she really has a full calendar. The night we went to the theater, Liz McGuire, a girl who went to Trinity was with us, insisted we go down to the Village for a beer before going home.

Jane got quite a kick out of that as well as a visit to "Ralph's" before the show. She went to a party last night with a young man from Pittsburgh. This morning she went riding in Central Park with Anne Darr. Bess was taking a group of them to the Westchester Beach Club for lunch and then Dave Foster is taking them to dinner.

Jane mentioned plans to see Katherine Hepburn in *Dragon Seed* at Radio City. I don't know her other plans except that she has to leave for Pittsburgh on Sunday.

Our Bill telephoned last week—the first we've heard from him since Easter. He wanted me to look for a radio-phonograph for him.

He's very busy at the Point as most of the officers are away so he can't get to town except late in the evening.

Nell cabled yesterday for "her bank balance" so I sent her the available cash immediately. I suppose she is on her way into France any time now since she gave Civilian War Relief American Red Cross as her address, her transfer to Margy's group must have finally gone through. I hope she will like the new work.

Love and much luck, ROSE

In Germany on July 27, Hermann Goering was directed to adapt every aspect of German life to the necessity of total warfare.

Mary Eleanor Morin
American Red Cross
Civilian War Relief
July 27, 1944

Dearest Rose, Biz and All:
Your package, cable and cards from Anne & Patsy arrived between last Wednesday and yesterday. The package is super—the hose are perfectly lovely, also the Clark bars and chewing gum are peachy. The box of Hershey's not only left me speechless but gaining a ton or so in anticipations of chewing them up whole.

Margy, Molly and I had dinner the other night and afterwards passed a scale and bounced on for lack of something better to do—to discover that Margaret weighed 10 stones (140 lbs.) and your proud beauty, 10 stones 7. Margy swears that it was eleven, but that couldn't be. I'd just about decided to sue the doctor who did my physical and, without weighing me, put down 160 lbs.

Having been tied down in clubs for months, it's marvelous to go to restaurants, shows, etc. I've been in a training course for two weeks. It really has been interesting. Margy held forth a couple times and did so most credibly. It's alternately exciting and terrifying—wondering what the new work will be.

Rose Dolan is with us. She is perfectly insane and everyone is crazy about her. Last night Molly, Rose and I left the office and started searching for a nice comfortable pub. We went in and out of several places before finding one we liked, had a couple drinks and decided to go some place different for dinner. We took a cab to a Chinese restaurant thinking we would be otherworldly and alone—only to meet Bill Giblin, Margaret, Marjorie Baumberger and several other people we've been seeing daily for the past two weeks.

However, we had one of the best meals I've had in ages. Rose Dolan says she likes me because I'm the first person she's ever met who talks more than she does.

I've given up on the packages. There's not much good in sending additional stuff now, it will be just that much more to cart around. As for the suit, I'm sure I can get on without it.

We're anxious to hear about Patsy's baby. It would be a fun if she was born tomorrow. Gosh, we're going to have an awful lot of children to set examples for. Maybe it's a good thing that the four of us adopted "careers"!

I'm wondering if Martin received the Scotch I sent him. He's doing better than we are—I haven't seen a fresh egg in weeks.

Best love to you all, NELL

Prime Minister Winston Churchill announced that V-1 "buzz bombs" have killed 4,735, wounded more than 14,000 and destroyed 17,000 homes.

Rose Mary Morin
New York City
August 1, 1944

Dear John:

Well I see by the letters from Nell and Margaret that you and Pat Mente were visiting in London. I hope you had a wonderful time and were not too much disturbed by the local menace. I know Nell must be happy to be back in London with Margy's group. It would seem that Pat has also been to France if he were able to speak to Martin a few weeks ago. The world is so large and the war so extended I marvel at the coincidence of all of you being so near to each other.

I'm sure Jane enjoyed the balance of her trip. She loved *Oklahoma!* Friday evening we did ourselves proud with a lobster dinner. Jane said she had never had one and wanted to try it so we went to the Seafarer and it was excellent. After dinner we took a Fifth Ave. bus from Washington Square up the Drive to 168th Street—the end of the line. It was eleven o'clock, so we had to come back by trolley and the el.

Saturday she saw *One Touch of Venus* with Anne Darr (Bess got the tickets) and that evening she had dinner with them and stayed at their apartment. I gave her the balance of your money to take Anne to lunch and to buy gifts to take to Eleanor and George—the latter had ordered a gun and Eleanor wanted a pinafore. Some friends from Pittsburgh had invited her for dinner and were taking her to a movie before putting her on the train.

Much love and best of luck, ROSE

Martin's 2nd Amored Division went up against the German counter-attack at the village of Avranches south of St. Lô.

# IN MY MIND AND PRAYERS

Mary Eleanor Morin
American Red Cross
Civilian War Relief
August 7, 1944

Dearest Rose, Biz and All:

Rose, I didn't forget your birthday. In fact it was on my mind for several days, but I was in a place where it was impossible to send a message to you. Happy Birthday—anyway. The same to Patsy, because I'm sure the same condition will exist next week.

We finished the course and I didn't feel like striking off to a strange place on my own, so I went back to the town where I had the Donut Dugout. The girls who have the club at a nearby camp asked me to stay with them. They have a little thatched-roof cottage and are nice to be with. I also know several of the men at the camp and it promised to be great fun.

The trip down was hectic. I arrived tired, starving and worn to a nub—only to discover that there was no transportation available. The boy who came to meet me broke the news that we had to walk three miles to the camp! We got a lift about a half-mile from the gate so it wasn't too bad.

Then the organization the girls were concerned with suddenly got moved to another place and took off lock, stock and barrel. They actually took every stick of furniture out of the place. There I was with nothing even to sit on. However I've found a nook in the hotel (which is jammed to capacity for the holiday) in the servant quarters.

It isn't as bad as it sounds—the room is comfortable and the people have been grand to me.

Edna Oxford will be calling you. I told her you would put her up on the davenport if she gets stranded in N.Y. Her father died suddenly and she had to go back to take care of her mother. She felt very bad about it. She served with Mart's crowd and is sorry not to be going on with them.

Margaret spoke to John and made some tentative arrangement for me to visit him on my leave. However, the time was short and I couldn't get a train. I've tried to get him on the phone since, but there is always a long delay and someone screeching behind me to hurry.

I'm anxious to get an assignment, lazy as I am, it seems pointless to just sit around. It seems the more rest I get, the more tired I get.

Hope you and Patsy will have a very, very Happy Birthdays.

Best love to you all, NELL

John's Bomb Group prepared to move to France.

Rose Mary Morin
New York City
August 8, 1944

Dear John:

We arrived home from the beach at midnight Friday—sunburned after four hours in the water and very sorry to come back to the heat of New York. A storm Sunday brought the temperature down to the 80's, and today it's even cooler.

On arrival we found a wire from Tom announcing that Patsy had a baby girl on August 2nd. The baby weighed 7 lb. 5 oz. and both were "swell." There was also a letter from Nance saying she had stopped one day in Washington to see her new grandson, Basil, and had gone on to Pittsburgh to stay with Aunt Jenny and Uncle Bill until Bill Mente's return to Washington.

Janet's mother sent us a clipping from the Columbus paper saying the Army had lifted a two-year veil of secrecy to honor the "Armored Anvil" on which Gen. Bradley's forces have beaten thousands of Rommel's best men. That anvil is the 2nd Armored "Hell on Wheels" Division. This should reach you in time for your birthday—I hope it is a happy one.

Best of luck and much love, ROSE

John's Bomb Group moved to an airstrip outside the little French village of Lessay.

Rose Mary Morin
New York City
August 15, 1944

Dear John:

Patsy wrote last week that they have borrowed my name for the new baby and will call her the full name, Rose Mary. They are doing splendidly and went home from the hospital August 9 (B-day plus 7 as Patsy put it).

Tom returned to duty in Los Angeles the Monday after the young lady arrived, expected to get back by Friday to take them home. He was surprised to find they had been home two days. Out there hospitals are crowded to the doors and don't keep any one that is able to go home.

The heat here has increased in intensity and is continuing. There were three bad fires in the vicinity over the weekend—Luna Park at Coney Island, Palisades Park, and one of the Hoboken docks. Casualties were few, but the financial losses ran into the high figures.

A letter from Pat Mente yesterday told of his recent visit in London with you and the girls. He mentioned just missing a buzz bomb after leaving them at the hotel. He expected to go into France momentarily and was looking forward to seeing Martin and long conversations with him if time allowed.

From what we have been reading in the papers of the speed with which they are moving, there doesn't appear to be any time for conversation.

Biz saw our Bill at lunch on Sunday and said he is fine, but quite thin. He kept the group interested with stories and theories on present affairs.

Much love, ROSE

# Chapter 22

## The Man of the House

The summer was almost over and soon I'd be going back to school to the third grade. Who would be my teacher now? Sister Agnes Vincent was the only teacher I knew in both the first and second grades, and I dreaded getting one I didn't know.

But that turned out to be the least of my worries.

Mother delivered the bad news under the cover of Grandmother's special Sunday roast beef dinner.

The table was covered with the good white tablecloth and silver knives and forks that we used for special holidays or when relatives from New York came to visit.

As "the man of the house," it was my job to do the carving, be it roast beef or turkey. I had learned through past Thanksgivings and Christmases how to hold the roast steady with the big bone-handled fork and slice piece after piece and lay each one down on the serving platter Grandmother or Mother held for me.

"Who wants the end?" Grandmother asked and Nellie said, "I do." Grandmother put the slice on Nellie's plate and passed it on to Mother, who added potatoes, a puffy slice of Yorkshire pudding, asparagus, a spoonful of hollandaise, and ladles of beef juice and passed it to Nellie. And so it went, no one touching a knife or fork until all the dinners were in place.

We then folded our hands and I said, "Bless us O Lord and these thy gifts which we are about to receive from thy bounty through Christ Our Lord, Amen."

Before anyone took a bite, Mother said she had something to tell us. She looked straight at me.

"The landlord has put our house up for sale. We will have to move very soon."

Move? We can't move, I thought.

"We've started searching. Jane thinks the Civic Center area near Forbes Field and St. Paul's Cathedral might have something nice. Aunt Ruth and I are looking in Crafton and Ingram."

I stood up, a piece of roast beef still skewered on my fork and asked, "Why can't we buy our house?"

"We don't have enough money," Mother said.

"What if we just eat hot dogs and baked beans?" I said.

"Even if we did eat only hot dogs and baked beans, we still wouldn't have enough," she said.

I felt tricked – trapped. I stood up and slammed my fork on the table. "I'm not going to move. I'll go live with someone else."

I pounded up the stairs and threw myself on my bed. Now I wanted to go back to school – back to Holy Innocents – with my friends.

Later Mother came up with a plate of roast beef with all the trimmings, wisps of steam floating off it. Her eyes were pink and moist. I sat on the edge of the bed with the plate on my lap and slowly took one bite, then another.

She waited until I was almost finished, then said, "I want to explain why we can't buy the house."

I kept looking at my plate, picking at what remained.

"All the money we have is what I earn at Dravo, what Jane can contribute, and the small amount the Army sends from your father's pay. That's enough to cover our rent and buy food and for things like lunch money, streetcar fare and clothes for school. That's all.

"We have nothing in the bank and no bank would lend us money because we don't have enough wherewithal to pay it back."

I knew she was telling the truth because I watched each month as she sat on the sofa with a pile of bills, her checkbook, a pack of Luckies and a glass of beer worrying over the list of who she couldn't pay that month.

I felt sorry for her and sorry for myself. What would I do without my friends? Where could we live that would be better than Pritchard Street?

# Chapter 23

## Pushing On

General Eisenhower moved his command headquarters from England to France for the Allied invasion of southern France on August 15. John's Bomb Group also relocated and came under attack by a scourge of bees and flies, making eating a meal practically impossible.

>Rose Mary Morin
>New York City
>August 22, 1944
>
>Dear John:
>
>This will hardly reach you on time to say "Happy Birthday" but I hope you will have one anyway. It has been an awfully long time since we have had any word from you, but I take it to mean you are too busy with your work to write.
>
>Jane sent me a lovely pair of white gloves and enclosed with it the attached card that she designed herself. Clever child you have there. She seems completely interested in the field of advertising and should be a great success.
>
>The weather has changed and has been really delightful since the weekend. The heat lasted for nine days whereas in Washington the heat would go on for much longer.

I told you last week that Pat Mente had written about the visit to London before he left for France. I loved the story of his whistling at the waiter. Was it at Manetta's? It certainly must have caused a stir and Pat was having too good a time to be bothered by conventions. I haven't seen his outfit mentioned in any of the reports as yet.

No doubt you have received a letter from Pittsburgh Plate Glass telling of their post-war plans for employees in the service. A copy was sent to 1726 Mass. Ave. Washington, D.C. addressed to Mary Jane Morin, so I forwarded it to Jane.

Best of luck and much love, ROSE

As American, British and Free-French forces approached Paris, enemy strong points, such as the occupied seaport of Brest, were the focus of John's 383rd Bomb Group.

Mary Eleanor Morin
American Red Cross
Civilian War Relief
August 23, 1944

Dearest Rose:

I'm afraid I haven't been very good about writing. There is too much excitement to settle down to do anything. We were thrilled to hear about Rose Mary. I'd love to see her. Paul sounds like quite a bundle of energy. They must both be very sweet and completely absorb all of Patsy's time.

I met Rose Dolan and Molly for lunch yesterday. They brought the package with the gown. It is grand. Thanks a million, Rose, I can't wait to wear it. Molly and Rose raved about it. If I take to living in sin you'll be at the root of it all.

I've had a couple of letters recently from Bill and a snapshot that I was happy to have but it doesn't do him justice. He sounds in very good spirits. I wish they'd send him over.

A good friend of mine arrived back unexpectedly from France day before yesterday. He brought me a bottle of Scotch as a belated birthday present. We had a good dinner at Manetta's and then we packed my bedding roll—consuming the Scotch meanwhile. The bedroll is as big as the side of a house, but should be comfortable if I get the blamed thing unrolled.

We expect to use them all the time and not just carry them around as I've been doing all these months. I put pounds of "DDT" powder in it and plan to cover myself with it before taking off.

Margy is taking driving lessons and doing very well. I started but discontinued the same day. I didn't even touch the wheel and figured I couldn't learn enough in two or three days to have it count. Maybe I'll get another chance later on. We are all hoping we'll get going soon.

This past month has seemed an eternity. We have been safe from the buzz bombs and I hope will continue to be. They certainly are devilish things.

Very best love to all, NELL

On August 25, Paris was liberated.

Rose Mary Morin
New York City
August 30, 1944

Dear John:

I keep wondering if Margaret and Nell have gone into France. The account of the victory parade in Paris yesterday was wonderful and brought back to memory so many familiar scenes of the long, long ago.

Sunday evening the Flanagans asked me to stop by the Pennsylvania station to pick up their reservations to Cincinnati. I had asked the ticket man about the reservations when several officers asked if they could interrupt as they were anxious to catch the Pittsburgh train leaving in a matter of minutes. They turned out to be four A.A.F. boys back on leave after 22 months and were most anxious to be on their way home. They were from around Cincinnati and Columbus. Two were able to get reservations on the 10:35 and the other two would try for the 11:40. They were certainly nice looking boys and unanimous that London was a good place to get away from these days.

How do you manage to get in there so frequently? Or was it just luck that you saw the girls so soon after your July visit with Pat Mente?

Keep safe—much love, ROSE

In the first week of September, the cities of Verdun, Antwerp and Brussels were liberated.

Rose Mary Morin
New York City
September 5, 1944

Dear John:

Nell's enclosed letter would indicate she was getting ready to take off momentarily. I know both Nell and Margy must be on pins and needles in anticipation of going into France. Newspaper accounts mentioned last week that American Red Cross headquarters were opened in Paris. That may be where they are by now.

We had a very quiet Labor Day. Our office was open until five as usual and we managed to keep busy. In the evening I went down to see the Moriartys before they left on their trip to West Hampton this morning. Biz went to the beach Friday night and came home about midnight of Labor Day. She said it was very nice. They have two more weekends in their cottage.

I read in the paper last week that a lieutenant colonel that was in one of the armored regiments in Martin's outfit was among the first to enter Verdun so the fair-haired boy must be in that general location. I do hope he is getting along all right. I guess Pat Mente is also in the same vicinity.

Bob Brown hasn't heard from his draft board since the company requested deferment was up in July, so Anne and Bob don't know what plans to make about moving. The house in Arlington hasn't met their expectations and they are anxious to go back to an apartment if they can find one. I doubt Bob will be called since he is thirty, in a war industry, and a pre-Pearl Harbor father.

Hope all is going well with you and the rest of the gang.

Keep safe, much love, ROSE

Cousin Alvin "Pat" Mente delivered a front-line report of the advancing American armies and described the hard living conditions with an armored division on the move.

> Lt. Col. Alvin L. Mente, Jr.
> CCA 7th Armored Division
> September 6, 1944
>
> Dear Rose:
>
> Your letters have been coming through with such speed that it's nothing short of phenomenal, and they have arrived at the most opportune time—just when our morale has been lowest. The effect has been great.
>
> We have been in contact with the enemy for three weeks and have been having a merry time chasing him, rather pushing him all over France. In fact, spearheading General Patton's Army has been our job for the last two weeks. We have had the last two days resting and catching up with ourselves. Two changes in our staff were made. I was switched to exec. of C.C.A. and the officer there became G-3. He was a friend of Billy's having attended Leavenworth with him. No reason was given for the change but I welcomed it. In two weeks I had four nights' sleep. I was practically out of my mind writing orders, directing operations—Lord what a relief. Also the chief of staff was changed so if we were socked we both got it. However, the division has been cited twice for our efforts.
>
> During the last day and a half I've slept nearly eighteen hours, had a haircut, eaten my first hot meal in Lord knows how long. Also I had a hot shower, the first hot bath in over a month. I've bathed out of my helmet and once in an icy brook but I feel almost new again, clean clothes and all. Last night we had a Red Cross donut wagon call on us—the first of those we've seen. And this is the piece de resistance—every one of us were issued a bottle of captured German Cognac—not bad, eh?
>
> Where are we? Well, remember the apartment you lived in when you first moved to Washington—well we are 30 miles east of there. Next time I write it will be from Germany—I hope soon.
>
> We have lost a lot of people but our tank columns have been moving so fast they hardly have time to get a good punch at them. We've been hit hard

once or three times, got some good artillery fire, sniper and machine gun fire quite regularly. I've never been close to it—except occasionally. Now, however, my new job brings me up into the thick of it—something I prefer a million times to being G-3.

Can't actually say when it will be over, but I'd guess about mid October—say the 22nd as a wild guess.

Love to you and Biz, PAT

U.S. troops reached the heavily fortified Siegfried Line and crossed over into Germany.

Margaret F. Morin
American Red Cross
Civilian War Relief
Continental Headquarters
September 13, 1944

Dearest Kids:

I arrived here the day before yesterday. What a trip—everything from luxury liners to tents, to bare rooms, etc. It was very interesting, however, and a beautiful chance to see the country. I didn't tell you I was learning to drive. All our cars are military and I learned on a truck chassis. I drove part of the way from the beach, and into the city. I'm very pleased with myself. However, after an attempt in this bicycle traffic, I've decided to take it in easy stages.

I'm assigned to the city and have seven people on my staff. Everything that I've heard about the place is true. I expected to be disappointed, because all of our people who have been here before had raved so, but I take it all as gospel truth, just being here these few days.

Nell is assigned to one of the army groups. She should be on her way now. She was in town the first night and loved it. I'm glad that she had the chance before she went off.

Eva Dahlgren arrived. She went off with an army group also, as did Rose Dolan. So much has happened since my last letter that I can't begin to write about it. Most of it can't be told anyway, however I shan't forget it and Nell and I can collaborate when we get home.

Things are in pretty good condition here compared with some of the other places we've been. There is not much food, but the people aren't starving. We are not allowed to eat in civilian restaurants. A few people have and the prices are exorbitant. Our mess is now on C-rations, so I'm not too worried about the few extra pounds I'm carrying around.

Our general supervisor just came in and said that all the people were on their way, which is a great relief to all. Nell is going to be with the same army as Pat. And Lee the supervisor says that there's a big reception planned for them, with "Blood and Guts" presiding. I probably won't see her for some time, until things quiet down and she can get back here, or I can make it over there.

I can't tell you how pleased we are that we are finally in operation again. My assignment is super and Nell was very pleased with hers, so all goes well.

Will write soon again, MARGY

John's Bomb Group shifted its bombing to support the ground battle along and behind the Siegfried Line, Germany's last-ditch effort to protect its homeland.

Rose Mary Morin
New York City
September 13, 1944

Dear John:

A card from Mrs. Westwater says that Janet had a V-mail from Martin on September 8th saying things are moving at a terrific rate since July 25th and that his outfit has been continuously in the thick of it—and still are. He says they will probably remain so for some time, but it suits him if it will bring the war in Europe to an end. I'm glad he had a chance to write.

Bob Brown was in New York Friday on business (in Brooklyn). He called when he arrived at eleven in the morning and came to the office on the completion of his mission. We met Biz at the Stork Club and when she left to catch the train for her weekend in Connecticut, Bob and I went to the Sea Fare for a delicious fish dinner. He took the 9:30 p.m. train back to Washington. Anne had wanted to come along but couldn't get anyone to take care of the children. He told some cute stories about Nunsey and Robin.

Among them was one about buying new brown oxfords for Robin—he has always worn white high shoes. He thought they were wonderful because "they were just like Daddy's." Bob said he was a little taken back when he heard what they cost, but the next morning decided he wouldn't have minded if they cost $150 because when he went into the children's room to see them, there was Robin sound asleep with the new shoes on.

Bob says both the children get along famously together. Nunsey takes a few hard knocks because Robin doesn't realize she is a little younger than he is, but she is able to take care of herself and never misses an opportunity to get back at Robin with a taste of his own medicine.

Patsy writes that they baptized Rose Mary last Monday, Tom held the baby as Godfather in Martin's place and she slept peacefully through it all. The dress fit her better than it did Paul because she was a little younger at the time.

Bob also told us the newspaper reported that William Hoaks, the farmer at Marion's Virginia farm, was killed accidentally by his eleven-year-old son while they were out hunting.

It will be a great loss to his family and to Marion. I doubt she will be able to replace him at least until the war is over.

Hope all is going well with you. Take care of yourself.

Best of luck, much love, ROSE

John's Bomb Group moved to an airfield in Chartres, France. Then on September 21, British and American forces launched Operation Market Garden, the biggest airborne operation ever attempted.

Mary Eleanor Morin
American Red Cross
Civilian War Relief
September 19, 1944

Dear Rose, Biz and All:
And I do mean all. At the rate we are going it will never be possible for me to write more than one letter a month. There are either too many people

around, or there isn't any light, or no ink in the fountain pen, or typewriter under a lot of foot lockers or just too much to see and digest to concentrate on writing. I've wished a million times that you were all here. You'd love it. From beginning to this point we have had a wonderful time, seen more things, and been so many places that if my memory doesn't fail, I'll take a year to tell you about it.

If our particular group doesn't settle before long and organize some costumes to wear besides these beat up battle dresses, G.I. shoes and assorted layers of dirt we will wind up in a refugee camp ourselves.

We left England thinking that we'd wear the battle dress for about four days at most and I give you my word, I haven't had it off for two and a half weeks. We've even slept in them several nights!

The sight of a bathtub with hot water and some of Biz's bubbles brings me right to the door of Section 8. Helmets are fine and dandy tucked in the car, but as a bathtub or headgear leave me with goose flesh or staggering under the weight of one.

I thought I'd be catching up to Mart, but discovered that I'm with the wrong team. However, I'm very apt to see Pat at any moment because he is not very far from where we are.

We've stayed in all kinds of places, tents, houses, cars, all types of hotels (read Bob Hope's book *I Never Left Home* for the best description of a place we stayed at for a couple of nights), one abandoned seminary, and yesterday we had got set up in a lovely Chateau, replete with swimming pool, when the Army decided someone who outranks us—a little—wanted it for his HQ.

We are in a little house now and have made it very comfortable. I never thought I'd get to the point where I could really sleep and be comfortable in a sleeping bag, but my little canvas cot and cocoon last night felt as good as any Simmons I've ever rested on. We either prepare our own K rations or get some hotel to do it for us. Believe me they do a good job. So we have nothing to complain about on that score.

If Anne doesn't want my black coat, you may as well send it as it is going to be darned cold in these parts in a few weeks. Is it hard to get Nescafe?

If not, please send some of that too. I've been scrounging it from Molly and Barbara Howard and feel that I'd better get around to paying them back.

Your cigarettes came a couple weeks ago. They were sure appreciated. We have difficulty getting them now, so any you can send will be appreciated even more.

Give everyone my love and please have them write.

With all my love, NELL

Mary Eleanor Morin
American Red Cross
Civilian War Relief
Received September 20, 1944

Dearest Rose, Biz and All:
Much as I hate this lousy paper I must use it since there is nothing else available. I'm writing with someone else's pen, leaning the paper on a mess kit, sitting on a cot under a nice wet canvas, and it's raining like Niagara outside.

Maybe Father was right in discouraging Margy's and mine wild desire to go off to camp. We've lived in one for several days now. By the most remarkable coincidence, we met John Dwyer the second day here! Molly and I hitched a ride to go sightseeing and John spotted us driving through the main street of a nearby town. We stayed and had dinner with him that night and Margy, another gal, Molly and one of the officers who is putting us up temporarily went in the next day for lunch and had a gala time all day and evening.

Yesterday Molly and myself went to see General Roosevelt's grave.

Our vehicles have finally caught up to us so we will be taking off almost immediately. We are all mad with curiosity to know where we will eventually be assigned. The next few days will disclose that. Margaret is a supervisor and will be at our headquarters. I'll be some place in the field. Molly will be at headquarters, too. Eva caught up to us in time to come along. We are all fine and have had a marvelous time. I plan to wear my black chiffon gown my first night in Paris.

Best love to all at home, NELL

Operation Market Garden, the Allied effort to enter Germany through Holland, wasn't going well. One retreating British force was down to a handful of men and no ammunition. Its last radio message was, "Out of ammo, God save the king."

> Rose Mary Morin
> New York City
> September 21, 1944

Dear John:

I thought you would like the latest news on Nell and Pat Mente as per enclosures. Isn't it strange about Nell running into John Dwyer first thing?

Alvin's experiences sound anything but pleasant, so I guess Mart's are the same. Janet had a letter written on Sept. 5th from Martin sending a kiss to Molly for her fourth birthday, Sept. 15th, and in which he said they are rolling along since July 25th without respite and that his "fate is in the hands of Providence."

He also mentioned wanting razor blades and warm gloves for Christmas, having lost the gloves Nell gave him when he was getting ready to leave. Janet was up a tree wondering what to put in his boxes, as he had made no special requests. Neither have you—so I guess you'll have to take just what you get whether you like it or not!

Much love and good luck, ROSE

On September 25, the Allies withdrew from Operation Market Garden in defeat.

> Rose Mary Morin
> New York City
> September 26, 1944

Dear John:

Miss Hall telephoned Friday evening. Biz answered the phone and dropped it like a hot potato when she heard the British accent and insisted that I take the message. When I did start talking, I missed a lot of what Miss Hall had to say as the others had gone on with dinner conversation. However, she did say that she saw you three weeks ago and that you were well and sent your best to all at home.

She said she expected to be back in New York in a month and would get in touch then. She explained that she had only met you before she left and that you were a friend of her sister.

We have had some perfect fall weather since the first day of the season—a bit nippy but clear—a great inducement to get into the outdoors.

Gerry McLaughlin called and said Bill McLaughlin is still in England but that she doesn't have any idea of what kind of work he is doing. I think she has been a little hurt at not hearing from Margaret who used to spend most of her time at the McLaughlin's.

Have you heard anything from the other members of the family since they are in France? Margaret seems to have given up writing—like you of course—but Nell is a little more faithful in that respect. I guess it is a question of having more time and when Margaret knows Nell has written she probably figures that's enough. Her birthday is Oct. 20. She should be able to celebrate in Paris.

Much love, ROSE

Mary Eleanor Morin
American Red Cross
Civilian War Relief
September 30, 1944

Dearest Rose, Biz and All:

Nothing wildly spectacular has happened since I wrote you last week. The group I'm with is still unassigned and being held in reserve. Our boss, George Kulp, was in town to a meeting and reported that the crowd there is very busy. We will very likely go some place this week. I imagine to a refugee camp or some place to help Civil Affairs get set up. The people on other teams have been having a pretty interesting time. We have one man who speaks Russian fluently, but the rest of us are perfectly helpless on that score. However, the Russians are marvelous workers and it doesn't take them long to catch on.

I must report that my French hasn't improved one iota. It is a combination of signs and something that sounds like pig Latin, so you can imagine what the French think of it. I think I told you that we live in a little house that has become quite comfortable. The only furniture we have is our cots, an odd table or so and some utility chairs. We have running water (damned cold). I've become so used to washing and bathing in it, I only barely remember what hot water felt like. The people who owned this house must have had a luxurious tub, shower, john, sink and sitz bath, but someone came along between their occupancy and ours and left only the sink and bath with a queer looking earthenware john. We've made a deal with the Army people in town to have a hot bath in a real tub at their place, but something always comes up to prevent it.

The lights go out at unpredictable hours, but we have candles, storm lamps and flashlights. When told about our light situation, the kids in town sent us an enormous candle, like a Christmas candle you'd see in church. Of course we have mice a dime a dozen. Traps click merrily all through the night.

Barbara swore she saw a mouse on my cot the other morning so now I shine the flashlight in the sleeping bag every night before I dare to climb in. On the subject of sleeping bags, they are very comfortable. I only use one blanket and keep the other one for the snowy, blustery winter that everyone assures us we can expect. We eat in a little hotel not far from the house. We have Army rations that the women there perform miracles with.

This is fine training for a career in pantomime. The French have endeared themselves to me by being patient and not laughing in my face as I try to explain to them what we want to eat.

The other night while I was in the kitchen asking about breakfast the next morning, an officer in the adjoining dining room came to my rescue and got the idea across. He asked a couple of us to join them with some Champagne—as easy to get here as Ruppert's beer is in New York.

It developed that he has the farm next to Marion and Bill's place in Virginia. His name is Al Hinckly and they were pretty good friends. He's had us to their mess for dinner and drinks and we had him over to our place the other night. As the evening wore on and more Champagne and Cognac was polished off, they confided that this was the best time they've had since leaving the States.

Barbara and I are going to a dance at their place tonight.

Tell Bill that Hinckly was very emphatic about being remembered to him.

I'm sending a package to you and want you to distribute the things to the kids. I can't make lots of little packages and there isn't any nice paper available to wrap things in. I don't think they will mind. They are all pretty cheesy as this is not the part of the country to do any shopping in.

Robin and Patrick probably will take one look at the belt buckles and push them in back of the Christmas tree with the remark that Po' Ol' Aunt Nell's had it.

Well, Rosey, it wouldn't be normal if I closed a letter without asking for something so here goes. My shoes have taken a terrific beating so will you send me high heeled black oxfords as often as you see them? I also need some black lined pigskin gloves and some black dress gloves. Also bedroom slippers and moccasins. The latter would be peachy in bright red, but anything you can get will be fine. That's about enough for the moment.

Best of love to all, NELL

The Allies entered Greece as German troops withdrew.

Margaret F. Morin
American Red Cross
Civilian War Relief
Continental Headquarters
October 4, 1944

Dear Kids:

It's been over two weeks since I last wrote. I remember in England when I complained about not having any work to do. Well, these weeks have been hectic. Because of the increasing liberated areas three of my staff have been taken away from me.

It will be more work for all of us, but it's so interesting and such a wonderful city that I really don't care. We had been living in a hotel that has now been taken over for an enlisted men's club, so I had to get busy on an apartment. I found one owned by a Mrs. Tigniani who is now in America with her grandson. It's the nicest place. There's a large sitting room, very nicely decorated and a smaller dining room, then my bedroom, really lovely. And Molly's room—comfortable but not as nice as mine. We moved in ten days ago. The electricity is now on but the apartment has a coal heater so we don't have any hot water or heat.

Nell's supervisor was in last week and says she is fine. She's drawn the extra job of mess officer. I'd love to see her telling the French cooks how to fix Army rations.

I have a fancy driver. She's French but speaks perfect English as she lived in New York for a few years. She married an American, who she is prepared to divorce as soon as the war's over. I haven't attempted to drive the command car in this traffic. It would be mass murder.

The general consensus is we should take vitamin pills here. That tremendous bottle that Bill McDonald gave me was in my bedroll that incidentally I haven't seen yet. Perhaps you could call him at Merck & Co. and ask what type he would recommend and send them to me. It looks like a long cold winter.

Please tell everyone to write. I suppose I don't deserve to receive any mail because I'm so lousy at it myself, but I'll promise to do better.

Love to all, MARGY

Since the beginning of the 383rd Bomb Group stay at Chartres bad weather allowed only 6 of the 26 missions briefed to be flown.

Rose Mary Morin
New York City
October 4, 1944

Dear John:

The biggest news this week seems to be that Bob and Anne are moving to the South West after Christmas. Bob has been given a sales district for his company in Oklahoma, Texas and Louisiana, and he thinks his headquarters will be in Texas. They are both quite excited over the opportunity.

Knowing so many people in Texas and Oklahoma should make it very easy to like once they are settled. The date is not definite yet, but they expect it will be about the first of the year. Anne telephoned and wanted to be sure that Biz and I plan to be with them for Christmas. She likes the idea of being so much nearer to Patsy.

Al Smith passed away this morning after being ill since August. His original illness was announced as heat prostration, but a lot of people think he has not been well since Mrs. Smith passed away, and that the shock hastened his death. I suppose Margy and Nell are still too busy to write their impressions of Paris.

Much love, ROSE

Martin's 2nd Armored Division received some ink in the *New York Times* on October 5 for smashing through German resistance and capturing the French port city of Elboeuf on the Seine river. The division destroyed 97 enemy tanks in the advance.

On October 7, the battle for the German city of Aachen began.

Lt. Col. Alvin L. Mente, Jr.
C.C.A. 7th Armored Division
October 8, 1944
Holland

Dear Rose:
Seems that I have received innumerable letters from you this past month and I've never had time to answer even one of them. Thanks, in particular, for the birthday card.

Many changes have taken place with us since I last wrote you. We were in the vicinity of Metz, France, about three weeks ago in General Patton's Army, since then though we have been changed and are in the same Corps as Martin. We did a lot of traveling since Metz going through Belgium and well into Holland, where we have moved about more than I'd like to, since my little amount of mail always gets side tracked.

First of all the 7th Amored Division (C.C.A. in particular) took Verdun. McConnell was in the 2nd Amored Division, like myself, but he too is now in the 7th A.D.

We never have been close enough to Martin to see him. However, he's making history at the moment. His outfit is fighting and breaking the Siegfried Line north of Aachen. I cannot say more. The newspapers are full of it, and I hope and confidentially feel that by 1 November Martin's outfit will be on the Rhine. That doesn't seem like much after the race through France, but it's different now. These so and so's can certainly fight when they have their backs to the wall—as they do now.

I don't entertain hopes about an early peace because instead of crumbling they seem to fight harder and certainly more fanatically.

Sometime between now and Easter it will end, maybe 1 Nov., Thanksgiving, Christmas, Heaven knows when. After five days under constant artillery fire it seems that it will never end.

Glad to hear Margaret is in Paris. Nell from the letter was near St. Lô if she visited Roosevelt's grave. Nearest we got to Paris was Arpajon and Melun and were there a week before the unit that went in. (Politics we calls it.)

In fact Rose we haven't seen a big town. We went around the big ones while the infantry mopped them up. Verdun's only a small place so is Chateau-Thierry. We're not going to know how to act when we see a big town. Martin's lot is much worse—he has been in France for 60 days longer than we have.

Excuse the writing, the stationery, the composition, etc. Remember us to Biz.

Love, PAT

Mary Eleanor Morin
American Red Cross
Civilian War Relief
October 10, 1944


Dearest Kids:

My correspondence to date has been inadequate. There just isn't time in the day to write. We are up with the birds and from all accounts will beat them to the punch next week. The C.O. of this organization is a nice guy, but a human dynamo type. We started off nice and easy having breakfast at eight, being at work at 8:30. Now it's breakfast at seven and we wind up the day after dinner with a meeting ending at 8:30.

I keep wondering why I was never able to get myself into Catholic Charities before 9:15. I think, unconsciously, I must fear the C.O.'s gun and knife dangling from his waist. Miss Barrett should try that—it wouldn't look too smart on Madison Ave, but it would sure solve lateness problem.

Before I get too involved in this—HAPPY BIRTHDAY, ELIZABETH! I'm ashamed of myself for not doing anything about it—and on time, but suffice to say, things are a trifle more difficult in these parts.

I thought of you, God knows. Did you have a good birthday? I hope you had a bang-up party and enjoyed a few "very dry martinis."

The package I spoke of in my last letter has gone up Salt Creek. I was going to send it off then, but decided to wait until I collected a few more things. When we moved to this place I stuffed everything I had in my barracks bag, including quite a lot of cigarettes. Well, to make a long story longer—and more painful—our house was broken into last week and most of everything in both bags carried off!

One of the soldiers in the office came back before lunch with my sewing box that he'd taken from some kids playing in a lot next to the house. It had been at the bottom of my barracks bag—under all the cigarettes and things. The next day a tiny little boy arrived at the office and said he knew who had done it. A stool pigeon at age six! The C.O. sent me off with the child, our French liaison officer and a gendarme to rout out the culprits.

It turned out to be the kids, and they all got their ears boxed, by the gendarme, their mothers and anybody within striking distance. Cigarettes appeared from every place: under beds, on top of wardrobes, out of cellars, barns and pockets. The balance of them had been sold or given away. The other things were all gone. So tell everyone their Christmas presents are gone. I'm so mad about it, it's taken me so long to accumulate gifts for everyone.

I've been assigned to Civil Affairs that is concerned with displaced persons. We have a number of camps and I'm in charge of supplies, food and clothing. I like it very much and all the people in the office are good to work with. Thank God, because there's nothing else to do in the little town, or no one to do it with.

All the pubs close before we finish our evening meeting, so don't worry about me drinking myself into any early grave.

I'm comfortably settled in my excellent bed no later than eleven and usually earlier. The building we are now living in is the cleanest I've seen anywhere. We generally have electric light and water. There is no running water, but they bring us pitchers of it and we have a basin and washstand arrangement.

They give us hot water in the morning and cold at night. There is a bathroom with tub at the office, the pipe is broken at the moment, but will be repaired soon. Last week, I had my first real bath since leaving England!

I have a heck of a cold now; it may have something to do with being civilized again. Still haven't seen or heard from Pat, but haven't lost hope. The possibility of seeing Mart until it is all over is very slight. Lord only knows when I'll see Marg, Molly and the others.

We have six teams of French girls working with us to do the actual management in the camps. They are mostly very attractive—and the G.I.s are picking up French quickly from them. The girls all seem to get on to English more easily than we do French.

My vocabulary is improving, but courage to utter a sound beyond good morning, thank you, etc., fails me. We have some French doctors all done up in the most beautiful uniforms with wonderful bright red velvet hats. They can't speak a word of English so the French girls have to act as go betweens at meals and when we're together.

They are the politest people I've ever come in contact with—so much bowing, saluting and bounding around to be of the slightest assistance.

I've just finished a clothing survey and it took two interpreters. There is an awfully cute girl in our office that helped us and we found a Russian in one of the camps who speaks French fluently.

Between the English, Americans, French, Russians and assorted nationalities, we are having a wonderful time. One of the G.I.'s in the office, who is less adept than I am at the native tongue, couldn't resist writing to his girl and telling her that he was speaking French habitually.

He nearly had a heart attack in the office the other day when her reply came back that she had started studying French in night school so she'll understand him when he gets home.

How is Mary doing on the knitting of those socks? I have to wear the boots a lot and they are darned uncomfortable without them. Tell her to break the long silence and write—I know she owes me a letter.

Give my best to everyone! Aunt Mazie, Uncle Dan, the Moriartys, and all the others. Be good and write soon.

Best love, NELL

John's 383rd Bomb Group moved to Northern France. Bad weather allowed only two missions during October, but the taxiways and runways still had to be maintained. Morale was never lower.

Margaret F. Morin
American Red Cross
Civilian War Relief
October 13, 1944

Dear Kids:

The mail has been dreadful. I've received one letter since I arrived here—Rose's of Sept. 16th. Nothing before or since for close to seven weeks.

I've been driving in the city the last few days. My nerves are practically shattered, but I'll learn, by Heavens, or else! There are no taxis but the bicycles! Did I tell you I might have a station wagon assigned to me? That will be much easier to drive.

I had about thirty people in last Saturday. It was great fun. The apartment looked lovely. I had it filled with flowers. We served brandy, soda and Champagne.

I'm going on a field trip Sunday or Monday, which will keep me away for four or five days. Everything is going well.

Love to you all, MARGY

P.S. It can't be true that Christmas is so near. Could you send some coffee?

Rose Mary Morin
New York City
October 13, 1944

Dear John:

Marg & Nell's enclosed letters and the article about Mart's division will be interesting to you although you probably have known all along what they are up to.

Janet telephoned last week to say she had a letter from Martin dated Sept. 21st from somewhere in Germany. That made us question if he was with the same army group as Pat Mente, but the enclosed article from the *New York Times* puts him definitely with the First. He wanted a "trolling" coat from Abercrombie-Fitch so we got something of the sort off to him this week. It will be warm as well as waterproof if it ever reaches him.

I asked Bill about Pat's new designation: Executive Officer C.C.A. He said Pat should not feel bad about being transferred from G-3 since it is only due to the new regulations that no one can be a staff officer who has not attended Command and General Staff School. Bill knew Charlie Leidecker who has changed places with Pat.

Tom's brother Paul has been in town since Monday evening and has really entertained Biz and myself royally. We met him at the Hotel Pennsylvania and spent the evening with a few drinks discussing Patsy and her family. He said there is nothing young Paul sees that he cannot imitate. One evening he sat between Tom and Paul on the sofa, reached for a cigarette, tapped it on the table, put it in his mouth, lit a match to the cigarette and took one drag. He put the cigarette down and coughed himself out of the room. They swear no one taught him and Patsy is really ashamed even to mention the incident.

We went to see *One Touch of Venus* Wednesday night then back to the Hotel Pennsylvania for midnight supper and a few dances to Frankie Carl's orchestra. Last night he had dinner at the apartment and took us to see *Catherine Was Great*. Mae West outdid herself in lavish costumes, setting, etc., but I liked the Mary Martin show better even though it has been running a year. Paul is leaving today for home.

Much love and best of luck, ROSE

The German city of Aachen finally fell, the first German city to do so. A total of 2,807 planes dropped 10,000 tons of bombs in the effort.

Mary Eleanor Morin
American Red Cross
Civilian War Relief
October 16, 1944

Dearest Rose, Biz and All:

I still have had no mail since we left England and the possibility of getting any seems slim. It is held at headquarters until our supervisor goes in town for a conference. By now there should be a healthy accumulation and I'm dying to get some.

I had a marvelous piece of news last night. I'd given up all hope of ever seeing Martin until after it was all over, but a major stopped in said Mart's outfit was not far from here. In fact our C.O. goes very near there to our camps and I often go with him. The C.O. promised to take me the first chance he gets.

I had the craziest dream last night. The war was over and the whole family was around in civilian clothes. Anne and Bob had a place in Paris and we were all there. Rose and I were out buying me civilian clothes—that God knows is realistic enough—but you should have seen what we were buying! I was concerned about a *slip*. I picked out material much wilder and funnier than the top of that gypsy housecoat you gave me. It had stripes of flowers in bright red, royal blue, green and yellow and I had picked out a screaming shade of turquoise to edge it. You kept telling me that wouldn't be very practical! Mart and Bill were there, trying to get away from us to go to some shady place. They kept talking in French so we wouldn't get the point, but, clever as we are, we did. Mart kept asking Bill to reassure him that they'd get breakfast! Can you imagine such a dream?

We had a little party Saturday night for the English officers who have been recalled. It was fun in a weird sort of way and of course got out of hand. Everyone made maudlin speeches. We started off with one bottle of Cognac, one of Myrabelle, and eight of Champagne.

That would have been a pretty dignified party of 12 people, but a friend of the English officers appeared with a case of assorted wines, Cointreau, rum and even a bottle of bourbon.

When so much liquor showed up the officers decided that the French lieutenants should come and all the enlisted men. The major who told me about Mart and a couple other officers roamed in thinking it was a cafe. Such a mixture of languages, accents, etc., I've never heard the likes of!

Good-bye for now, best love to all, NELL

Rose Mary Morin
New York City
October 18, 1944

Dear John:

Cousin Kimmy came on Monday evening from Pittsburgh and will be with us until Friday afternoon. She looks marvelous, more and more like Aunt Rene, and she says and does so many things just like her.

It is hard to believe that Blair and Sue are fifteen and twelve years old. They are apparently very good kids and well trained. They go to Sacred Heart school now. Kimmy's former husband is an M.P. and overseas. She and the girls live on Negley Avenue and Aunt Annie and Uncle Eddie have the house on Fifth Avenue. Kimmy was saying Annie had just finished washing down all the walls. It is hard to recall the poor health she used to have several years ago, she is so active now.

Did you know one of the Keisel boys is in the South Pacific with the Marines and the other one is married and has a child?

Kimmy had a whirl in Atlantic City and says the hurricane damage was terrific. They are still pumping water out of some buildings. There is no boardwalk above Heinz Pier or below the President Hotel. Kimmy had Blair in shopping one day and saw Jane in Gimbel's. She said Jane looked wonderful and made a big hit with Blair.

Bill thought he might get a ride down to see us yesterday but we waited until seven thirty before going out to dinner and never heard from him. We had dinner at a Swedish restaurant *Gripsholm* and tonight plan to go to a

Hungarian restaurant for some goulash and Viennese music. Kimmy insists we are her guests and sounds just like Aunt Rene saying it.

                Much Love, ROSE

Mary Eleanor Morin
American Red Cross
Civilian War Relief
October 22, 1944

Dearest Rose, Biz and All:

I don't know where to start. The supervisor showed up on Wednesday with the mail. There was a stack of *New Yorkers* the first I'd received of last year's subscription, a letter from Molly Morin, and one from Jim Kuhn, and yours of 8/30, 9/6, 9/23, and 10/4.

    I've developed a passion for mail and will certainly perish from the face of the earth if I don't get lots and lots of it!

    Before I answer your letters, I want to tell you what just happened. We were all sitting in my office figuring out how many pounds there were in a bushel of potatoes, when we heard a terrific noise that sounded to me like a plane about to crash.

    Everyone rushed out of the office in the street to see. I ran into the back office and held my ears, praying for the millionth time I'd be spared from explaining to people that I wasn't a Red Cross nurse and was no good at fitting pieces of people back together. Then one of the lady lieutenants came to find me. I said to go away that I didn't like to observe plane crashes and she shrieked, "But it's a German!" The sound turned out to be ack-ack.

    On the package situation. I guess it would be simpler to tell you what I've received: A box of candy way back in March or April, a box with mushroom soup and olive oil in May or June, chocolate bars and a box of Lucky Strike Flat Fifties in September, and the nightie last August. I can't think of anything else.

    I went to a party last night where all of our French coworkers hang out. We had to be home at eight o'clock because of the curfew. There are two

French military doctors and they are trying to learn English. All during the dance they insisted on addressing me as American Red Cross, "Danz wiz mee Baybee?" And finally one of them let out a line of English words the like of which I've never heard.

He was very proud of his demonstration, bowed and clicked his heels at me before I could get my breath. I suspect one of the G.I.'s of pulling his leg.

I ran into Bill Davidson the newspaper reporter and he promised to look up Martin when he got to the division. He may also see Pat. If you've read any of the *Yanks*, you have some of his articles. He'll come back through here and let me know how they are. He is interested in our setup and might write that up too.

I went to introduce him to Major Richman and Major Lamet today and for a minute couldn't remember either of their names!

Well, I guess I'd better close for now. I hope I'll be hearing from you soon again.

Best love to you all, NELL

On October 23, the *New York Times* again wrote up Mart's 2nd Armored Division, reporting that "Hard-Boiled Harmon," Major General Ernest T. Harmon, would be returning to the division, having traded in an assignment in Texas to be back at the front.

On October 18, all German men aged 16 to 60 were ordered to become the last-ditch defenders of the Reich. Pat Mente passed on news that Nell was seen in Verdun.

Lt. Col. Alvin L. Mente, Jr.
C.C.A. 7th Armored Division
October 18, 1944

Dear Rose:
Last night I stopped by our rear echelon to pass a little time with some of my friends. They gave me some news that I know will interest you. They said that while they were at Verdun they saw Nell. She saw the 7th Armored Division patch and asked for me. From what I can make out, it was while we were in Metz that would put it about the 10th or 15th of September.

They had no other information to relate. Nell may have been there on business, permanently or just visiting—these dopes failed to ask her. By now she might be anywhere. It's been over a month now.

Haven't seen or heard any news of Martin. They are just south of us, but we never get a chance to see or visit them. I asked a Red Cross doughnut girl to look up Martin the next time she served his unit. I'll probably never see the girl again but if I should I'll immediately inform you.

Holland is the coldest, windiest, wettest place in the world, believe me. I'll be oooh so glad to get into a warm barn and out of the pup tent—it leaks.

Best to Biz.

Love, PAT

Lt. Col. Martin J. Morin
41st Armored Inf. 2nd Armored Div.
Somewhere in Belgium
October 25, 1944

Dear Rose:

As usual it's been too long since I last did this. Why it should be difficult to write from this end I don't know, but for me it is. One would think I was living in the past and future: the former very dim and the latter highly speculative.

To tell the truth there hasn't been too much substance to my existence for the past three or four weeks. I was admitted to the hospital to undergo an urgent major dental overhaul. The job was completed about two weeks later. In the meantime, I have been expecting to be released daily, but so far, no luck. This will end someday soon I hope.

I haven't seen Pat, nor Nell, nor Peg, nor John since leaving England late last spring. It's sort of a madhouse over here, if you get what I mean, still I keep feeling that I'll run into any or all of them any time.

Both Army and Notre Dame seem to have powerhouses this year. If you can possibly manage it, don't miss their clash on the 11th. *Stars and Stripes* keeps all of us well informed on such matters.

Love to you and Biz, Mart

Rose sends John news of Johnny Harris, his former show-business boss. Johnny Harris and John were among the eleven founders of the Variety Club, a show business charity for children.

>Rose Mary Morin
>New York City
>October 25, 1944
>
>Dear John:
>Not much news from this source today, but the enclosed copies from the girls should keep you occupied for a while. They arrived last week after I had written you. Strangely enough Nell's earlier letter of Sept. 30th had arrived much sooner than the enclosed.
>
>The *Colliers* magazine this week has an article illustrated in color about the *Ice Capades*, Johnny Harris's ice show. It gives your old boss quite a buildup. According to the article, Johnny rates his "Ice-capets" higher in precision skating than the "Rockettes" are in precision dancing! Margy and I saw the show year before last and it was quite good—but I'd rather see Sonja Heinie.
>
>Anne writes that their choice of a place to "alight" in Texas will be in or near Dallas or Forth Worth, but they won't decide until they hear where the most housing is available.
>
>Bill telephoned last week. He had quite a bad cold, but did not seem worried about it. He is coming in Saturday of this week for the Army-Duke game that according to the newspapers promises to be a very good game. I think Army is the favorite. We are going with him to the Army-Notre Dame game on November 11th.
>
>What goes on in your part of the world? You haven't written in ages.
>
>                    Best of luck, much love, ROSE

# Chapter 24

## Centre and Craig

Jane and Mother went with the moving truck as Grandmother, Nellie and me swept out the house while waiting for Uncle Charles to pick us up and drive us to the Civic Center, wherever that was.

I was in the enclosed back porch where I had spent hours playing Jane's records on her windup Victrola. My favorites were, "Chattanooga Choo Choo," "Boogie Woogie Bugle Boy" and "Blues in the Night."

Uncle Charles beeped his horn, but I didn't want to go. Then Grandmother yelled for me. Finally, Nellie came running back and yanked me by the arm and said, "Come on, we have to go." I let her drag me through the house and out across the front porch. At the top of the porch stairs, I stopped to take my last look at Mr. Clancy's house, the city steps, Frankie and Dickie's houses and Margie Patterson's father's Ford.

Uncle Charles was in his car facing down the hill. He leaned over to open the front door for me, "C'mon, Georgie, get a move on."

I slumped in the front seat and pulled the door shut, but didn't say anything. Then, as Uncle Charles drove down Pritchard and Kelvin Streets and made a sharp right turn onto Chartiers Avenue, Nellie and Grandmother told Uncle Charles all the good things they'd heard about the new apartment. It was so close to everything. Streetcars outside the front door, restaurants across the street, St. Paul's Cathedral were the Bishop lived, and the schools we would go to, just two blocks away.

Uncle Charles elbowed me as he turned onto the Point Bridge leading to Downtown Pittsburgh. He laughed, trying to sound like he was kidding, and said, "Those city boys are tough, Georgie. You better get some meat on those bones."

By the time we got to the third-floor apartment, the moving men had put all the furniture in place and Jane and Mother were unpacking the glasses and dishes in the kitchen. The kitchen door led to a cement porch and iron fire escapes.

From the porch I could see St. Paul's Cathedral and the University of Pittsburgh's Cathedral of Learning in the distance. They were both black, not light gray like the color of Holy Innocents Church.

Beyond the black spires of St. Paul's, I saw the light stands that bracketed Forbes Field, where the Pittsburgh Pirates played baseball. At night, behind it all, I could see the fiery reflections of the steel mills that lined the shores of the Monongahela River flowing between Oakland and Homestead.

My room was on the other end of the apartment and looked onto the streetcar tracks and Belgian blocks of Centre Avenue – one pair of tracks going up and another coming down. Directly across the street were the Gold Bar, Schwartz's Dry Cleaners, a barbershop, and Hannah's Bar and Grill. Looking right at me from Hannah's roof were two large Pittsburgh Outdoor Advertising billboards. One was for Coca-Cola and other for Camel cigarettes. It showed a soldier wearing a helmet with a rifle slung over his shoulder smoking a cigarette and saying, "I'd walk a mile for a Camel." That was my favorite.

Craig Street crossed Centre Avenue in front of Hannah's. On Centre, under my window, a concrete island in the middle of the street was the streetcar stop.

After dinner Jane asked me to take a walk with her to see our new neighborhood. More than ever, Jane was my big sister. Now she worked in the advertising department of Boggs & Buhl Department Store. She wore a black cape and held her hair back with silver barrettes. With her lipstick and makeup, she looked nothing like the freckled-faced sister I used to know.

Sometimes she had to work on Saturday mornings and would take me with her. She'd clip a big sheet of paper on a drawing board and give me a box of colored pencils to draw with. She also showed me the ads that were going to be in the paper that week. I would look at every page in the newspaper all week until I found the one I saw in her office.

Now she was going to show me the Civic Center. Walking along Craig Street seemed strange and unfamiliar, I never thought I could find my way back. There were houses on one side of the street and apartment buildings on the other side. Streetcars were coming and going both ways. Several cars were stopped at the red lights. We passed a gas station on the corner of Bayard Street and kept going. I thought we'd never get there until I saw St. Paul's Cathedral rising into the early-evening sky. It made Holy Innocents seem very small. We turned the corner on Fifth Avenue and walked past the front entrance of the Cathedral. I looked up at the black spires and could hardly believe I would be going to Mass there from now on.

We walked past the Webster Hall Hotel where men with peaked hats and uniforms opened the trunks of cars and loaded luggage onto shiny brass carts, just like in the movies.

Across the street was the Mellon Institute, surrounded by fat, black stone columns. Pitt's blackened Cathedral of Learning now loomed across the green lawn in front of us. From our back porch the tower seemed large, but looking up at it from the sidewalk, it was gigantic, the tallest building I had ever seen.

We went into the Webster Hall Coffee Shop. Most of the tables were filled with two and three people, talking, drinking coffee and eating. One man sitting alone cut pieces of pie with his fork and slowly delivered them to his mouth without taking his eyes off the folded newspaper he held in his other hand.

We sat at the rectangular counter with stools anchored to the floor and seats that could spin very fast. After I took a couple of twirls, Jane asked me to stop.

The waitress wiped the counter and handed us menus. Jane ordered tea with lemon. I didn't know what to get. Jane said, "Have anything you want."

I looked at the waitress. "Do you have chocolate milk?"

The waitress smiled. "I think we can arrange that. Would you like a piece of coffee cake with that?"

"Yes," Jane said – and then whispered to me, "They're famous for their coffee cake."

Famous coffee cake! I couldn't wait to tell Tommy and Bobby.

It was dark by the time we walked home. I strolled easily along Craig Street with Jane, now feeling that I might get to like this Civic Center, the place that everyone called Oakland.

On Monday, Jane walked Nellie and me to St. Paul's Cathedral Grade School, one of two school buildings across Craig Street from the church. The other was the girls' high school. The convent, where the sisters lived, was in front of the grade school on Craig Street.

As we waited outside the principal's office on the first floor, a nun came sweeping out of a classroom and practically flew past us. I almost fainted. She had an enormous white headpiece and an immense white collar framed by her black, floor-length habit. The sisters at Holy Innocents had little black bonnets on their heads. I wondered how these nuns could even move their heads.

I was in the third grade and Nellie was in the fifth. We had started school at Holy Innocents and were now entering our classes more than a month after school started for the others. I didn't know anyone in the entire school and remembered what Uncle Charles had told me about how tough these city boys would be.

# Chapter 25

## News, News, News

During October John's 383rd Bomb Group made successful daylight missions as well as a number of Pathfinder night attacks.

>Rose Mary Morin
>New York City
>November 2, 1944
>
>Dear John:
>Your letter came last Saturday and we were of course glad to hear from you. Jane had come for the weekend and she got quite a kick out of the letter. She had just told me they had not had any word from you for some time and she was wondering if you had received the cigarette case.
>
>The house in Sheraden was sold and they are now in an apartment at 4514 Center Avenue, corner of Craig Street. Nell and George go to the Cathedral school and all in all it seems a much better arrangement.
>
>Dot gets a ride to work and Jane's trip is about the same as it was from Sheraden. She thinks it is much nicer than a house. Jane decorated one of the bedrooms for her and Eleanor, painted the wall gray, has a dark blue rug on the floor, covered two studio beds with the same shade of blue and

painted a dressing table and other furniture chartreuse green. Oh, yes, she also made blue swags for the windows.

Georgie has a small room to himself and Dot and Mrs. Wilson have the third bedroom. Jane was saying she had tried to impress on George that the bishop was at the Cathedral and she described his different robes, headdress, etc. A few days later he came in all excited—he had seen the bishop—when asked to describe him, he said he was wearing a black hat turned up at the sides with a feather, evidently some Knight Templar!

Jane got in on Saturday morning and we took her along to meet Bill for lunch before he attended the Duke-Army game.

She left Sunday on the Trail Blazer so she would get in to Pittsburgh in enough time to sleep before going to work Monday.

I shall pass your message on to Bill—he doesn't seem to write to anyone. In fact Saturday is the first I've seen him since the night he left to go to school at Ft. Leavenworth.

He is on a nice trip this week. Having been the Production Engineer on the C-69's while in Washington he was invited to fly to Los Angeles in one of the planes on Monday and will come back the end of this week in another of the C-69's on a "maiden flight."

He seemed quite excited over the prospect of his first trip to the coast—flying out in nine hours—and of course seeing Patsy and her family. He was going to surprise her.

He has heard no rumors of any move from the Point and is sure he and the group he attended school with are being "saved" for the Japs. Be sure to write Jane and the kids.

Best of luck and much love, ROSE

P.S. I almost forgot the biggest piece of news—Bess Darr married Dave Foster, hardly a year after her sister Margaret's death. The whole family is quite upset! Dave Jr. is being married Saturday of this week to some girl from Rye who he met in kindergarten. Dot may come over for the wedding.

Margaret F. Morin
American Red Cross
Civilian War Relief
Continental Headquarters
November 3, 1944

Dearest Kids:

Martin and Nell arrived in town a few days ago. We have had a wonderful time. At this point I'm worn to a nub but you'll hear all the details from Martin. I had a very good birthday. I wrote you about my trip through Brittany and Normandy. I arrived back the night before my birthday. There was a dinner party with too much Champagne, flowers, etc.

My mail is the very worst ever. Nell has received much more than I have. However, I'm not giving up hope that it will all catch up. We are in the process of reassignment. Lord knows where I'll end up. I hope I can see some of the forward areas, but can work out of here. We are really comfortable except for the lack of heat, which Martin probably told you about.

How are Patsy, Anne and Billy? You haven't mentioned any news of Biz in your recent letters. I hope you're all well. I'm hoping to get you all Christmas tokens. So far, every time I plan to shop, something comes up to take me somewhere else. I may also need some money. The Bank in England gave me an awful blow by saying I was $70 overdrawn. I haven't had time to check my stubs but if you get a RUSH request, that will be the reason. Everything is exorbitant here. You can't imagine the prices of things.

I must get a monthly report in today. I hate the damned things, but such is life. Will write soon again,

Best love to you all, MARGY

Mary Eleanor Morin
American Red Cross
Civilian War Relief
Continental Headquarters
November 8, 1944

Dearest Rose and Biz:

I had an unexpected and very wonderful trip to Paris last week. It was a complete surprise. The Red Cross man with me had been sick for a couple of weeks and none of the treatment we had around here seemed to help so the C.O. decided he should go in.

Eva had to have new glasses made and pick up some warm clothes, so I got permission to go along for the ride. I ran into some of Marg's friends, found out where she lived and went to stay with her and Molly.

You should see their apartment. It is really lovely. It is in a nice part of the City. They have a small dining room nicely furnished and with an open fireplace. Marg's room is comfortable and pretty. Molly's is sort of a sitting room or den. They have a large sitting room done in soft shades of green with an open fireplace and English furniture. There is a bath and separate W.C. and a nice kitchen. Both bedrooms have fireplaces. The only drawback is they have no heat.

I hope they will be able to get some wood to burn because they can only use a little electric stove and it doesn't begin to heat the place.

Hot or cold, I'd be delighted to spend a good deal of time there. The kids are very blasé about it, but I'm absolutely dazzled.

Paris is the most beautiful city in the whole world. (The world traveler speaks!) I could ride or walk around and just look at it for days on end.

We heard Mass at Notre Dame last Wednesday. Margy drove us to church to add to the excitement of it all. That is the first time I've ever heard Mass with the priest facing the congregation. I was fascinated by the old gentleman who led the priest out and seemed to take over the whole place. He was done up in short pants, white hose, cutaway, and enormous hat with white fur or feathers on it.

We went to the Ritz nearly every day for a drink before lunch and dinner. It was marvelous to sit there and watch the crowd go by. I wouldn't have recognized a soul, but the kids recognized everyone and pointed them out. The ladies all have nice hairdos and are attractively dressed, but the hats are out of this world—simply gargantuan things with feathers, plumes, veils, birds and lord knows what all. It wouldn't surprise you a bit after seeing a few of them if someone staggered by with a Sherman tank balanced aloft.

Margy and Molly had plans for dinner each night and included us. One friend of theirs had asked Margy to dine with him on Tuesday night. She called him first thing in the morning and told him that her sister had arrived in town unexpectedly and would it be all right to bring her along. He said, "Sure thing!" About noon Margy had a friend of his call to say that someone else had shown up to be included!

The friend got on the phone and said: "You know the gal you asked to dinner tonight! Well, her sister, brother, and two cousins from the Free French Resistance have turned up—may she bring them all?"

We went to a small but very good restaurant and had a delicious dinner. All the men were correspondents—and very amusing. Margy's friend was particularly nice.

Toward the end of the evening the restaurant decided we had enough to eat and drink and wanted to hurl us out of the place. We begged and pleaded for another Cognac. The waiter refused, bridled and said it would be pretty expensive, but finally brought us one, "The last!"

Margy's friend made an elaborate and painstaking speech of gratitude in French, to which the waiter replied in English, "Don't mention it!"

Butch had a dinner party at his place another night. He had four bottles of Champagne and a bottle of Scotch, which I appreciated, but it was sort of bringing coals to Newcastle. I think we must have gone through a year's liquor ration.

On the last night we went to a party at the Ritz and from there we went to a party that one of our girls gave in the apartment of her friends who were the proud possessors of a large wood fireplace.

It was meant to be a cocktail party, but went on until 10:30. Nobody was interested in going out for dinner and stayed having martinis and enjoying the fire. I hated to leave the next day to come back, but as someone, whose throat I felt like slitting, said, "C'est la guerre!"

Well, Rosebuddy, I'd better close and get this off. Give my love to all the kids, the McKetricks, Moriartys and all. Have a Happy Thanksgiving!

Very best love to you and all, NELL

P.S. We now have a stove in the day room so I brew up an old fruit tin of water each night and bathe in that. If, in view of post-war planning, you think we should cut expenses to the bone and the four of us facing a life of single and impoverished blessedness, there is one suggestion I can make:

Get a cold water flat. Give up bathing in tubs and try it in the sink. After a few weeks, try it in a basin. What I'm driving at is—you really don't *need* a house with a bathtub.

M.E.

On November 7, President Roosevelt was re-elected for a record fourth term.

Rose Mary Morin
New York City
November 8, 1944

Dear John:

Martin swears to Janet on a stack of bibles that there is nothing wrong with him except that he was hospitalized for a dental overhaul, but it's kind of hard to convince her. However, his letters sound cheerful enough and he is certainly back with his outfit by now.

Election day was most exciting. Our office got an unexpected holiday so I took a tour of the shops to see what there is to buy for Christmas giving. The prices are exorbitant for what they have to offer, but we are lucky to be able to buy anything.

We are having a spell of wonderful fall weather. I hope it keeps up for the game Saturday. Not that I mind sitting in the rain, but it always makes one look so messy, especially if we are to go on someplace for dinner. It should be a good game from all reports.

Best of luck and love, ROSE

Making up for the 26-0 spanking by Notre Dame in 1943, Army's football team trounced the fighting Irish 59-0.

Rose Mary Morin
New York City
November 14, 1944

Dear John:

If you have been to London recently you no doubt received the message Martin left at the hotel for you when he was en route home. He had asked for you in the hope you may be in the vicinity. Then he arrived here last Thursday. I never had such a shock—you could have knocked me over with a feather.

He looks very good, although there are a few more lines in his face than when he left. They removed all but two of his teeth and gave him some fine replacements in the hospital in Belgium. I didn't see a Purple Heart so he sustained no injuries; however, he is wearing the Silver Star and the Bronze for four campaigns. I still can't believe that we have seen him. It was such a complete surprise.

Then he left Friday evening for the Redistribution Center near Columbus, Ohio. He had not notified Janet nor was he sure how much notice he would give her. She is very excitable and he did not want to get her upset in advance—and then be delayed a couple of days.

He will have twenty days at home then to report to G-8 in the War Department, Washington. For how long he doesn't know. He seems to think he will eventually land in the Pacific theater.

On Thursday evening we celebrated with cocktails at the Ambassador and steak dinner at Christ Cella's. We intended to spend Friday at Belmont for the races, but it rained quite hard so we called it off. We met him for early dinner before he took the 7:30 p.m. train for the last leg of his journey.

When he went to Paris to locate Margy, whom did he find sitting in her office waiting for her? Nell! The three of them and their friends had a gala three days. He says the girls look wonderful and seem very healthy and happy. Nell isn't too pleased with her present assignment, but there is promise of a better one any time now.

And now if you can take further shock—Bill was married on October 27. He married Lois Tebbett from Albany who was with him at lunch the day Jane arrived. In fact, they had been married the day before the Duke-Army game and intended to break the news then, but when the crowd descended upon them, they got cold feet. Then, of course, he left the day after the game for Los Angeles and was there a week. We heard nothing further until a letter came from Bill inviting Biz and me to lunch Saturday before the Notre Dame game and news of the wedding.

Lois couldn't be nicer and she's most attractive and they both seem very much in love. She has a three-year-old boy by a previous marriage that ended in divorce so there is quite a tangle as far as religion is concerned. However, they hope to be able to work something out and go through a proper ceremony as soon as possible. They are now living in Bill's (bachelor) apartment at West Point but are hoping to be assigned a house so that the little boy can be with them. The boy is now living with Lois's family in Albany.

Lois is Anne's height and build and quite blond. Bill has told her so much about all of us that she talks as though she has known us for years. The 59-0 Army-Notre Dame game was almost anti-climax compared with all the other excitement of the week, but was wonderful as well. To quote Bill, he lived for that day since he was a plebe.

Best of luck and most love, ROSE

# Chapter 26

## Getcher Paper Here

There was more to Centre and Craig than just the view from my bedroom window or the bars, drugstore and restaurant on the corners.

There was also Wieners. He was a round, bald, tanned little man who ruled the corner newspaper stand with the drive of a Marine drill sergeant. His headquarters was the battered metal stand with a jumbo orange umbrella on the curb in front of Hannah's, on a corner where the streetcars turned.

Yellow-and-black trucks from the *Pittsburgh Press* and red-and-gray ones from the *Sun-Telegraph* backed into Wieners's corner and threw off bales and bales of papers. As soon as a bale hit the ground, Wieners snipped its metal wires and stacked the papers on his stand. All the papers were on the stand ready for action as the trucks pulled away.

Then he loaded up his corps of newsboys and dispatched them to the streetcar islands on Centre and Craig. The boys boarded the streetcars and rode them to the next stop where they hopped on a one coming back. As each boy returned from his foray, Wieners rushed to him with a fresh sheaf of papers.

Throughout the afternoon and evening chants of, "Paper, here, getcher paper here, getcher *Press, Sun-Tele*, paper here," blended with the screech of turning streetcars.

When the war news was extra good or bad Wieners's operation intensified. I was walking home one Saturday afternoon a week or so before Halloween and heard one of Wieners's boys yell, "Extra, extra read all about it, German troops surrender!"

I thought the war was over. I dug my last nickel out of my pocket and got in line to buy a paper. The paperboy could hardly pass out papers and collect nickels fast enough. I ran up to the apartment, two steps at a time, and took the paper to Grandmother in the kitchen, yelling, "The war's over, the war's over."

She wiped her hands on her apron and sat on the couch in the living room to read the news. Then she looked up and smiled, "Well, it's not over yet, but this is very good news."

I sunk in a chair. "It's not over?"

"No," she said. "But the German soldiers are starting to surrender, so maybe it will be over soon."

She handed me the paper and went back to the kitchen. I read the story and felt like returning the paper to Wieners to get my nickel back – but I knew he wouldn't give it to me.

Across Craig Street from Wieners's stand and Hannah's Bar was the Luna Restaurant & Bar. It was a white brick building with blue neon that formed a crescent moon and spelled "LUNA" in cursive letters. Mother said that *luna* meant "moon" in Italian. Inside were polished wooden booths with soft leather seats along the walls. A group of soldiers, sailors and marines huddled at the center of the bar holding tall mugs of beer. They talked loud and laughed a lot. One of the sailors stood back a little from the group and recited, "The cabin boy, the cabin boy, the sneaky little nipper," then lowered his voice so only his friends could hear. When he finished they erupted in laughter. Every time a beer mug was empty, the bartender filled it up from a pitcher of beer on the bar. When the pitcher was empty, the men in civilian clothes on the ends of the bar took turns signaling the bartender to fill it up again.

Our waiter's name was Louie. He was chubby with gray hair and wore a light blue vest and long white apron.

As he handed us our menus, I asked if he had spaghetti and meatballs. He smiled and said, "The best."

My meal came in a silver pot with handles on the side. Louie held the handles with a napkin and tipped the steaming spaghetti and meatballs onto my plate. "Very hot," he said. Mother spread the spaghetti on my plate with a fork.

The first forkful burned my tongue, so I tossed it around inside my mouth and I sucked in air. I continued by blowing on each bite before delivering it home.

When I ordered apple pie for dessert, Mother added, "a la mode." I didn't know what that meant until Louie came back with a wedge of pie and a ball of vanilla ice cream on top that was just starting to melt.

# Chapter 27

## Before the Storm

Another holiday season away from home approached and Margaret, Nell and Rose kept the letters flying over land and sea.

> Margaret F. Morin
> American Red Cross
> Civilian War Relief
> Continental Headquarters
> November 14, 1944

Dearest Kids:

Just today I received your letter of September 23rd with enclosed birthday card. It was very sweet of you and the message was perfect. This was the first birthday that I've really minded.

    I was sorry to hear of your difficulties with cigarettes. This week we get none. All are reserved for combat troops, which as it should be.

    It was good to hear from Pat. Nell is getting a very good job that she wants and should be very pleased.

    This is terrible. Now that I have a secretary I can't ever get to the typewriter. I can't write at all anymore. Please call Gerry and tell her not to be angry. I'm a stinking correspondent. I'll probably not have a friend left when I get back.

Rose, I surely made a mess of my bank account in England. I miscounted one check and need $100 to make it up. I'll try to borrow so that I can send it off right away, but would you send me the $100 now? Thanks so much, Rose, for all your trouble. Please write to me soon—all of you.

Love, MARGY

On November 20, French troops reached the Rhine River through the Belfort Gap, the same route Julius Caesar had used to push German tribes across the river in 55 BC.

Mary Eleanor Morin
American Red Cross
Civilian War Relief
Continental Headquarters
November 20, 1944
V-mail

Dearest Rose:

I'm sending you this "V-mail" so that it will reach you very quickly, but not to establish a precedent. I hate V-mail and like to have regular letters from you all.

The purpose of this, and I'm deadly earnest, is to ask you to send me a box of cigars—real quick! I foolishly made a bet with the colonel, head of Civil Affairs in our Army, and lost. I'm supposed to pay it as near to 12/10 as possible. I don't know the first thing about cigars, but ask Bill or Spence what is very good, and send them. He reminds me of our friend, LaGuardia, but I don't think he likes the same kinds of cigars. If you read *Bell for Adano*, you'll recognize the character as the general's aide. I know it sounds silly but it is one of those things that might make or break a career.

I'll write a real letter later in the day. I'm visiting at the moment and slightly AWOL, so can't take more time.

Lots of love to you and all, NELL

Margaret F. Morin
American Red Cross
Civilian War Relief
Continental Headquarters
November 21, 1944

Dear Kids:

It's an unusually dull day in the office today. I'm supposed to get a new job shortly, and I surely hope that it comes through in a hurry. After going like a beaver the first six or eight weeks, this inactivity is annoying. Besides which it's as cold as you know what in these buildings. I could be much more comfortable out of doors.

I've had a cold for so long that today is the first day in weeks that it has finally subsided.

Yesterday being Sunday I went out to the golf course, about ten miles out of the city and walked 15 holes of golf. The guy who "brung" me is unusually good and joined up with an officer and two French civilians, who all played well, so it was fun, as well as the first bit of exercise I've had in months.

I suppose you have seen Martin by now. Were you all surprised? I wrote you what fun we all had when he and Nell were here.

Rose, could you please get me some material for a new uniform? You remember the color that you sent Nell. Well the same shade in gabardine would be wonderful. Molly seems to think a lightweight wool would not wear as well as the gabardine. I'd need enough for two skirts and a hat as well as jacket. I'm going around here looking like a sack. The uniform I got in England and the Italian one are ready to fall apart from constant wear. An added bother will be the lining, thread, zippers, if possible, and seam binding. I'm not too sure of the practicability of the red lining. I supposed it will be a case of whatever you can get. My good and faithful Mrs. Godfrey is going around in a thing she got in 1939, and it is impossible for her to get anything here. Could you find something for her in beige or blue? She wants the same color as mine, but headquarters frown on French personnel looking like they are wearing ARC uniforms. You might get mine first, and while doing that see what you'd suggest for her. She's about an inch taller than I am, but wears the same size clothes, so she would need the same amount.

I know this will be a terrific bother for you. It looks, however, that we will be wearing these things for some time, and mine are impossible. The uniforms from Hecht's did not arrive.

I explained to you that my raise would not be coming in until September. They gave me the difference in England. I'm still not too sure of my status in the bank, but will know in a week or so. However, if there is $100 in the bank there, you'd better send it to me.

Must run now. Excuse this begging letter that seems to be all I do.

Love, MARGY

Mary Eleanor Morin
American Red Cross
Civilian War Relief
Continental Headquarters
November 23, 1944
Thanksgiving

Dearest Rose and Biz:

It has been a couple weeks since I've had a letter from you now, but I guess they are jammed up someplace.

I've been transferred from my other job to this place to make a survey. It is a large and rather attractive city. It has rained constantly so that you can't see it even if you could get around. The survey is being done without my assistance as I've contracted, of all the simply divine things one can contract—scabies! I'm having a treatment that is supposed to clear the stuff up—and if it doesn't I'm going to denounce the inventor. It is damned unpleasant and smells to high heaven. It's only a mild case, according to the doctor.

If you should see Msgr. Ready tell him to make a special and fervent novena that I never get the serious type. I'm very self—conscious because several million people had to know just why the hell I couldn't make the survey. I have a feeling that they are inwardly shrinking from me. Can't blame them, I'd run like the devil from Walter Pidgeon if I thought he had the same thing.

At lunch today one of the officers at the table with us turned to the guy next to him and said, I'm getting out of this place—it smells! Then turning to me, chivalrously remarked, feminine company excluded of course! I like ta died!

Norman Hackney, our supervisor and a gentleman from the Deep South, assured me that it was just the officer's way out—that I didn't smell at all. Well, it will be all over in the morning and I'll be able to go on a job as soon as I can get transportation.

I'm going to an exciting place that will have simmered down by the time I get there—I hope. I'll tell you about it in a fireside chat when it is all over. This new job promises to be interesting. I think I'll like it much better than the last.

It seems less like Thanksgiving than ever before. Last year at this time we were beating our brains out in the club to show the kids as good a time as possible on British rations. The boy in the mess this morning showed me the menu for dinner tonight, and if it isn't all "a fissure of his imagination" as our friend Molly stated once, we will all be groaning in the clutches of indigestion. I guess they set 5:30 as dinner hour with that in mind. The words "with pie and chocolate ice cream" didn't take a war for me to kill for. And I'm supposed to be on a diet. Oh well, I keep telling myself, I'll lose it all on the ship going home.

I'm living in a real, honest to goodness chateau. It is a lovely, big impressive house and must have been charming in peacetime. It is colder than Birds Eye halibut at the moment, though it is refreshing to go out in the morning before it is quite light and feel yourself enveloped in the warm air. In addition, I'm the only one there with the exception of the lady who owns it. She doesn't speak a word of English and lives in the hidden recesses of the cellar as near as I can make out.

My little friend from the mess is called "Mississippi." This morning I stayed sipping coffee after the others left and we whipped up a conversation. He said it was a logical nickname because that was where he lived. It turned out he was from Vicksburg. He knows the Morrisseys and thinks they are sensational people. A friend of his took Tootsy out. He's writing home today to tell them what a small world it is and enclosing a note to be delivered to the Morrisseys for me.

Someone just went through the hall beating on a washtub, calling the enlisted men to mess. I guess I'd better close and get ready to go down as they'll be calling us soon. That is one thing I'll never learn to like about war—having dinner so early.

I give you advance warning that "I will not dine 'til nine" when I get home.

Also, I wish we'd suddenly acquire some wealth so I could afford someone to waken me with tea. I miss that so much since we've been away from England. It is a very good practice and should be adopted in every country. It not only breaks the shock of getting up, but also fortifies against the cold.

Goodbye for now. Give my love to all the family, the McKettricks, Moriartys and anyone else that's interested.

      Love again, NELL

Rose Mary Morin
New York City
November 23, 1944

Dear John:

Please find turkey enclosed! I am at the office but there isn't much to do and we expect to leave early. Biz and I are having turkey at Cavanaugh's with Mrs. Moriarty and Mary. It was next to impossible to buy a bird for private consumption and it seems such a lot of trouble to prepare the "fixins" unless there is a crowd to enjoy it.

We got word from Patsy after I had written you last week that Tom was ordered to sea duty. He left last weekend. She feels he is headed for the Philippines. I guess it will be pretty lonely out there for her. Fortunately she has the two babies to keep her busy. Tom was promoted to Lt. Commander before he left which seems like a nice thing for him. It's the second promotion he has had in three years.

Gerry McLaughlin telephoned the other evening. She is worried about Bill having heard from him only twice since the invasion, with no word at all in several weeks. Do you still see him, is he well? She was going to move to a house the family owns in Brooklyn, but decided to stay in Bay Shore for another winter. If you should run into Bill you might mention that she was wondering why she had not heard from him recently.

We received a copy of the *Bulletin Index* yesterday and there is quite a nice article in it about Jane and her new job at the Playhouse with *Outlines*. It also carried a rather good photograph of her. I'm sure she will send you the magazine or at least the clipping. You should be very proud of her.

I don't suppose Martin and Janet will be coming to New York. We have not heard from them directly, but several notes from Mrs. Westwater indicate they are planning to remain in Columbus until he has to report to Washington. Anne has heard from Bill and Lois that they expect to go to the Army-Navy game next Saturday and are planning to see Anne over the weekend. I know at the Notre Dame game he was trying to figure a way to get to the Army-Navy game even if it was at Annapolis.

Hope everything is continuing to go well with you.

      Best of luck & Love, Rose

Rose Mary Morin
New York City
November 29, 1944

Dear John:

Dot wrote that she and her mother had come over for young Dave Foster's wedding, but their train was several hours late and they had to go directly to Rye for the services. They called Sunday morning before taking the train back to Pittsburgh, but both Biz and I were away from the apartment. I had gone to Glen Ridge when I had not heard from Dot Saturday

Dot also said that they had an 18-pound turkey (anyone who was able to get a bird this year had to take a large one) and you would have enjoyed carving it. They are all very fond of their new apartment although George and Nell don't have as much space to get around as formerly.

Patsy wrote last week that Tom had left and is to be assigned as a liaison officer.

Janet wrote the other day that she and Martin would not be coming to New York. She is thoroughly enjoying having him around the house and is trying to forget that he will have to leave again.

In fact, his leave terminates next week. He is to report to the War Department but thinks it will not be for long.

Our Thanksgiving dinner at Cavanagh's was wonderful and we enjoyed it thoroughly. The portions were huge but, of course, eating out is never quite like having a festive meal at home with members of the family.

      Much love and best of luck, ROSE

Lt. Col. Alvin L. Mente, Jr.
C.C.A. 7th Armored Division
December 1, 1944

Dear Elizabeth:

Got your Christmas package yesterday and as might be expected—but, what's unforgivable is that I ate up half of one box immediately.

Thank you so very much. I shall save the rest for some festive occasion. You probably got the word from Margaret that I was on 48-hour leave in Paris. It was great fun for a country bumpkin like me. I was simply enthralled by it. In fact, after seeing nothing but agrarian French people, fat muscular Hollanders, and cows, mostly dead ones, for over three months, I must say I practically drooled at the smart looking Parisiennes. Nothing quite compares to the way I stood in the Rue de l'Opéra and ogled beautifully millinered, gorgeously furred, attractively shod, and stylishly dressed women. I was absolutely bug-eyed at it all. I was put in my place though. It was St. Catherine's Day, a sort of Sadie Hawkins Day, during which girls chase men all over the streets and kiss them. After an hour of waiting nothing happened, so I went over and bothered Betty Baker, Bill Giblin's secretary.

That night Margaret, Betty and I went to a quaint cabaret, drank Champagne and listened to French songs that Betty tried vainly to explain to Margaret and me. I guess I must have gotten more or less under the weather for I awakened at 0630 Sunday morning in the Red Cross Club where we were put up. It was formerly the Hotel Deux Mondes in the Rue de l'Opéra. Sunday Margaret walked me along the right or was it the left bank to La Cathédral de Notre Dame where we arrived too late for Mass. Sunday afternoon we had dinner at Prunier's after which we all retired to Giblin's gorgeous apartment where I announced that I intended to get boisterously drunk.

At 0200 Monday I was coming close to it when Giblin took his guests home leaving me with my choice of walking later or going quietly then. Next morning in the state of complete exhaustion I returned. Boy, do I love Paris.

I got your letter, Rose, last night and was glad to hear that you finally got Martin's location straight. I tried hard to hint at it but you seemed determined to put him with "Guts and Blood." We are no longer in Holland, nor France, nor Belgium but next to Martin's outfit and that ought to place us.

Incidentally, wasn't it grand that Martin got a chance to go home? I bet he frightened you half to death on his arrival. I went over to his outfit about a week ago and was thrilled to hear how well he was liked and how much the officers and men missed him. I hope he gets himself a regiment or at least a promotion.

Germany doesn't promise much. It's all wrecked houses and buildings and odors and mines. One place near here has a sign on the side of the road: "Lousy with Mines." That starts to describe it. But the shells both incoming and outgoing are the worst of it. I shan't go into the smells, but they aren't Chanel Numéro Cinq, believe me.

Thanks again Biz for the caramels. They are swell. And Rose, keep up the letters. It's good to hear from you.

       Love you both, PAT

Mary Eleanor Morin
American Red Cross
Civilian War Relief
Continental Headquarters
December 4, 1944

Dearest Rose, Biz and all:
Let me think what I can write that will possibly interest you jaded people sitting around N.Y. I think I told you that I had a new assignment. It is much the same as the first one except it is in a large city. There isn't much that military security will permit me to say about the place other than it is pretty beat up. It looks like it will take ages to get back into shape. They say it was a very gay place indeed, prewar.

There is a French officer with us who lived here before the war and he says it is hopeless in contrast. An American Red Cross man and I concern ourselves with Displaced People and Refugees. Both are well taken care of. There is a French team of WACS running the camp. The refugees are in the very capable hands of a French captain who used to live in the vicinity and has a magic wand in working out their problems. He gets them places to stay, food, clothing, etc., and while that is a monster undertaking, he manages as though it were nothing at all.

We have a "Grand" office in what was the City Hall. Catholic Charities will have to find a much more pretentious place than the Belmont House if they want me to be contented. I'll surely get delusions of grandeur from this one.

There are two Louis XIV chairs in the room upholstered in pale green damask and painted gray to match the walls and woodwork. An enormous French window looks out on the square and affords a constant view of the Cathedral. The clock in the steeple is always right so I don't even have to wind my watch. Mary Moriarty would loathe the place because it is alive with pigeons. They fly and swoop around all day long, egged on by the kids, in the street who have a wonderful game of chasing them around, sneaking up on them, but never succeeding in actually catching them.

We have electric light and generous steam in the office. The billet isn't so hot—ha, ha—as Marion would say, it is blistering cold, but they promise light, heat and running water in a few days.

I've slightly beaten the elements by filling my canteen with water, setting it on the stove in the lobby, and putting it in my sleeping bag to warm it while I'm getting undressed for bed. That takes about two split seconds. It keeps me warm until I get to sleep and I keep it slightly warm until morning, when I use the water to wash in!

I had a bath about eleven days ago and that is a good and unusual thing to be able to say in this part of the world. As far as cleaning or pressing goes, that is just something to remember and talk about like people use to about the Old Country.

I wear my oldest uniform all the time. It is accordion pleated with wrinkles and a sight to behold, but I hate to get my others all dirty. They've been packed so long they'll be beyond pressing.

I average about 9 1/2 hours sleep at night. The first couple of nights I found myself in bed at seven or seven thirty. Everyone darted to their rooms from mess because was too cold to hang around downstairs and no place to go outside—it was horrible. I'd wake up about twelve and pray for morning to come so I could get up.

We found a stove in the garage that worked and pulled chairs from the lobby to sit, talk and keep warm. The garage is an unbeautiful place, filled with muddy jeeps and the floor covered with water or grease, but it was mighty cozy.

Two officers came in to see me one night, thoughtfully bringing a bottle of Cognac, and were stunned when I led them to the back and into the garage. But they got used to it and have been back a few times since to spend the evening. We now manage to stay up until 9:30 or ten and I'm bound to be asleep by eleven. The funny part is that I'm getting used to it.

There has been one dance since I've been here. There was no light or water anywhere, but the officers used a generator and the place was ablaze. It was in a building that looked like a palace. The floor was good, their orchestra good too. They served supper and several different kinds of drinks. By some miracle they corralled a number of local lovelies, a couple of nurses and ourselves. One of the officers knew Pat Mente pretty well. They had been together until Pat was moved out of this area several weeks ago. It was a lot of fun.

Nobody thought of dressing for the occasion. Or even getting washed. Old muddy boots, wrinkled clothes but they treated us as though we had been hours getting ready to put in an appearance. It was even more fun because there was no question whether you had on the right thing. Very simple, this life!

One of the officers in our detachment is from New York. We had an exhaustive discussion on the place last night. Took about two hours. We spent a good long time prospecting on the delights of walking around the city looking at things, talking about restaurants, etc. He can hardly wait to get back and spend the evening at the St. Regis.

Well, I must close for now and go to work.

Very best love to you and all the kids, NELL

Rose reported that a movie newsreel showed scenes of the Variety Club banquet in Washington, including the presentation by Johnny Harris to Secretary of State Cordell Hull.

>Rose Mary Morin
>New York City
>December 6, 1944
>V-mail

Dear John:

There was a letter from Margaret that I enclosed with a Christmas card I sent the other day. It will probably reach you before this does, or at about the same time. She has seen Nell again since Martin left.

Biz and I went to the neighborhood movie to see *Laura*—a very good mystery. The newsreel carried a few shots of the Variety Club banquet in Washington at the Mayflower Hotel where they made an award to Secretary of State Hull as the "Greatest Humanitarian." Johnny Harris made the presentation. Except that some of his hair is still dark, he is the image of his father. I was amazed at how much older he looks than when I last saw him a few years ago. I don't think he would like to hear that though, do you?

Did I tell you that our friend Monsignor Ready is to be consecrated Bishop of Columbus, Ohio, on December 14th? The ceremony is to be at St. Matthew's in Washington. I have been invited but haven't made up my mind whether I should go. Biz and I plan to spend Christmas with Anne and her family and it would be an extra trip. If I don't go I'll send a check to be added to the purse that they are no doubt making for the Bishop-elect.

I was speaking with Bijou Dwyer yesterday. Her brother John applied for discharge, but they have not heard that it has been granted. A friend who applied when John did is already home and in civilian clothes. What did you think of the Army-Navy game? We haven't heard from Lois and Bill whether they enjoyed it.

>Much love, ROSE

Mary Eleanor Morin
American Red Cross
Civilian War Relief
Continental Headquarters
December 11, 1944

Dearest Rose, Biz and all:

I was so glad to get the mail last week and word that Mart had arrived home safely. I don't know how I restrained myself from telling you that he was on his way.

I imagine the household in Columbus was in an uproar. Janet must have been in a state. The little red beret is from Molly Ford through Mart. I think she got it in Italy. I'm sorry I had nothing to send with Mart but the whole thing was so unexpected and then hectic in town that I didn't collect my wits long enough to get anything. His luggage was a big problem, as they limited him to a certain amount. However, I could have gotten something that he could have carried in his pocket. Didn't he look well?

I think being over here helped him considerably as he didn't look at all well in England in those sordid pictures we sent home. I'm glad he's safely out of this, but I will miss him. I devoted a large part of my time dreaming up ways to get to see him. Now I'll just have to concentrate all my energies on Pat.

I nearly fainted when I read about Billy's marriage. I'm glad though and would love to see Lois. Keep after Bill to send us pictures. Eva and I had long conversations about him. I shouldn't really describe them as conversations because Eva is inclined to carry the ball for herself and the person she is talking to—and in several languages. She was planning to go home, but I heard the other day that she changed her mind and is in a R.C. club somewhere.

To get back to Billy, I wrote to him last week as soon as I received your letter. It must have been painful for them when you showed up with about ten million people for lunch. Have they enlarged the Sherry Netherlands? Boy, would I love to queue up for lunch there today!

I'm glad that you sent along John's letter. I've been wanting his address and enjoy hearing firsthand, what he is up to. I don't know where he got the story about the cocktail party, but it was slightly confused. Rose Dolan wasn't there. Barbara Howard and I were though.

I miss Rose Dolan. She was a lot of fun and a very good worker. She can speak French faster than most French people. I've had French civilians and French officers tell me that! I don't think I'll be seeing her because of the change, unless we accidentally meet someplace.

I've been hoping that some business or other would take me over Christmas. It would be marvelous to be with Margy and Molly and the others, but the chance is very, very slim.

I received two Christmas packages from you and one from Betty Brown. I opened one package and found the little tree that is adorable. It will brighten things up considerably wherever I happen to be. Thank you for all the things Rose. It is hard for you to take so much time to shop for all that and I can't tell you how much I appreciate it. Thanks a million.

Patsy must have been thrilled when Billy showed up. Why is he surprised that children like him?

Jane is sure becoming an artist. Her decorating scheme sounds grand. I'll bet those poor nuns at the Cathedral got a blow when more Morins showed up.

I wish we would find an apartment down in Mary Moriarty's neighborhood when the war is over and we come home. It might be a good plan to start looking and stake a claim on a place now. Any old railroad flat will do—but 86th St. is just too far away from everything.

Did Mart tell you about "the" party at the hotel in Paris? It was sensational. Molly invited Lamet, my friend who had my watch repaired. We dined in a private room after we had gallons of drinks in the suite. We had a wonderful dinner, more drinks and eventually wound up at Margy and Molly's apartment. It got out of hand, as it always does. Margy claims that she and an English officer were in her room putting in a phone call when I tiptoed in, closed the door softly, and in a whisper, pleaded with her to stop fighting with Mart!

At another point Molly said me and Mart were seated on the davenport silently sipping Champagne in coats and gloves.

Lamet was the last to leave—I remember pushing him out the door and burying myself under the pile of blankets Molly had put on the settee in the dining room. I was fully clothed and must have died for a few hours because my clothes were hardly wrinkled when I woke up and went to bed.

Margy, Molly, Mart and I got together in the Ritz Bar the next noon and tried to review the events of the night.

It was really a fine party. To assure me that everything was still okay Lamet sent me five pairs of stockings! I don't know whether they are silk or rayon and they're in all different shades and sizes, but it was very thoughtful of him. At the moment though I'm wearing those wooly kind. It's too cold and damp for anything else.

To get back to Mart's arrival home—please go to Christ Cella's and have the outside crispy slice of roast beef and some broccoli with Hollandaise sauce for me.

The day of the Army-Notre Dame game we got together here to hear it. Jim Riordan came over and he, Fred Barker and myself gathered around the radio with a bottle of Armagnac to listen. It began to feel pretty cold while we were waiting for the game to come on, so Fred, who was never a boy scout, decided to build a fire in the peculiar old stove we had in the day room.

The room was bare of anything but a few odd wooden chairs and tables and a nice cold stone floor. Fred had all kinds of trouble getting the thing going, while Jim and I sat and looked on complaining about the cold. In desperation, Fred went and got a container of Jerry gasoline and threw some on the fire. It flared up and as Jim jumped back the gasoline jumped out of the container onto the floor and we had fire all over the room. In all the confusion we forgot all about the game.

I was wild the next day when we heard the score. It is just as well John Dwyer wasn't home to give his famous party after the game—it would have turned into a wake.

I can't think where you got the idea that the crowd I was with was fun. There are plenty of very nice amusing people in Civilian War Relief, but I haven't had the good fortune to be with them on an assignment. They all live to eat dinner and jump into bed. I have a terrible time trying to find someone to sit up and talk!

I can always wangle the French officers and girls into staying up and we have a lot of fun. A few of them speak English and translate for me so we get along very well together.

It's marvelous about Father Ready becoming a bishop. I'll write him the first chance I get. I hope someone will propose to me when I get home. It would be very nice to be married by a bishop. Maybe he'll be a cardinal by the time that happens!

Well, Rosy so long for now. Hoping to hear from you very soon.

Loads and loads of love, NELL

Rose Mary Morin
New York City
December 11, 1944

Dear John:

I thought you would be interested in the latest copies from the girls. Nell seems to be having quite a time contracting the "itch." It is a good thing she has such an easygoing disposition and takes everything in stride. She must be very near Metz if not already there.

Martin left for Camp Atterbury last Sunday the third, then stopped off in Columbus on Monday to have dinner with Janet and the children before proceeding to Washington. They have not heard about his assignment or where he is living. I think he planned to go to Anne's until he was settled.

We are leaving here the 23rd for Christmas weekend with Anne and will likely see Mart unless he does get off to go to Columbus. I hope he can after being away from them for two Christmases already.

We had no word from Lois and Bill about their weekend at the game and at Anne's. No doubt they will spend Christmas with Lois's family in Albany as her little boy is there.

I hope some of your boxes have arrived by now and that you will have a Merry Christmas.

Best of luck and much love, ROSE

Lt. Col. Alvin L. Mente, Jr.
C.C.A. 7th Armored Division
December 14, 1944

Dear Rose:

Received both your letters of 28 Nov. and 5 Dec. and the clipping about General Drum. I had known about his nephew who is a very close friend of mine. The injury wasn't as serious as it sounded. He'll have to salute the wrong way if you get what I mean. It happened in that town you mentioned in Holland.

Also, I have been in that town numerous times lately myself; our command post is only a few miles away. I doubt if the picture is of me because I can't remember stopping long enough to have a picture taken.

I have run into several officer friends of Martin who have been absolutely superlative in their description of the many deeds that Mart did. He must have a chest full of medals for his many exploits.

Greatest recognition came from some enlisted men. I passed a command half-track on the side of the road the other day. The name of the vehicle was "Jamestown." I immediately recognized it as Martin's so I thought I'd talk to the crew. All they could do was talk of Colonel Morin and say, "Boy we wish he was still here."

And that Rose, isn't idle chatter, and is honest proof of humble but better grade admiration. When the enlisted men like you enough to want to talk about it, you have something that cannot be topped by typewritten prattle.

Rose, I listened to every minute of the Army-Navy game. It was marvelous. What I enjoyed more than the game, however, was the fact that Army beat Navy in the manner your Dad would have deemed it.

Uncle John would certainly have been pleased as punch with a team like that. I'm glad everyone got a chance to either see it or hear it.

We finally read where the 7th A.D. fought like lions somewhere in Holland. Again, Rose, it was CCA and our strength was of the strength of ten because our hearts were pure. It's been so long ago no one seems to remember.

I'm sorry to hear Tom left for parts unknown. If he stays close to the China coast we may see him. I figure we'll get mixed up in that place before we get home to stay. I hope we get home before we go there, but I'm just a plow-hand in these parts. No plea of mine will change the minds of the Joint Chiefs of Staff anyway.

Do continue to write us all the news. It's great hearing from you. How's Biz?

Love to you both, PAT

# Chapter 28

## The Oakland Boys

On my first day in class at St. Paul's Cathedral, Sister Fredette made me stand up and introduce myself. I stood up okay, but that was the best I could do. I didn't know what to say.

One of the girls giggled. Sister asked, "What is your name?"

"George," I said.

"Do you have a last name?"

"Yes."

More giggles. "What is it?"

"Morin," I said.

"Now, George Morin, where do you live?"

"4514 Centre Avenue, Apartment 3-C."

"How close is that to Craig Street?"

"It's on the corner," I said.

"Well, isn't that nice to live so close to school? You certainly won't have any excuse for being late."

Now everyone laughed. I fell into my seat – my face on fire. Sister said, "CLASS!" and the room fell silent as fast as if she clicked off a radio.

"Welcome to the third grade of the Cathedral, Mr. Morin, we look forward to your contributions to our class. Now everyone open your catechisms to chapter three."

Desktops squeaked open and close and the room murmured. Sister plopped a catechism on my desk. It was the same catechism we had at Holy Innocents, only we had been on chapter 5, but I kept quiet about that.

After catechism it was time for grammar.

Sister wrote a sentence on the blackboard in neat Palmer Method, a little tail on the last letter of each word. She pointed out the nouns, verbs and prepositions. And then asked which word was the subject and which the object. All the girls raised and shook their hands feverishly to get Sister to call on them. I'm glad she didn't call on me because I thought the words that turned out to be the subject and object were nouns.

Lunchtime was a relief. I sat with Nellie in the lunchroom as she talked and talked with girls from her room, as if she had grown up with them.

What I dreaded most was after school. I remembered what Uncle Charles said about city boys being tough. When school let out I couldn't find Nellie, so as I walked along Craig Street; I held my books under my left arm and kept my right fist clenched. I heard someone running up behind me, but before I could turn around he said, "Hey, Morin, wait up. You and me live on the same street."

I turned to see a skinny little kid who looked anything but tough. "I'm Mike Trent," he said. "I live right up the hill from you."

"Where?"

"In the Bellefield Dwellings, on Centre and Dithridge."

I had never been in the building, but from the outside, it looked like rich people lived there. The front doors had wrought-iron designs over thick panes of glass framed with panels of white marble. It seemed like it had five times the number of floors my apartment building had.

"Too bad baseball season's over," he said, skipping backward in front of me. "You could come with us to Forbes Field and sneak into the games free. It's easy." He turned and walked beside me, looking in my face. "We run past the guard when he's not looking and climb all the way to the top the right-field stands – and go over the rail.

"It's scary the first couple times, but you get used to it. Do you have tenny shoes? You need them so your feet don't slip climbing up the slats."

In Sheraden, people always listened to Rosy Rosewell on the radio announcing the Pirate games. On warm summer days you could hear the game all over the neighborhood because everyone kept their doors and windows open. Every time a Pirate hit a home run, Rosy would yell, "Open your window Aunt Minnie, here she comes." Now here I was, living just a few blocks away from Aunt Minnie's window.

"Gordo Goodman is the fastest climber," Mike said, "And I'm next fastest. Danny Serger and Jimmy Leighman are slower. They go to Liberty Grade School. I'm the only Catholic. My mother's Catholic, but my dad isn't, he's English. They have their own church. He's in the war, in the English Red Cross."

"So's my dad," I said, squeezing in a word. "He's a captain in the Eighth Army Air Corps. Do you like airplanes?"

"Wait till you see my room," Mike said. "I have posters of airplanes on my wall and model airplanes I built hanging from my ceiling. I'll show you when you come up to do homework."

"Do you have a B-26 Marauder?" I asked.

"You mean the one that blasted the beaches on D-Day? I wish."

After I dried the dishes that night, I got my books and headed up to Mike's apartment. I walked into the high-ceiling lobby and a man came out from behind a shiny wood desk and asked if he could help me.

I said, "I'm going to do homework with Mike Trent."

"Hop aboard, fella," he said, sliding the elevator doors open., "That's 8-F." He pushed the handle on the side of the car forward and I felt a quiver in my stomach as we picked up speed. The numbers of the floors lit up as we passed each one. We slowed passing seven and stopped at eight – with a jerk.

"Home work hard," he said as he opened the doors. "Turn right to the end."

The floor was covered with thick carpets and the walls with pale green fabric with curlicue designs. I rang the bell at 8-F and eyed the door's peephole. Mike's mother opened the door.

"Hello," she said, "you must be George. Mike is so happy to have you nearby to study with."

I mumbled, "Thank you for, ah, letting me come, ah, to your home." She was taller and younger than my mother, and not skinny. I liked her dark hair and pretty face.

Mike, standing in the middle of the hall behind her, motioned with his head to follow him. We went down the hall past the living and dining rooms to his bedroom in the back. The wall facing the door was covered with posters of a B-17 Flying Fortress, a B-24 Liberator, a P-51 Mustang, an American Flying Tiger and a British Spitfire. Two model airplanes hung from the ceiling. Over his bed was a large poster of Stan Musial wearing a red-and-white St. Louis Cardinals uniform.

"I thought you liked the Pirates," I said.

"I do," he said. "But Stan Musial is my man."

Mike propped himself on the pillows at the head of his bed and bounced a pink rubber ball against the far wall, catching it in his first baseman's mitt. Soon his mother stuck her head in and said, "Mikey, stop it."

Mike put the ball in his glove and laid it on his dresser.

"You like the Lone Ranger?" he asked.

"Yeah."

"It's time," he said.

He had his own Zenith radio on the corner of his desk. He clicked it on and after a few moments a voice faded up saying, "The hoof beats of the great horse Silver." Then a voice in the distance echoed, "Hi Ho Silver, away!"

And away we went for the next half hour, lying on our stomachs staring at the green light behind the radio dial, listening to the adventures of the unconquerable masked man and his faithful Indian companion.

As the last hoof beat on the radio faded, the door opened and Mrs. Trent's voice floated in, "Don't forget the homework, boys."

The next morning, I rushed out the front door of my building just as Mike was coming down the hill from his. It was my second day at school and I didn't want to be late. Mike said we had plenty of time so we walked together, still charged by the adventures of the Lone Ranger and boasting about how fast we knocked off our homework. Mike said he and some friends were going to play touch football on Saturday on Schenley High School's lawn, did I want to come?

"Yes," I said.

I went up to Mike's on Saturday morning and waited till he finished breakfast. He got his football and we went down the elevator to the lobby. Jimmy Leighman, who lived in 4-B, was waiting. Mike tossed the football across the lobby. Jimmy caught it with one hand and tucked it against his chest like he was ready to run. We crossed the lobby and Mike said, "This is the new kid I told you about." Jimmy reminded me of Frankie Newman, with curly brown hair and freckles.

"I'm George," I said.

"I'm Jimmy."

Schenley High was across Bellefield Avenue from Mike's apartment building. Gordo Goodman and Danny Serger were already there, sitting on the grass, hunched against the building.

Gordo had straight black hair and his brow was slightly wrinkled, like something was worrying him. He said, "Hi, I hope you're going to like it here."

Danny, tall and slender with straight brown hair, said, "Nice to see you. Now we can play two against two."

We paired off. Me and Mike against Gordo and Danny. They had the ball first. Danny hiked the ball to Gordo. Mike rushed Gordo who juked out of the way and tossed the ball down the lawn to Danny, who I was chasing. He caught the ball and skipped into the end zone – the sidewalk – as I stumbled after him.

Now we had the ball. Mike was the passer. I hiked the ball to Mike like Danny had, but it bounced on the ground and Gordo picked it up and ran past me for another touchdown.

We played like that until Gordo and Danny had about a million touchdowns. Then we stopped and just tossed the ball around. Mike threw it to me easy and I caught it and threw a wobbly pass back.

Later, Gordo said, "Don't worry. The Steelers can't play football, either." That season the Steelers lost every game.

# Chapter 29

## Counterpunch

On December 16, 1944, Germany launched what became known as the Battle of the Bulge, a huge German counteroffensive with twenty-four divisions against six U.S. divisions of untried or battle weary troops.

As she wrote on this date, Nell was unaware of the development.

> Mary Eleanor Morin
> American Red Cross
> Civilian War Relief
> G-5 HQ, 12th Army Group
> December 16, 1944
>
> Dearest Rose and all:
> I don't know how far I'll get with this but I'll try. I've moved again, and this time I like it. It is the job I've been hoping to get and had just about given up hope on. I came here a couple days ago and so far, so good. The kids, Margy and Molly, are expected here about Monday. They are going to deliver the mail and visit the people in the forward areas for a couple of days.
> I envy them. I'd love to go up where Mart was. The trip might take them where Pat is too. I heard Pat was in town, but haven't heard any particulars of the trip. I can hardly wait to see the kids and hear what they've been up

249

to. I hope that we can cook up sort of a dinner party and have some fun, but I'm afraid they'll be tired from the drive and won't be here very long.

In case their trip should instill some worry in your mind, forget it. They will go with our general supervisor and he won't let them get into territory that might be dangerous.

Mart met Lee, the man I'm working for, at the party Dorothy Reader had when we were in town.

Lee is a peach and very nice to work with. It is a big camp. The only tent I've seen is the powder room. That isn't as bad as it sounds, and it's a whole lot better than some of the indoor arrangements.

Great plans are on hand for Christmas. I am on the committee for the party for our section. It is going to be the afternoon of Christmas Eve. The officers are giving it for the enlisted men. Some are even contributing gin, Cointreau, fruit juice and food from Christmas packages. We're going to try to get some donuts out of the Clubmobile girls. Remembering my Clubmobile days, I'm afraid we won't get any further than trying.

I nearly got into town to do shopping for the party. Everyone on the committee was very enthusiastic about going but me. I expected Mart and Margaret to be here, but they didn't get permission so everything's okay.

My only complaint is my cot. It's comfortable except that my head seems to be dangling down the back without a pillow. I can't imagine why I left England without one. I guess I subconsciously didn't take using cots very seriously.

Love, NELL

Rose Mary Morin
New York City
Tuesday, December 1944

Dear John:
You will doubtless enjoy all the nice things Pat is saying about Martin in his enclosed letter. I do hope Pat is coming through the present events safely. The papers and radio keep mentioning the outstanding service being performed by the 7th Armored as well as Mart's old outfit the 2nd Armored. We haven't had any word from you in ages. What have you been up to?

Nell's letter is very enlightening. I am glad she has the time to give us so much of the details of her life overseas. I suppose she gets in her letter writing when the others crawl off to bed.

Margaret on the other hand hasn't written in two months but her social life must take all the free time she has after office hours.

Patsy had some interesting letters from Tom. He seems to be getting a big kick out of the natives and has enough time during leisure hours to have acquired the name of "Mr. Hoyle" by his prowess at poker. His quarters seem to be in a very nice building situated in the midst of many small native huts. On a recent trip he slept on a hammock suspended between palm trees.

Biz still has the cold she brought back from her Christmas trip. Anne writes that she is just about over a case of ptomaine but aside from that everything is well.

We had an announcement from Jane yesterday of her *Outlines* program for the month. It looks like a very interesting setup.

Much love and best of luck, ROSE

Rose Mary Morin
New York City
December 20, 1944

Dear John:

Merry Christmas & Happy New Year.

Lois was just here delivering Christmas packages for Biz and me and Anne and Bob. We had planned to go down to Washington on Saturday morning—by reserved seat coach—but I'm beginning to weaken on getting there a bit earlier and taking the six o'clock train Friday evening. That will allow us to help Anne on Saturday when she will have an awful lot to do.

Patsy writes that she has heard from Tom and that he arrived safely and is with a grand bunch of men. He is second in command of whatever he is doing and says it is most interesting work and the best assignment he has ever had.

Biz and I went to the LaGuardias on Saturday for a cocktail and stayed for dinner, at their insistence, of course. He prepared hamburger like I've never had it before. It was wonderful. Of course, while he insists he is doing the job he requires the services of everyone by handing him condiments, plates and platters. But it was fun. They asked for all of you.

Mr. Keegan, the commissioner who attended father's funeral passed away Monday. He had a heart attack on his way back from Washington Sunday evening and died the next afternoon. He had the condition for some time, but it was very sudden, and of course, an awful shock to everyone.

Will let you know all about our weekend when we get back. Perhaps we will have some news on what Martin is doing in Washington. We have not heard from him but I suppose he is very busy.

Much love and best of luck, ROSE

On December 26, General Patton's Third Army arrived to turn the tables against the Germans at Bastogne. John's 323rd Bomb Group was awarded the Presidential Unit Citation for attacking enemy positions through rotten weather and fierce anti-aircraft barrages.

Rose Mary Morin
New York City
December 27, 1944

Dear Nell, Margaret and John:
This has to be a quickie and one letter for all because two days of the week are already gone and I may not have another opportunity to write you about our visit at Anne's.

We decided to go down on Friday night and take our chances instead of going in our reserved seats on Saturday.

During the ride I regretted that we had changed our plan because people were standing in the aisles from Philadelphia to Washington. We had seats and were not too badly off.

I gave my seat to a girl with a crying baby in Baltimore, but didn't mind standing for the rest of the way because the train was an hour late and I was tired of sitting in one position.

When we arrived at the house we sat up for hours—not getting to bed until nearly five o'clock. Anne had marketing to do Saturday morning and I went along to help with the children. That afternoon while they napped she and I went to town for some last minute shopping. She bought Nunsey a doll for the cradle she had found the day before which she had painted light blue.

Well, there wasn't an infant doll in the town so we settled for a Kewpie doll that we dressed in an infant dress. It turned out all right. Biz and Anne made a fancy pillow and cover for the cradle out of a pale pink lace with a blue bow. I concocted underwear and socks out of a pair of Robin's old socks. It all looked quite professional when finished.

A friend of Bob had shot some teal ducks that we had for Sunday dinner. They were wonderful. I had phoned Mart at his office Saturday and he said he would try to make it for Sunday dinner, but wasn't sure he could.

He didn't make it or even have time to let us know. The Browns came in to help trim the tree and stayed with the children while the rest of us went to Midnight Mass. We finished fixing the things around the tree after the children had gone bed.

I think the older ones were more excited about the tree and toys than were the children. We couldn't wait until it was time for them to get up. They had been talking Santa Claus for days and all Robin really wanted was a wagon. Bob found one just like the big boys use.

After they had breakfast they went into the sun room and all Nunsey could say was "lights, lights." Robin's eyes were as big as saucers. It was several minutes before he discovered the wagon. He also got quite a kick out of the football Biz and I had brought him.

Nunsey discovered her "Bebe" right away and played with it constantly.

We had planned dinner for four-thirty or five so the children could eat with us but they began to get cross so we compromised by letting them eat at the big table with the candles but before we had dinner. Thinking Martin would not be too much delayed, we dilly-dallied until seven. When he had not arrived we went ahead. When Martin had not been heard from by nine the Browns left. He came down the street as they drove away. After a Scotch, we fixed a plate for him and he finally got his Christmas dinner about ten.

He looks well but is still thin. He's working very hard, every day including Sunday and holidays from 5:30 until 8 or 9 o'clock when he arrives back at his room and goes straight to bed.

He said he has a nice clean room in an apartment at 17th and R Street. His office is in the Pentagon. He likes the work immensely. His immediate boss keeps such long hours Mart feels he has to get there at least ten minutes before him and not leave until at least ten minutes after.

He spoke to Janet from Anne's on Christmas and we all had spoken to Patsy earlier in the evening.

Martin left about midnight to be at work the next day at 5:30.

Patsy said they were having a good Christmas and that Paul was pleased with all his gifts.

Anne and Bob raved about the affair given for Bishop Ready. The reception was in the Chinese room of the Mayflower, they had a bar the length of the ballroom with drinks of every description. Our friend the bishop sipped tomato juice while everyone else drank everything in sight. Nell, I am sending you the souvenir program.

I hope you all had as nice a Christmas as possible and will let us know about it.

Much love and Happy New Year, ROSE

P.S. I don't suppose you have heard from Pat since his trip to Paris. I do hope he is getting through the present crisis safely if he is in the vicinity. R.

Pat was wounded at Bastogne. Nell wrapped up the year.

Mary Eleanor Morin
American Red Cross
Civilian War Relief
G-5 HQ, 12th Army Group
December 30, 1944

Dearest Rose, Biz and all:

Before the year is out, I want to thank you for all the wonderful presents, cards, toys and trimmings. There were far too many.

I had a wonderful Christmas and all your thoughtfulness made it so. The staggering project staring me in the face is to itemize all the things so you will know that nothing went astray.

In my buoyantly enthusiastic way I wrote you on the 13th or 14th and told you that Marg and Molly were on their way here and would go on from here to the field with Christmas mail.

Then everything happened and I could see you receiving the letter in breathtaking time and hearing the reports simultaneously. I hope you weren't worried, though Lord knows I was, and furious with them when they came back.

After no word from them from Monday until late Friday afternoon, they swept in full of their trip and all the excitement and said, "Whatever were you worried about?"

It wasn't bad enough that I worried, but I drew anyone that would listen to me into worrying as well. I knew that Lee would take good care of them, but there is always a chance that they might have wandered away from him.

We had a party the first night they were here at the "quaint inn" you thought you had stayed in. I'm sure it must be the place. It is the only place in town that could be considered quaint.

The dinner was very good and after that we went to the officers club for drinks and Marg and a Lt. Col. played the piano. We all got heaved out of there at 11. It was a lot of fun for us.

Marg's driver, Skippy Godfrey, whom she has written you about, had driven up to get another girl who was going out to the field. We had dinner in the mess here and a very good evening.

The Christmas Eve afternoon party started everyone off and we just milled around from place to place. The colonel who plays the piano so well has asked me to have dinner at the town mayor's home some night soon. I'll get all done up in my new little black dress that you sent.

We gave no real presents here. Just wrapped up little things like cigarettes, candy and so on. Not that cigarettes are so insignificant anymore. We are rationed now to five packs a week. They are all going to the kids at the front now, which is as it should be. However, we'll be emulating the displaced persons pretty soon and drying little bits of weeds, grass and God knows what, to make into cigarettes.

Had a letter from Jack O'Donnell yesterday—all about how he was surprised out of his life by running into Mart in the Pentagon. He said, "I met Marty (Col. Morin, to you)." I know he was being funny but I hope Mart will get those eagles soon.

Father Ready, now Bishop Ready in Columbus, will have the pleasure of confirming Pat and Molly. He can't escape getting involved in the family.

I had my battle dress trousers cut into a skirt by the woman in the tailor shop here on the post. You should see it. It looks like something you'd cover a birdcage with. The clothing problems get wilder and funnier here. I only have two uniforms to wear. I refuse to take chances with the blue gabardine, though I may wear it tonight—it's New Year's Eve!

And it's a beautiful day. It snowed through the night and is bright and sunny now, but the snow isn't melting. This is the loveliest weather I can remember since I've been away from home.

I'm still from South Ireland though when it comes to the girls' room and washing in that liquid ice that flows from the spigots in the stopper-less sinks.

I didn't know until the last mail came in that Tom had gone to the Pacific. Poor Patsy must be desolate. Is she going to stay out West? I suppose the Hansons would sue her for kidnapping if she dared bring the children East. We have a couple naval liaison officers, why couldn't they send Tom to us? Then we could dance round and round, singing, "Hut-Sut Rawlston sittin' on the rillerah," and fall on our faces. Unless my memory fails me again, that was our holiday of '41.

Crumbs almighty, I just went to copy Tom's address and saw that he's a lieutenant commander—I've been bragging and boasting about him being a lieutenant senior grade.

I just got in a conversation with the sergeant who sits next to me (we've been having long conversations, when he isn't working like crazy for the colonel) and I don't know how it came out, but we were in the same grade at St. Paul's Cathedral. He had a crush on Janet O'Brien when I was going through my Carl Vilsack stage. His name is Rowland Keating. He knows all the people I remember from that dim, far away place—even Jim Kuhn and Binx Dangerfield.

Isn't it a small world? (Forgive me for that!) You knew his sister, it seems to me. If any of them should ask you, he is in perfect health and an awfully nice kid. He won a bottle of gin at the Christmas party that we had. Even though we learned we went school together, I still call him sergeant and he makes with the respectful—Miss Morin.

I've been hoodooed in an effort to get something home to you. First it was those brats pinching everything, then the French liaison officer rooked me on the perfume—I found out when I bought Molly a bottle of "N" in town that was three times the size and cost only half as much. Well, that's all for this year.

Much love to all and Happy New Year, NELL

*1945*

# Chapter 30

## The Beginning of the End

The Germans, having lost the Battle of the Bulge, pulled back from the Ardennes forest.

In the Pacific, General MacArthur took over U.S. ground forces in preparation for the invasions of Iwo Jima, Okinawa and Japan. Tom Hanson reported from the Philippines.

>Lt. Commander T.H. Hanson
>G-2 Section (CCD)
>Advance Echelon USAFFE
>Philippine Islands
>January 5, 1945

>Dearest Rose:
>
>Your Christmas card and note arrived yesterday and I'm deeply grateful to you—funny, but I had no idea how important a piece of mail could be. As is probably natural under the circumstances the postal system will be lucky if the accumulated sacks are delivered before the war in this theater is over. I've been more fortunate than most, having received three letters from Patsy and one from you. Excuse the pencil and paper. The Aussie ink we have available, with the dampish paper, is inclined to run all over the place. It

was swell that you mentioned the cheerful tone of Patsy's letters to you. I don't worry about her being able to get along, and with the two youngsters to care for she will not have time to do much in the way of fretting over her lot—summing it all up, she's wonderful. It is my hope that you will be able to see the children before too much time elapses.

I certainly hope that Martin's assignment is as he wants it. Seeing him out here would be swell, but as far as I'm concerned he's entitled to a good long tour stateside. In my opinion this campaign is one of the most successful ever made, and General MacArthur and his staff proved their greatness right here. All concerned are optimistic about future operations.

We arrived on November 30th, flying all the way (Lt. Commander K. T. Ripley came with me—he wrote travel, etc., for several magazines before the war.) It was pretty rough for a while—air raids, paratroop landings, and what have you, but the issue was never in doubt, and at this point the mopping up process is almost over. We are digging out and killing a thousand or so stragglers each day, with negligible losses to ourselves. As my address indicates, I'm attached to the Army now—for the time being I'm doing what amounts to counter-intelligence work, but will ultimately be executive officer of the organization responsible for the security of telecommunications in the Islands. It's all very interesting, separation from my family being the only drawback.

My love to you, Biz and the rest. Mention me to everyone, and let me hear from you as often as possible,

As ever, TOM

Staff Correspondent for the *New York Sun*, Judy Barden, reported the exploits of Margaret and Molly when their command car took a wrong turn and ended up on the outskirts of Bastogne in the midst of an artillery bombardment. On the advice of startled G.I.s the two Red Cross civilian relief workers and their driver got out of there fast.

# THE BEGINNING OF THE END

Margaret F. Morin
American Red Cross
Civilian War Relief
Continental Headquarters
January 6, 1945

Dearest Kids:

Please forgive me for not having written sooner and more often. The last three or four weeks have been very hectic. My area has been enlarged so I have to be out in the field a great part of the time. Then the week before Christmas, I went on a field trip with Molly that turned out to be most exciting. You will hear about the details from Bill Giblin who plans to go home for a while next week. He says he will get in touch with you in New York.

Christmas came and went, and I can't say that it was too much of a success. Everything was confused and as I had planned to go to Cannes with Molly for a week's leave, which I didn't do on account of the changing picture. Makeshift plans had to be made.

I went to Brussels the Saturday before New Year's and returned this Friday. Marje Bromberger is stationed there. I loved it. It really is a lovely city, and the people are most hospitable. We had an audience with the Queen, which we expected to be very sticky. We went at five o'clock and left at seven-thirty. She received us very informally and we had a sit-down tea. She had Marge, Bill G., and the head of the Belgium Red Cross, and myself at her table. She seemed to enjoy our foolish talk so much that she must have forgotten about the time. The fact that I had been in Bastogne during the first bad days made me a great success with everyone. I hadn't realized that I was such a heroine before.

It's funny, Rose, that you should have asked for Pat. I saw him here the day I left for Brussels. Bill G. can tell you the details that you can believe implicitly, because he was with me. Pat left that same day for England. I'm going to write John when we hear of Pat's exact location, so that John can keep in touch with him and us. I wrote Nance, but one can say so little that I hope she can get some little comfort from it. He was most fortunate, because I was there and I know. He looked very well in spite of his present discomfort. He still has an awful lot of moustache which I always said makes him look like a German.

I saw Nell on our trip to the front. She is very well and much happier in her present assignment. It is a mixture of personnel work and liaison between headquarters and an Army Group.

Must run. I've got the car and want to get back before dark. It's a station wagon. Pretty fancy.

Love, MARGY

TWO STAR MESSAGE FROM WASHINGTON, DC
MISS ROSE M. MORIN, 425 E. 86TH ST.
REGRET TO INFORM YOU YOUR COUSIN LT. COL. ALVIN L. MENTE JR. WAS SLIGHTLY WOUNDED IN ACTION TWENTY ONE DECEMBER IN BELGIUM YOU WILL BE ADVISED AS REPORTS OF CONDITION ARE RECEIVED
DUNLOP, ACTING THE ADJUTANT GEN.

Lt. Col. Alvin L. Mente, Jr.
D.O.P. Hospital Plant 4150
January 6, 1945

Dear Rose and Biz:

Undoubtedly by this time you have heard that I'm the dog it shouldn't happen to. Guess I should have voted for the other party or something. At the moment I am very comfortably a bed in a marvelous hospital in England. Comfortable, but bored as the very devil—and with two holes, one in each leg, both of which ought to heal before long. I'll be back with the 7th before the winter snows thaw.

Somewhere between here and my outfit is probably a letter which I ought to get in a month or so. I thought I'd write while I have time. I saw Margaret in Paris and she gave me a couple of bottles of Champagne, besides a soda bottle filed with Scotch. Anyway I feel well and Margaret certainly looked well.

There's nothing much else going on, just lying back and waiting.

Love, ALVIN

In the Pacific, MacArthur's Sixth Army invaded Luzon in the Philippines and carrier-based planes raided Japanese bases in Indochina.

Lt. Col. Alvin L. Mente, Jr.
D.O.P. Hospital Plant 4150
January 14, 1945

Dear Rose and Biz:

Been nearly a week now since I last wrote so I thought you would like to know how we have been doing. A sort of bedside bulletin on the case of "Old Sulfa and Penicillin." We are still flat on our back and have shown no signs of getting up yet. The wound on our right thigh is closing by itself without benefit of sewing. Latest X-rays show a comminuted fracture of our navicular (bone in instep). Now what do you think of that? Better get out Webster for I don't know too well what it means. Anyway, don't tell Mother. I'm keeping the fracture a secret.

What's the latest news on Martin? Not that he'll be able to help, but I'd like to get a job back home for a little while and then return to combat duty. I'm not convinced one way or the other, but as long as I'm going to be away from my unit, I'd like to get well in comparative ease. A job in the states somewhere for about six months sounds ideal, but nothing like that could ever happen. I'd love to go back to the 7th tomorrow but that is quite out of the question.

I'm anxiously awaiting word on what the latest news is. How have you and Biz been? Well, I hope.

Love, PAT

As Margaret was writing, the U.S. First and Third Armies linked up after being separated by the Battle of the Bulge.

Margaret F. Morin
American Red Cross
Civilian War Relief
January 16, 1945

Dearest Kids:

I was shocked in your letter of Jan. 4th to hear that you had not heard from me since Nov 15th. I don't write much but certainly more often than that. I expect Bill Giblin has seen you and given you all the gory details. We all envy him his trip so much and I'm sure he'll make the best of it. What do you think of the picture of our laying the wreath at the Tomb of the Unknown? It's rather peculiar, but if you put in a frame which gives depth it shows off to the best advantage. I told Bill to explain all this to you. I can hear the remarks when you first got it—as I got the same from everyone here.

No, Rose, I've never received the copy of the Quentin Reynolds book—nor do I want it from all accounts.

Have you heard from Bill Robinson yet? If not, give him a ring at the *Herald Tribune*. He's probably lost your number. He's a wonderful person. We had lots of fun while he was here and I miss him a lot.

I still haven't got out to Marymount, which probably seems unbelievable to you. I will go. Right now we're perishing with the cold. However, spring will come, I hope.

Love to you both, MARGY

Lt. Col. Alvin L. Mente, Jr.
D.O.P. Hospital Plant 4150
January 18, 1945

Dear Rose and Biz:

Got your letters of Dec. 19th and Jan. 5th today and was really glad to hear from you. One line in your letter to the effect that one who escapes from pockets should get the Congressional Medal of Honor. All I got was a P.H. and don't mean Pearl Handle. As you might expect, I'm glad to be aboard.

I'm walking on crutches now. Walking hardly describes it. It's more of a slow drag. The leg I must walk on—the other being in a cast—is my hurt one. It's really painstakingly slow, but it's better than a wheelchair. I'm still awaiting my transportation back home. I'm getting a bit bored waiting, but I'm not going anywhere anyway. I'll phone as soon as I can.

Nothing else new. Hope you are both well and not too greatly bothered by the cold.

Love, PAT

On the Eastern Front, Russian forces captured Warsaw and soon liberated the Auschwitz concentration camp.

# THE BEGINNING OF THE END 267

Rose Mary Morin
New York City
January 19, 1945

Dear John:

You may have already heard from the girls or from "Pat" himself that he is in a hospital in England after being wounded in both legs in Belgium on December 21. Nance had written about it last week, just before we got Pat's letter. When the War Department wire came to me yesterday I was scared to death. I had forgotten about Honey telling me Alvin had given my name for any such notification, and having already heard from the patient himself when I saw the "stars" on the wire, I naturally thought of you or the girls.

I'm glad Margaret was able to see him while he was in Paris en route. I thought you would also enjoy Nell's letter and Tom's. Nance said one of Pat's injuries was in the foot and the other in the thigh. There can't have been any bone injury as he expects to get back so soon. You may know where his hospital is located and get down to see him and cheer him up—he seems bored to death.

We've had considerable snow of late and that means slushy streets for New York. The officials are making every effort to have it removed but with lack of manpower it takes time. I was awakened in the early hours this morning by men calling back and forth to the person driving the snow removal machine.

When you get a moment let us know what goes on.

                                    Love and good luck, ROSE

Lt. Col. Alvin L. Mente, Jr.
D.O.P. Hospital Plant 4150
January 21, 1945

Dear Rose and Biz:

This will probably be the last letter you will get from me before I phone you or drop in to see you. The next time I go through the Port of Embarkation I hope they give me enough time to call you at least.

This morning I got official word that I was being sent back. By what means, Lord only knows. By boat, I suppose, but air evacuation is very popular. When? He only knows that, too. My guess is some time after the first of February. No one knows anything, particularly those who are supposed to know.

As yet I am still in bed, but it rarely snows in it. No matter how bad one feels, he can always be darn glad he's not in a snow covered foxhole. I am due to get up on a couple more days and that, my friend, is real progress. I was hit a month ago today.

Will phone at the earliest opportunity, if I get that close.

        Love to you both, ALVIN

Mary Eleanor Morin
American Red Cross
Civilian War Relief
G-5 HQ, 12th Army Group
January 23, 1945

Dearest Kids:
This is going to be very brief—good thing I typed out that volume right after Christmas to make up for the time elapsed and this: I've had some trouble with my eye. First thought I had a cold then the doctor decided conjunctivitis and then discovered I had an ulcer on my right eye, a corneal ulcer—very fashionable sounding don't you think? So I was slapped into a local Army hospital for two or three days, but a bit over two weeks later, I'm sitting up in bed writing this to you. They say I'll get out eventually, but I've come to doubt that.

It is all under control and the last few days the inflammation has cleared miraculously under penicillin drops. Today, they tried a new treatment and I think it is cured altogether.

Lord only knows how I'll be able to face the barracks after all this time between linen sheets, beautiful white blankets and more care and attention than you'd ever believe possible.

This is my first successful attempt at writing. I'm afraid to overdo it, so I'll cease.

        With best love to all of you, NELL

Margaret F. Morin
American Red Cross
Civilian War Relief
Continental Headquarters
January 24, 1945

Dear Rose:

Yesterday I received your letter of the 10th. I'm very concerned why you haven't heard from me in so long. I know that I never write very often, but certainly more than you have received.

You may be amused to know that I wore a pair of the white gloves last Wednesday, when Molly and I placed a wreath on the tomb of the Unknown Soldier for the American Legion in France.

It was fun. We had to march up the Champs Élysées, after a bad snowstorm and the streets were covered with ice, carrying a huge wreath right behind the color guard.

We were laughing so hard that we almost dropped the thing. It was just at six-thirty in the evening and nobody saw us marching. You know, Rose, how the French have a parade at the drop of a hat. One gets accustomed to it. A few people we know were at the Arc de Triomphe so that we do have some witnesses. We signed the book too, the one that only "Presidents and Ambassadors sign," so maybe someday we'll be famous. Molly got me into it. One of the men came into the office and asked her if she could find another girl as tall as she, it would be very picturesque. The choice was obvious!

Aunt Margy (kneeling) at the French Tomb of the Unknown Warrior under the Arc de Triomphe on Champs Élysées.

I got a notice from London yesterday that my long lost bedding roll has arrived and is on the way over here. I can't believe it, after almost a year. I hate to think of opening it and finding everything stolen or ruined. I'll let you know what the outcome is.

I've been waiting for the past two weeks to go on a field trip. But the French take so long to get things going, and there's no sense in going until our ARC clothing gets there for distribution. I'm not looking forward to this one, because it will be all through Normandy and Brittany, which is none too comfortable at this time of the year.

We've been reading so much in the papers over here about the new draft rules. It sure would be funny if "The Brain," that's one of the names for Giblin, got caught. He'd fire me if he thought I could see anything funny about it. Goodbye for now.

Love to you both, MARGY

P.S. I received the $100 in December—thanks again!

In France, John's Bomb Group prepared to move to from Athies to Prouvy so their bombers could fly deeper into Germany.

Rose Mary Morin
New York City
January 24, 1945

Dear John:

Doubtless by now you have heard from Pat Mente or from Margy as to his location in England. While everyone is writing to him it will probably be some time before he has it coming regularly. He writes to Nance every day to keep her informed of his condition. I think it is sweet of him to keep the news of the fracture a secret from Nance. She would be worried but I think too that she is so grateful that he is not too seriously injured and getting along nicely that it probably wouldn't upset her too much. However, you can be sure we will keep his secret from her.

What do you think of Margy's references to her recent experiences? I'd like to have had a picture of her with the Queen. I bet she looked even ritzier than she did in that picture taken with you, Mart and Nell after she arrived in England last year. And having been in Bastogne at such a critical time. I wonder if she will ever come down to earth again after all she has seen and done. We are anxiously awaiting a call from Bill G.

Even if there isn't time for him to come to see us I surely hope he will telephone and give us the news. Margaret is so casual about everything. Thank Heaven Nell keeps us quite current as to what she is doing.

I haven't heard from Anne so don't know what Martin is up to in Washington. He probably is still on the same schedule of long hours and hasn't time to write. Nor have we any recent word from Bill and Lois. Her last letter said they were getting a house and would let us know when they have moved so that we could go up and pay a visit.

Best of luck and much love, ROSE

# Chapter 31

## Doomsday

In the winter it wasn't unusual to wake up when it was still dark outside, but it had been always light by the time I left for school. So one rainy morning in early January I couldn't understand why it was still dark when I headed down Craig Street to the school two blocks away. Reflections of the streetlights streaked down the trolley tracks and cars had their lights on as they splashed over the Belgian blocks.

It looked like the middle of the night. Mike and I never waited for each other when it rained, but I caught up with Donny Gilford and Rachel Young. Donny was the biggest kid in our class and Rachel was the prettiest.

"Why is it still dark out?" I asked.

Donny said, "Duh! Maybe the sun ain't up yet."

Rachel said, "Don't worry, it'll be light soon."

"We never had mornings like this in Sheraden," I said.

"No wonder, Sheraden is in the sticks," Donny said. "You're in the city now."

Sheraden was in the hills away from the rivers and I couldn't see steel mills from my back porch, like I could in Oakland.

Our school slowly appeared through the murky haze as we approached from half a block away. Every light inside was on and spotlights outside bathed the schoolyard.

A substitute teacher, Sister Bertha, was waiting at Sister Fredette's desk as the class came tumbling in, hanging coats in the cloak room and putting books in the desks. Sister Bertha was the smallest and sternest sister in the school.

"No talking, settle down," she said.

When the 8:30 late bell rang it was still pitch black outside the windows. Class went on as usual. First the Our Father, then the Pledge of Allegiance, then, "Take out your catechisms." Religion was the first class every morning.

Nobody said anything about the darkness outside, so after we put away our catechisms and took out our grammar books, I raised my hand.

"Yes, Mr. Morin," Sister said.

I stood up and said, "Sister, why is it still dark out?"

Sister looked at the windows as if it was the first time she noticed it was dark as midnight.

"Why do you think it's still dark, Mr. Morin?"

"I don't know, Sister."

"Well, maybe it's a message from God that we must change what we do here on earth."

*Uh-oh*, I thought, *more catechism*.

"We have wars and we disobey His commandments and are surprised to find ourselves cut off from His heavenly light. Do you think we should have wars?"

"No," I said, apologetically, as if I had started World War II from the schoolyard.

"Of course we shouldn't have wars! How can you think we should for one minute? All of you should think about that. Where is this darkness coming from? What are those mills making over there in Homestead? Peaceful things to make the world better? No. They're making war materials to kill and maim our fellow human beings."

She lowered her voice and said darkly, "A day like today is God's warning that we must stop or we will destroy the earth and all the people on it."

I sat down, silently withdrawing my question, hoping she wouldn't roil on. As if reading my mind she said, "Open your books to page 54, the 'Principal Parts of Speech.'"

It was still dark when school let out at three-thirty. Donny came up as Mike and I walked along Craig Street. He said, "That'll teach you to ask stupid questions. We're lucky she didn't talk all day and make us stay after school to make up."

"Yeah, too bad," I said, "I still don't know why it's dark out."

He raised his hands and wriggled his fingers like the Angel of Death., "Oooo, it's doomsday, we're all going to die!"

Then, out of the corner of his mouth, "It's not the first time, stupid, this is Pittsburgh."

# Chapter 32

## The President's Last Chapter

Rose Mary Morin
New York City
February 1, 1945

Dear John:

Bill Giblin met us for cocktails at the Ambassador last night and Biz and I both think he is wonderful. How lucky the girls are to have anyone so nice for a boss! He is going through town from Washington to Boston to spend some time with his family. All his reports about the girls are so good. Marg and Molly's escape out of Bastogne was most exciting. They apparently sat in a command car waiting for Lee to get some directions while shells whizzed all around them, then got out by the last road to Namur.

Bill's description of their visit to the Queen in Brussels was also very amusing. Apparently Marg got along very well with the Queen due to their mutual interest in music. Bill says the girls are all doing a beautiful job.

Amy just telephoned on her return from a visit in Washington. She was out to Anne's on Sunday and just raved about the children, especially Robin. Bill Giblin told us the story not to be related to Nance, of Pat being taken prisoner but escaping and finally being wounded when fired at by our soldiers as he approached our lines. Incidentally, as you will see in his enclosed letter, he is expecting to leave for home at any time now.

Janet was in Washington visiting Martin to find a place for them to live—so apparently Martin has some idea that he will be there for a while and is moving the family.

Let us hear from you, Love, ROSE

President Roosevelt, Prime Minister Churchill and Josef Stalin met at Yalta from the fourth to the eleventh of February.

Rose Mary Morin
New York City
February 8, 1945

Dear John:

No further word from Pat Mente but I guess we'll be hearing from him soon even if he returns by ship. Maybe he will be here at about the same time Bill Giblin comes back. I would hate to miss seeing them.

Tom is apparently still on one of the first islands invaded, as he makes no mention of having moved on. He did say in a letter written to Patsy early in January that he was going to fly to Australia and New Guinea.

It must be very hot there now as Tom said he gets little or no exercise. The news of the entry of our troops into Manila was thrilling, and the many tales appearing in the newspapers about the released prisoners most exciting.

Janet has had no luck so far in finding a house in Washington or vicinity. I guess it is a case of hearing of someone moving and being on the scene before someone else can grab the vacated property.

Anne won't turn her house over to them because it looks now as though it will be six months or more before Bob goes to Texas. In a way I'm glad because she doesn't seem too anxious to get started in view of difficult traveling conditions, housing, etc.

This no doubt will arrive a little too late for Valentine greetings, but best of luck and love.

ROSE

In the Philippines, on February 3, the U.S. Army attacked the Japanese in Manila and were fighting to recapture Bataan.

> Lt. Commander T.H. Hanson
> G-2 Section (CCD)
> Advance Echelon USAFFE
> Philippine Islands
> February 10, 1945

Dearest Rose:

Your greeting card (birthday, which I probably acknowledged previously) and the letter you wrote Jan. 26th (the birthday) has arrived, and I'm tremendously grateful to you for thinking of me. I know what a volume of correspondence you have over the other ocean, and I marvel at your having the time to care for it and take care of everything else you have to do.

Wish I had known that General MacArthur and your father were friends—I'd have talked to him the day we stood beside him on the wharf. I was half tempted to get his autograph, but the officers stood back for the enlisted people, so I had no chance to elbow up. If ever our paths cross again, I'll sure introduce myself. He's a genius, and if things bog down in Europe again, the folks at home will be screaming for him to be sent over there. (Sutherland and Krueger, plus all the rest of his staff, are a great help to him, I might add.)

The youngsters from all accounts are doing exceptionally well and I'd probably be insufferable if I didn't think that perhaps Patsy was a bit prejudiced in her reports of their doings.

I'm looking forward to receiving the copies of letters from Nell, Marge, Pat, et al., and promise that I'll get something in the mail to them reasonably soon thereafter.

I met a Red Cross man recently whom you may know—Johnny McVickers, who was with Raymond Whitecomb's travel agency for years, and more recently associated with the management of the Hotel Pierre. He thinks he has met Bill and is not sure if he knew Marion, although he knows many of the people in that set.

We're all packed and ready to move, and wait only for transportation. Things moved so swiftly that they are having a difficult time reestablishing a schedule. We should be away from here anytime though, and look forward to the new place.

I'm sorry Pat was hurt, but glad that it wasn't too serious. I'll look forward to details.

Nothing much else, and I have many letters to crowd through this machine while I have a chance at it, so I'll close. Take care of yourself, write me when you can, and know that we're looking forward to a reunion as soon as possible after this mess is done. Best to you and to Biz,

As always, TOM

After massive Allied bombing on Tuesday, February 13, and Wednesday the 14th, Dresden, Germany, was destroyed by a firestorm.

Lt. Col. Alvin L. Mente, Jr.
D.O.P. Hospital Plant 4150
February 15, 1945

Dear Rose:
Your letters of the 19th and 24th arrived and all I've done is read and re-read them. Patsy wrote. Janet and Mrs. Westwater sent some Omnibooks. You've really started something. But really, Rose, I'm all well now, fit as a fiddle, and ready to take off—just as soon the Air Transport Command gets on the ball. About that foot, it not only doesn't hurt, I walked on it immediately after being hit and it was so painless they didn't discover the trouble until the 15th of January, over three weeks later. No, Rose, I haven't had any pain in nearly a month now and what I had was so slight, I've already forgotten. Come to think of it, if Jack Flanagan is at the Kennedy General at Memphis he might be my doctor. One never knows.

John's location is miles beyond London and on the other side of England. I tried to phone him one night and it was so far I couldn't get his operator. I'd like to see him but this place is so distant and has no facilities, I couldn't even buy him a beer.

Rose, thanks for asking what I need. Nothing, absolutely, but keep at those beads and before long I'll see you and show you my operation.

Love, best to Biz, ALVIN

Margaret F. Morin
American Red Cross
Civilian War Relief
Continental Headquarters
February 16, 1945

Dear Kids:

I've been away for the past two weeks, off and on. Nell was down. She's probably written you about that. It was fun seeing her. The first trip I took was down through Brittany. We drove down in a terrific ice storm and after almost two days driving arrived to find almost spring weather. The weather has improved here too.

Last week I went up to Rheims. I've been there four or five times before, but for the first time I went through the Champagne caves—Pomeroy. Afterward the manager brought out a few special bottles for us to sample. What can one do with a bottle of Champagne except finish it? I was there five days and the officers decided they would give me what is known as the Class A treatment. When I got back I swore I'd never look at the stuff again. However, I felt better about it a few days later.

Rose, I finally received the moccasins. They fit perfectly. I also received the box of four packs of cigarettes. Thanks so much! If you could find a good-looking sports jacket that would go with my slacks—perhaps and unlined flannel—would you send it to me? Don't you think a box type would be best? I don't think anything too fitted would be practical. In any case whatever you think. About the color—perhaps a nice bright plaid or a plain color—Kelly green or yellow. It sounds wild, doesn't it?

My new uniform has been finished all week, but I haven't had time to pick it up. It should be very snappy.

Take it easy about Bill G. He can turn on that charm like a tap—and does. What's more he knows it all himself. Restraint, my chicks!

I'm so glad to hear that Pat's going home. I haven't heard from our John in ages. Met his old C.O., who is quite a guy. He had me to a buffet supper at his house here—where he lives with three other officers—which is really something.

As you can see my handwriting gets worse and worse, so I'd better stop.

They're planning an anniversary party on the 21st—two years overseas. There are five of us here who arrived together. Bill G. is the sixth, but from recent reports he won't be back then.

Love to you all, Margy

Mary Eleanor Morin
American Red Cross
Civilian War Relief
G-5 HQ, 12th Army Group
February 16, 1945

Dearest Rose and Biz:

I'll try to shake this spring fever off long enough to write. It has been simply awful this week; I've had to drive myself to do anything. It has been beautiful for the last few days. I've never seen or expected to see such weather in this part of the world. Between the weather and being away from work for so long, I'm in a hopeless state.

The hospital finally let me out. Believe me, you have no need to worry that they aren't completely thorough—22 days and they were still reluctant to discharge me. My eye is completely better. I'm going back to the clinic for a checkup this afternoon. The most important thing was that I didn't strain it by reading or catch cold when I first got out. I came back to the office long enough to catch up on some work here and get my clothes ready to go in town.

My boss volunteered to send me in town for a week or so. I stayed with Dorothy Reader for a couple days until Marg came back. She lives in an apartment of some friends of hers that is the most comfortable place, you can imagine. She met me at the train and took me to her place where she had a big fire and supper ready.

We had a few nightcaps and talked each other blue in the face before finally going to bed. You should have seen the bed—hot water bottle, gown, robe and slippers and only a stone's throw from a real bathroom. Marg came back Sunday. Dorothy had another of her parties during the week and John's old boss, Thatcher, was there.

It was good to see him. He asked Marg and me to have dinner with him the following Sunday night. Marg went but I left to come back Sunday morning. I was sorry to have missed it, as he is a peach. He asked all about John. That picture I sent of Dulcie and me on the Clubmobile was taken on his station when we met John for the first time. They were simply grand to us.

I don't think you've received all my letters, because I'm sure I said something about Lois and Bill. I had just written to Billy for his birthday and wrote again right away. How are they? What are they up to? Tell Billy to write.

I sure hope Bill G. and our Bill were able to get together. It was nice that he could get to see you all. He's heard so much about the various members of the family from all of us that I was sure he wouldn't miss seeing you if he could help it.

Poor Mrs. Moriarty must be wild with the possibility of Mort going overseas. I suppose she has forgotten the statement she made about being glad we'd finally gone into the war and she'd be proud to have her son the first to the front. It shook Mort but left Mary and me in convulsions. I think she added that she planned to go and drive an ambulance!

I guess I've told you before that we have the best mess in the entire theater. That is for the size and it is more than difficult to be birdlike at meals. They even do C-rations up well and the most insidious thing is that they bake all their bread, rolls and pastries with the assistance of the French. The result is perfect, as you would imagine with our rations of white flour, etc.

You must be hearing from Marg by now. She writes, I know, but perhaps her letters just don't get through.

Thanks for the cigars. Butch will like them, I know. He smokes constantly.

The kids saw Pat and from all accounts he was as well as could be expected under the circumstances. He's better off being out of it. I suppose by now he is home and I hope you will all get a chance to spend some time with him. We met his friend Cosgrave, Betty's beau, in town. She had a cocktail party at the Ritz for a few people. Betty is a peach and very fond of Pat. Cosgrave seems like a nice sort of person but very quiet.

Patsy must have been terrified when she saw Rosemary skidding off the sink. I'm glad the baby wasn't hurt and hope by now Patsy had got over having heart failure every time she has to bathe the child.

Bishop Ready will spare no energy making an impression on Columbus. The correspondent who shares the room with me said she had heard from her family in Columbus and they are quite taken by him.

I just went back to the barracks and Marie and Jose were there. She said her auntie had sent her a lot of clippings about Ready. I told her I thought he'd turn the house into a chancery and live elsewhere. That didn't surprise her in the least. She said it was a horrible old house and in a bad part of town. Be good, Rosebuddy, and take care of yourself.

Loads of love, NELL

P.S. I just dipped into my briefcase for an airmail envelope and there was a mouse in it. I escaped from the office before the kids could make good their threat to throw it at me. They killed it right on the floor. Those lists of gifts I was looking for got well chewed up before it found the only candy bar there. Lord, how I hate those hideous things. M.E.

Rose Mary Morin
New York City
February 16, 1945

Dear John:

I finally got extra copies at the office of the *Sun*. Margaret's letter enclosed will give a little more light on the wreath laying!

We have been wondering why no word from Nell, but her enclosed letter explains her long silence. I do hope she will be all right and that the ulcer won't leave a scar where it will affect her sight.

Biz visited Anne over the weekend since they gave her Saturday off and Monday also (Lincoln's birthday). She saw Martin and Janet. Mart developed a sacroiliac involvement about two weeks ago and has been in Walter Reed. Janet has given up house hunting for the time being and spends every day at the hospital. When Biz left Monday, Mart was able to move from side to side, but any other movement is still painful. She said he looks wonderful, after the rest and excellent treatment he has had, and was enjoying the opportunity of taking things easy. No doubt they will fit him with a belt and send him back to work very soon. Lois and Bill came in to shop Tuesday and had dinner at the apartment. They are moving into a four-bedroom house at the Point today and have been very busy with drapes, curtains, furniture covers, etc.

Best of luck and much love, ROSE

P.S. Tom wrote Patsy the beginning of the month that he was getting ready to move on to Manila. Pat Mente hasn't come back yet and I judge from his enclosed note that he didn't get the early start he was expecting. R.

On Monday, February 19, U.S. forces invaded Iwo Jima.

Rose Mary Morin
New York City
February 20, 1945

Dear John:

You certainly are giving us the silent treatment with no word since October! Lois and Bill came in Saturday and we had a highball with the LaGuardias before dinner at a neighborhood restaurant. The L's were having an early dinner before attending the opera. Biz spent the night with Mary Lou and Peggy. After church Sunday we spent a few hours in the Museum of the City of New York. Bill liked the pair of Lowestoft urns that had belonged to Revolutionary General John Morin Scott. Did you ever hear of him? I'm sure Grandma Hickey messed up there as she never included him in any of her stories, but of course he wouldn't have been an ancestor. Bill said he was one of the signers of the Declaration of Independence.

I spoke to Anne last night on the telephone and she said Mart was walking all around the hospital Friday, so he expects to be back at work in four or five days. The first couple tries they had to put him out on his feet, but Friday he got out of bed alone.

Bill and Lois moved to their new house last Friday and Lois went to Albany for her little boy yesterday and is expecting her mother to be their guest this weekend. All goes well here.

Much love, ROSE

On Sunday, February 25, U.S. B-29s dropped 450 tons of incendiaries on Tokyo.

Margaret F. Morin
American Red Cross
Civilian War Relief
Continental Headquarters
February 27, 1945

Dearest Kids:

I received today your letters of the 24th of January and Feb. 16. I had not had any mail in so long that I was beginning to wonder.

I've written you that Nell was down after she left the hospital. I spoke with her on the phone Friday. She sent us a lot of wonderful food. We are eating at home, almost all the time, so it helps. I've been on another trip—this time to Displaced Persons camps. You'll probably be hearing a lot about them soon.

We had a really bang-up party last Wednesday. It was the second anniversary of our arrival in Oran. There were about 60 or 70 people. The sitting room was jammed, but everybody had a good time. The famous secretary was there. I also got hold of Wawee Barkley who is here now.

We consumed 20 bottles of Champagne and 10 bottles of Cognac. The apartment looked wonderful. It was the first time we've used the dining room and sitting room since November. Godfrey found a little florist who came up and arranged the flowers. The "Brain" is expected back any day. We'll be deluged with stories. Things look pretty quiet for a while, but who knows?

Best love to you all, MARGY

Mary Eleanor Morin
American Red Cross
Civilian War Relief
G-5 HQ, 12th Army Group
February 28, 1945

Dearest Kids:

There is a tie-up someplace. I haven't had a letter in what seems an eternity. Actually, it probably is no longer than a week, but it sure seems longer than that. This as you've already figured out is a deliberate play on your sympathy. But please write as often as you can and encourage everyone else to do the same. I've had letters from Anne, Patsy and Janet, but I guess Biz and Mary Moriarty are holding out for bigger game.

I gave everyone in the office a good scare a few days ago by screaming blue murder when my groping hand in the briefcase came across a mouse.

By a strange chain of circumstances my name was drawn on the liquor ration for a bottle of gin. It really is strange because the officer who drew it also drew his own, his roommate's and our section executive's. Saturday night we decided to have a party in their quarters. In case you are questioning my judgment in being there—it is considered perfectly good form as long as there are three or more people there at the same time. There was a blinking light up in the smoke covered ceiling, two big windows with homemade blackouts that kept falling in, three cots, three hardwood chairs, standing utility wardrobe, a very good Jerry radio, lots of boxes of coal, chips, wood, buckets of water and a peculiar type of stove with the "chimney" out the window. No one had any idea how to build the fire and it was the orderly's day off so we fortified ourselves with gin and went to work.

That is, the lowest-ranking character in the room did, while the rest of us sat and heaped ridicule on his head for his efforts. It couldn't have been more than a half hour later that we were all choking from the smoke and peeling off tunics, driven out and forced back to the club.

During the evening it developed that one of the men had a birthday next day. I remembered that after regaining consciousness about 4:30 Sunday afternoon I decided to have a cocktail party for him. After I'd invited six people and arranged for exclusive use of the WACs and Red Cross part of the club, I realized that I had nothing to mix the stuff with, so I threw myself on the mercy of my chum, Blackie the bartender. He produced a liquid distinctly related to Vermouth and a large jar of king size olives. It turned into an elegant affair.

My guests came in their newly authorized battle jackets and low-cut shoes. Two new R.C. gals came in, beautifully timed, just as we'd filled our glasses for the last time. Someone got out Champagne and we went in for dinner—Turkey in quantities, and all the rest of it.

It's lucky for me in more ways than one that I chose social service work instead of strip tease. I had lumps and bruises up to my knees. All of which just goes to show that there are things to fear other than enemy activity. I'm already having misgivings over a promise I made to go to a dance next week with an engineer.

Lee has given me permission to spend Easter in Paris with the kids. I hope if you were able to get that black suit that it arrives on time. They say the Easter Parade there is really out of all worlds—Notre Dame, bells chiming, chestnuts in blossom—I can hardly wait.

Just called to see if there is any mail and discovered a package and letter from you. I opened the shoes at lunch and they are very nice. I think it's remarkable that you can pick them out to fit. The funny part is that the package was postmarked at Grand Central January 24 and they arrived here yesterday with the sales slip tucked under the <u>outside</u> string. How in the world could it get this far without falling off is a mystery to me.

Well, I guess I'd better close, as there is nothing very startling to relate. Give my love to everyone and tell them to write.

Lots of love, NELL

Rose Mary Morin
New York City
February 28, 1945

Dear John:

Nell's enclosed letter, Pat's and Tom's will give you the latest news we have on the overseas contingent. We have been awaiting a call from Pat Mente every day but so far no luck. I hope he was able to contact you even if you were not able to get down to see him off.

Bill Giblin came up for a little while Sunday evening. He was planning to return sometime Monday by plane so he must be there and at work again by now. He was not able to see Anne in Washington but spoke to her and to Nance (who is staying at Anne's) on the telephone.

We have not heard from Janet but Martin must be now about ready to leave the hospital to return to work if he has not already done so. According to Nell they make sure you stay long enough. Mrs. Swofford's reappointment was confirmed by the Senate yesterday.

I spoke to Anne and the two children Saturday night. They were having a party for Nunsey just before Anne and Bob and the Browns left to celebrate Mr. & Mrs. B's anniversary. Nance was going to stay at the house with Robin and Nunsey.

Why not let us hear from you? Your last communication was written after you had seen Bill Giblin in England—October, I believe.

Much love, ROSE

In the Pacific on Friday, March 2, U.S. forces recaptured Corregidor. In Europe on March 7, Allies took Cologne and established the Remagen Bridge across the Rhine River. Two days later, in the Pacific, fifteen square miles of Tokyo was firebombed by B-29s.

Mary Eleanor Morin
American Red Cross
Civilian War Relief
G-5 HQ, 12th Army Group
March 9, 1945

Dearest Kids:

Crumbs! The way time flies by these weeks. It's all I can do to keep up, whether I've written you or not. I made just such an absent-minded remark to my "acting" boss and he demonstrated the most extreme shock that I didn't whip one or more off daily. I tried to illustrate to him that sisters enjoy a somewhat different attitude toward one another than man and wife. He's a stubborn Dutchman though and will never see it my way.

Jim Riordan read about Bill F.'s brother's death in the *Paris Herald Tribune*. I would never have seen it as someone interrupts me each time I pick it up. The same issue also carried a notice of the death of the father of one of his best friends. So we sat down in unison and wrote Bill. Sent it V-mail airmail because I couldn't leave my desk as I was waiting for a call and didn't dare risk leaving it.

I had a grand letter from Pat written Jan. 22nd, said he was waiting for the boat then. His friend and Betty Baker are being married tomorrow.

The most exciting thing just happened. Had a call from Dorothy Reader who said she was going to put on an old friend. The next thing I remember is, "Is this Nell, the beautiful cloak model?"—Dwyer-ski himself!

There is no truth in the story of his getting married or going home—and he implied that he had entertained thoughts of getting out of the Army back in August as it looked then as though it would all be over soon and he was worried about Bijou. The assurance that Bijou is fine and doing a bang up job changed his mind.

He hopes to get a few days leave in Paris in April and wants me to go in at the same time. Lee has already given me permission to go over Easter for a few days, but it may be too long a trip by then so I'm trying to arrange to go in for St. Pat's weekend. Who knows? Fate may be kind and let me go twice. I hope the suit will arrive by then. Did I ask you to try to find me a soft, frilly blouse for it in white or pale blue?

Margaret got me into an interesting and amusing situation this week. She referred the new Ambassadress of Poland to me to talk about Polish Red Cross activities where I am. It took me hours to get dressed in my very best uniform, white gloves and was picked up at the barracks by a sedan. The executive of the section I'm in had an appointment with her too, so we worked it out together. When we reached the meeting place there were swarms of Poles but not her. We waited and waited and finally decided that we'd missed our cue and tried to leave but they plied us with Champagne until her driver showed up and took us to her hotel.

She eventually came trooping downstairs about 9:30, swept us off our feet with the most commanding charm, sank into a chair and ordered whiskey for all. The waiter got a glazed look in his eye. Well, if there is no whiskey bring us a drop a gin. Nope, nothing but ordinary red or white wine.

Bill Page came to the rescue by asking her to come back to our place. She dispatched a slave for her portmanteau and while we were waiting for that I studied her uniform. After all my pains there, she was showing me up as a complete "fool" (non-combat troop) by wearing fleece-lined boots to her knees, blue R.A.F. officer's tunic, WAF's skirt, stiff collar and black tie.

The coat was a classic—full-length suede, beaver collar and border and fleece-lined! It must have cost a million pounds. On the way to camp we learned she had eaten early and was starving, so I got some cold dry hamburgers from the mess and we made some coffee on the stove and then settled down to Champagne and international affairs. She went on in great length about Margaret and how perfectly delightful she is. Then settled down to business—no silly trusting to memory, right on the line in assorted notebooks. The Poles may not know it yet, but they will be cared for if it's the last act of her life. It would be marvelous to have so much interest, enthusiasm, ability and drive at any age but it is remarkable in a woman of her age. We got through the evening without incident, but as we were leaving I followed her down a flight of slippery metal steps and my foot slipped so to avoid upsetting the whole applecart I braced it between the rungs, regained my balance and nobody knew the difference but me. Two nice little cuts above and below my ankle. The things I suffer for the American Red Cross!

This Bill Page was in '25 at the Point and knew Bill McLaughlin very well. Said he tried but failed to get Bill into this. That is all we need. There's excitement enough without him to bring it to the boiling point.

Speaking of West Point, we saw a movie last night on the post and they showed an awfully good short on the place. It was modern and very thorough, even to shots of all the games for '44, so I got to see the famous Army-Notre Dame game after all. I was nearly wall-eyed throughout, however, trying to pick Billy out, and I knew he was in several of the scenes, but couldn't find him. Very disappointing. Why doesn't that big lug write to me? Better still, come over here? It would be marvelous if he could be with this group.

Let me think, there are always so many things I want to write. About the apartment, I hope you will get one in the fifties. Save you a lot of time and shoe leather between yours and Moriartys' place.

I know this won't come as a particular shock to you but I've only put in two of the five years I planned on when I left you. Margaret, unless something very unforeseen comes up, will feel the same way.

When the war is over we will have the biggest job of all to do until all our troops are home. Then I haven't seen a heck of a lot of the countries I've been in and missed a lot more, so I must do that, after going to Norway and get home by way of China. So I won't be cluttering up the apartment for some time to come.

# THE PRESIDENT'S LAST CHAPTER

Well, Rosey-Posey, so long for now. The mailman just brought in five letters for me so I'll have to stop. Also because there is a whole flock of people going to zoom in any minute and I want to have the desk tidied up.

Best love to you and Biz, NELL

With improved weather in March, John's Bomb Group made 43 successful missions, the most in one month in the Group's history. In the Pacific, the battle for Iwo Jima is all but over.

Lt. Col. Alvin L. Mente, Jr.
Ward 23-A. Kennedy General Hospital
Memphis, Tennessee
March 13, 1945

Dear Rose and Biz:

First of all, may I apologize for not writing in so long. As you may well note, we finally left England by boat—the USA Hospital Ship *Charles A. Stafford* and docked—not in NYC as I had expected, but in Charleston, a little hamlet thousands of miles away. There we stayed for three days. Then we came to Kentucky General Hospital after the slowest, dirtiest, most tiring ride. Lord, you made Georgia take too long!

Upon arrival here we were placed in a receiving ward where a nurse came in calmly announcing that the patients of the hospital had been poisoned—all 4,400 of them. Ye Gods, I thought, take me back where it was safe. However, it turned out they only had ptomaine.

Yesterday morning I introduced myself to Jack Flanagan, who, it seems would have been my supervising surgeon anyway. Just like you predicted in a letter last January, he is handling my case. He looked at my foot, directed X-rays, replaced the cast and recommended me for a 30-day furlough.

Tonight I'm going to his house for dinner. Rose, he's marvelous. If I don't get well under him, I'm never going to get well. I wish Martin were here. He'd have us both well in no time.

Nothing else is new. I'm sorry to hear about Martin. I'll write more later.

Love to you both, PAT

Rose Mary Morin
New York City
March 14, 1945

Dear John:

Pat Mente arrived in Charleston last Wednesday and left there Saturday morning for Memphis and Kennedy General Hospital. Nance went to Charleston for one day to see him. We phoned the Flanagans at Memphis Monday evening to tell them to look out for Pat and found that Jack (Major in Medical Corps) who has the orthopedic ward had already seen Pat and was taking good care of him: furnished him with a walking cast and recommended a 30-day leave.

We called there last night as the Flanagans had invited Pat for dinner and had a chance to say hello to him. He said he hasn't had so much attention in years. He hopes to come up to see us from Southern Pines during his leave. The Flanagans said he looks wonderful and he certainly sounded all right, although a bit excited at finally being home. Monday night when we called Anna May and Amy Froehlich (sisters-in-law of Jack Flanagan) were at the apartment for dinner and I was going with the two of them to see the new musical comedy *Up in Central Park* based on a story about the doings of the Tweed gang. It was an excellent show and had very nice music by Romberg, I believe. The girls had just gone for tickets that afternoon and got three in the first row center of the balcony that is a rare feat these days. Usually there is nothing available for several months. Why the silent treatment since October?

Much love and luck, ROSE

Margaret F. Morin
American Red Cross
Civilian War Relief
Continental Headquarters
March 19, 1945

Dearest Kids:

Everything's going well here. Spoke to Nell yesterday. She's very well and will probably be moving further away soon. She's planning to come in over Easter. We're going to have a big party—that is, if I can still get some Champagne in Rheims when I'm up there tomorrow. I was in Rouen for a day last week and saw John Dwyer. He's very well and treated us beautifully.

I haven't told you about my wonderful trip to Cannes. The week before last I flew down in a general's plane. We left from Rheims and only took 2 1/2 hours. The whole thing was like Hollywood. The sun and sea and all. We stayed at the Martinez Hotel. Ozzie Roberts, who used to manage the Mayflower, runs the place for the Air Force as a rest center. We knew him from Capri. Naturally, the general helped a little, we had a four-room suite facing the sea! The next day we drove to Grasse, which is delightful, and saw the perfume center.

I have some for you all but Lord knows when I'll get it to you. That afternoon we drove to Nice, which can't compare with Cannes. The next morning we said a sad farewell and flew back to Paris on time for lunch. We stopped over at Lyons for gas, but I didn't get to see the city. It was awfully short, but couldn't have been more perfect.

I'm leaving tomorrow for Rheims, Lille, and Deauville that will keep me away until Friday. Please investigate the possibilities of finding me a job with some travel agency after the war. I've gotten so now that I get itchy after being in town four of five days. But I'm always glad to get back, which is good. The weather is getting warmer and all the blossoms are out in the Bois.

Yesterday I walked nine holes of golf at the Club at St. Could, without a coat. It was lovely.

My love to you all, MARGY

Rose Mary Morin
New York City
March 20, 1945

Dear John:

Hope this will arrive in time to wish you a Happy Easter. Tomorrow is the first day of spring but today is more like a summer day. In fact for nearly a week we have been enjoying temperatures in the seventies but today must be eighty at least.

The enclosed letters came after I had written you last week. I don't know to whom Margy is referred as the famous "secretary" but it sounds as though they had a bang-up party in celebrations of their two years overseas.

We haven't had any more word from Pat since we spoke to him last Tuesday evening but he must be at Honey's by now to begin his 30-day leave. Honey's husband is overseas—or did I already write that news.

Anne telephoned Sunday evening. She has been too busy to write and wanted us to know that everything is well with them. She wants Biz and me to go down for Easter but we haven't yet decided—traveling these days is anything but pleasant and one hates to keep someone off the train that really should be going someplace.

Apparently the move to Texas has been postponed until after the war. It seems under War Manpower regulations, the company is not permitted to change Bob's job. Patsy had a letter from Tom written from Manila March 2nd. He said things are pretty well shot up, but they are setting up offices.

Love, ROSE

Margaret F. Morin
American Red Cross
Civilian War Relief
Continental Headquarters
March 23, 1945
Happy Easter!

Dear Rose:

This is going to be a quickie. April 20th is Bill G.'s birthday. There's positively nothing here within reason. I would like to get him a *very* nice dressing robe. You know one of the lightweight silk ones that pack easily. He wears a size 42. Would you go to a good shop and pick one out for him? I've seen some beauties here but they run $160-$200, no kidding. I think you should be able to get one for considerably less at home. In any case get something nice and send it to me. I'm keeping my fingers crossed that it gets here on time. Perhaps you could send it airmail.

Nell is coming in on Friday for the weekend. We have great plans. Will let you know the details later. Will write more during the week.

Best love, MARGY

P.S. About the apartment. I don't know what to say. There are times when I think we'll be over here for at least another year. My gosh that seems a long time putting it that way, doesn't it? However, this past one has gone so quickly. Did I tell you my new uniform is very smart!

Love, M

Lt. Commander T.H. Hanson
G-2 Section (CCD)
Headquarters, USAFFE
Manila, Philippine Islands
March 28, 1945

Dearest Rose:

Have time for a note, so I'll acknowledge the recent airmail V-mail from you. I've written you, but the mail may have gone astray, as Patsy hasn't heard from me since my arrival.

Hope that Pat Mente has arrived in the States by now and that his injuries were as minor as he indicated. It would have been terrible to have been in this mess as long as he has and then, with the end in sight, get smashed up. From the news today it appears that the show in Europe will be over sometime this summer—the Germans can't stand that pasting forever—with seven Allied armies over the Rhine there isn't any place for them to go.

Things out here are still ahead of schedule and, despite a minor setback once in a while, the tactical situation is apparently beyond all expectations.

We rented a house from a Swiss and will live here for a while, or until we are ranked out of it, which is a possibility—I'll kick like a steer if it happens. The place is in Quezon City, about ten kilometers from Manila, and is quite nice as well as wonderfully cheap.

Nothing much else, so I'll get this in the mail. Be sweet, take care of yourselves and let me hear from you.

My best to Biz, as always, TOM

Mary Eleanor Morin
American Red Cross
Civilian War Relief
G-5 HQ, 12th Army Group
March 29, 1945

Dearest Kids:

At this moment I'm so tired I could fall right to sleep at the desk. I've been having a very energetic week. Someone asked me to go for a walk on Sunday. We'd been up pretty late for several nights with one thing and another, so I said I didn't think I'd like to walk very far, but a little walk wouldn't be a bad idea. We went to the Visitors' Bureau in a jeep for a lunch that wasn't madly exciting. Then, with not much energy, started out. We walked up and down and in and out of every back street in the place. It is all up and downhill, steps and things. Then we struck out along the river road to the canal and followed that for two and a half kilometers. Then I sat down. I was puffing and blowing and tormented with the thought that there was only one way to get back and my feet were screeching with pain. The character I was with is eleven years older and does not live right but he was holding out beautifully and wanted to walk on to one of the forts—about three miles away.

We sat by the canal until I regained my health. He found some snail shells that match pretty well, so I think I'll try to have earrings made out of them for Marg. Finally we started back. This guy doesn't just look at these things, but discusses their history and at length. It was most interesting and enlightening, but I was about to collapse. Then we walked back to the station where I had to take my shoes off and relax for about an hour. I swore that I'd never make a date to walk with anyone again. As a consolation prize, he made me the most marvelous martini—with a real olive in it.

I thought I'd had enough sightseeing, but the next day a very good friend of mine had the afternoon off unexpectedly so we drove out to one of the most interesting memorials of the first war. It is a good distance away, but worth it. I've never seen anything so impressive. When we got back we were informed that we could have a new motor for the car if we went to get immediately. I spent the balance of the afternoon and evening making arrangement for a G.I. driver first thing Tuesday morning. Had to drive all the way to the headquarters of Ninth Army, forward. I expected the boy to know the way inside out, as he drives for the executive of the section. We weren't on the road very long until I discovered that he is a smooth driver, but as dumb as a griddle, couldn't read the map and had a peculiar fear of M.P.s.

I had to do it all and we had quite a time. We sailed through several countries, which was all very interesting, but I had to get to the headquarters before the section head left or we'd have had no place to stay. We made it in time to have dinner with our people and spent the evening. They got hysterical when they heard that I thought the car would be finished in time to take off in the morning. I had told the Col. when I asked for his driver that we would only be two days, so the boy's orders were for just that long. Meanwhile the Col. would have no orderly.

So they said they'd see what they could do. It was ready the next day at three, but only because the boys worked all night with flashlights to get it done.

When I saw the car was ready, I decided that I'd better take off. We got to a town in Belgium where some of our people are and decided to stay there. I was worried about the kid getting us really lost after dark.

It was a nice, though worrisome break in the trip. It was getting to the point where we were both going to be without food and since we couldn't eat in the same mess, I sent him off to the billeting officer for a mess ticket and a room and told him to come back after he ate. I met the kids and had dinner at their hotel, which is luxury to an extreme degree. My room was enormous, beautifully furnished and had its own bath with scalding hot water at any hour of the day or night.

We had steak for dinner and all sorts of things like raisin pie that I shouldn't eat, gallons of coffee and proceeded to wonder what was keeping the boy. My plan was to soak for about three hours, wash my hair and get to bed early for a change.

But my driver never came back and we couldn't find him in spite of spreading a dragnet all over town. He had my musette in the car with all my overnight things so I had to borrow soap and face the world with no eye makeup after a tortured night wondering if he'd been sniped or worse.

For all my pains he turned up as a cool as a cucumber at 8:30 a.m. No explanations. We had a wild drive that got us back here in time for lunch at one—the deadline for mess. I'm still rattled.

Now the thought of organizing my clothes and packing to go into town for Easter makes me almost wish I wasn't going. That combined with the realization that instead of spending eight or nine days as I'd planned, we must come back here Tuesday or Wednesday because we may be "going places." It is hardly worth going in for so short a time, just long enough to make you unhappy about coming back.

Instead of going Friday, we're going Saturday that means that I won't have time to get a fancy Parisian hairdo and will look like a country bumpkin in comparison to those two dazzling dames. But it will be fun. They are planning a large party Saturday afternoon.

Here's another item to add to the strange coincidences that are constantly happening: a full colonel seated next to me at dinner, a West Point product from Pittsburgh, and whose name eludes me suddenly, turned on me and asked if I knew a John Morin, to which I replied, "Yes, indeed, he was my father."

"What! It can't be true—we were classmates." (That will show you how much I've aged.) Anyway, he insisted on being remembered to our John and now I can't remember his blooming name. I don't think he and John were close friends anyhow because he's the grim, silent type.

Thank goodness Pat is home safely.

So long again, we are all well and thriving. My eye is all better. The doc told me he's satisfied and that's good enough for me.

Very best love, NELL

Rose Mary Morin
New York City
March 29, 1945

Dear John:

Well, here it is another Easter. We have continued to have summer weather and it is hard to believe that there may still be some cold weather in the offing.

We have had no further word from Pat Mente, but Helen Flanagan, his doctor's wife, wrote her family that Pat had asked her husband to fix him up in a hurry because he wanted to get married as soon as possible.

It must be the young lady in Louisville whom he met while at Fort Knox, as he was stopping off there en route to Southern Pines. No doubt he was such a splendid Cupid in the Betty Baker-Major Cosgrove match that he decided he should get busy with his own plans. Anne says she thinks he was engaged to the Louisville girl when he went overseas.

I read in the *Herald Tribune* this morning where Bill and Lois were best man and matron of honor for Sleepy Semple and his bride last Sunday at the Cadet Chapel. Sleepy was quite a friend of Bill while at West Point and was stationed in Newport with him. He resigned or was discharged because of physical disability while in the Philippines in 1937 and joined the Canadian forces when the war first began and then transferring to our Army after Pearl Harbor. We haven't seen or heard from Bill and Lois since the weekend they stayed at the apartment.

I suppose now that Lois has her son, Jimpy, with them it is difficult to them to leave the Post.

I saw *Bloomer Girl* with the Froehlichs last Wednesday and enjoyed it a lot. Celeste Holm who was the star in the original company of *Oklahoma!* played the lead. I called Anne last night to say I wouldn't be down for Easter but right now I can't decide what I want to do. I really want to go down to see them, but can't quite make up my mind to face the traveling hordes over the holiday.

Hope you have a Happy Easter, Love, ROSE

On April 12, President Roosevelt died at his home at Hyde Park, New York, and the Allies liberated the concentration camps at Buchenwald and Bergen-Belsen.

# Chapter 33

## Over the Wall

After my ninth birthday in January came and went, I had nothing to look forward to except the start of baseball season.

The paper said spring training wouldn't start until the middle of March because of the war. But that didn't stop Gordo, Jimmy and Danny from arguing about who was the best Pirate all during February. Gordo liked Frankie Gustine, Jimmy liked Bob Elliot. Mike didn't like anyone because the Navy had drafted his hero Stan Musial. Danny said he liked all Pirates.

I had never even seen a baseball game, so I didn't know who to like, so I went along with Gordo and liked Frankie Gustine.

When the snow finally melted from Schenley High School's lawn, Gordo, Jimmy, Danny and Mike got out their gloves, bat and ball – and put together a baseball diamond with four flat stones they found in a garden wall on Bellefield Avenue.

Gordo showed me how to keep my hands together and swing the bat level. He watched as I took a few wobbly swings. "Keep practicing," he said.

We played roundsies. Three fielders, one pitcher, one batter. The batter would stand with the high school's wall behind him and, if he didn't hit the ball, throw it back to the pitcher after it bounced off the wall. If he hit it, he'd run the bases until he was tagged out or made it all the way home and bat up again.

Gordo made it all the way home a lot because he hit the ball over our heads into the street almost every time. They all knew how to scoop the ball up with their glove, spin around and throw it in one smooth motion. I didn't have my own glove, so I borrowed the batter's – but when the ball came to me I either missed it or dropped it.

That night at dinner I told Mother and Jane that I needed a baseball glove.

The next morning at the kitchen table Jane had that I-have-a-secret look in her eyes. I sat down and – *plunk!* – a baseball glove appeared in front of me. It was shaped like a first baseman's mitt but not as large as Mike's. Jane waited for my reaction. I put it on and punched its pocket a few times, like Mike did to his. The leather felt dry.

"It was Grandfather's," Jane said. "He gave it to me to save for you." I punched it again. It seemed small.

"He played professional baseball in Montana," she said.

I punched it once more. *Maybe it's not too small*, I thought.

Later, Mike took one look at it and said it was too small. Gordo said, "Maybe if it was your grandfather's, people were smaller then."

It was the only glove I had, so I got used to it.

When April rolled around we couldn't think of anything except Opening Day at Forbes Field in just three weeks. But when President Roosevelt died one Thursday afternoon, all the excitement stopped. Even Mother, who always called him, "that damn Roosevelt," felt sorry he died. Pictures and stories were in the *Press* and *Sun-Tele* for three or four days. The radio never stopped talking about him. Everyone felt because of him the war was almost over, and it was sad that he didn't live to see it end. He was buried a few days after he died, and things slowly came back to normal.

Opening Day was still on my mind. After some earnest begging, Mother relented and said I could go to the Opener instead of to school. When the big day came, the five of us put tenny shoes on our feet and neat's-foot oil on our gloves and headed down Craig Street toward the ballpark. On Fifth Avenue we cut across the rolling green lawn of the Cathedral of Learning to Forbes Avenue where stuffed streetcars emptied and the crowds closed in on the ticket windows and turnstiles of the hulking concrete-and-iron structure on the edge of Schenley Park.

Gordo led the way across the worn grass past the outfield walls to the right-field stands. While the crowd lined up with their tickets to go up the right-field ramp, Gordo hooked his glove on his belt and pulled himself up the concrete wall to the base of the slatted wall of the stands. Then he slipped his tenny shoe between the bottom slat and the strip of metal that held it. He went up hand-over-hand, foot-by-foot, slow and steady, always looking up. Then Jimmy hopped up and followed Gordo.

Mike gave me a boost up the wall. I grabbed the metal strip and fixed my foot on the first slat. I paused and looked at the crowd inching toward the turnstiles. I could go down now, I thought, but I knew I *had* to go up.

I kept my eyes on each foot as I slipped it between the slat and metal strip, going up one slat at a time. I looked at Gordo who was almost up to the second tier, with Jimmy two body-lengths behind. I looked back at my feet and at the next slat, then the next.

I was going good until I reached the second tier. Now I must let go of the metal strip with my right hand, reach over and grab the railing on the side of the tier and climb over.

I glanced down. I could see the treetops – and hear my heartbeats. I grabbed the railing with one hand – then the other – and pulled myself up and over – landing safe on solid concrete, my back to the field.

When I turned around I saw a wonder I had never seen before: a major league baseball field.

I couldn't stop looking. Glistening green grass. Groomed tan infield. Pure white bases attached to the home plate by perfect, milk-white chalk lines that ran through the green to the outfield walls. I didn't know it then, but this would be my summer home for the rest of my boyhood.

Danny was the last one up, and we all set out to find good seats. Every time we did, people with tickets showed up and made us move. We ended up sitting on the steps next to the railing of the right-field stands that we had just conquered.

We came again the next day and the next, a Sunday. During the seventh-inning stretch, after the lady sang "God Bless America," the loudspeaker announced that Allied forces had entered Berlin.

I bet no baseball crowd ever cheered louder.

# Chapter 34

## V-E

Rose Mary Morin
New York City
April 4, 1945

Dear John:

You will be pleased to learn that Mart's promotion to Colonel came through last week and that he was back to work on March 26, apparently feeling in the pink. I spoke to him Sunday night. He sounded grand and said he feels fine, and both Anne and Bob said he looks very well.

Just before speaking to them Pat Mente telephoned from the hotel here in New York. He got a ride up by plane from Southern Pines, leaving there at one in the afternoon, making the trip in three hours. The train ride would have been thirteen hours—if on time, and it would be uncomfortable for him to keep his leg still that long.

He is staying at the Piccadilly, which seems to be Army Hqs. Pat came into the office to take me to lunch Monday and he looks wonderful. He manages very well with his walking cast and cane and when the going gets difficult, it's easy to capitalize on his shortcomings because buses wait and people give him their seats.

He expects to be married early in June to Jane Robbins from Louisville. Apparently it was all settled before he went overseas, but he kept it under his hat except to tell Betty Baker and Martin. From all accounts she is a grand girl and Nance is very fond of her. Pat has to return to Kennedy General Hospital in Memphis April 15 and will be there for about a month, then have another 30-day leave.

He took Biz and me to the Waldorf-Astoria Monday for dinner and yesterday went up to West Point to see Lois and Bill and a lot of his friends who are there. We are expecting him at the apartment this evening for dinner. He plans to leave for Louisville via Washington tomorrow, driving his own car from Washington.

Love, ROSE

Mary Eleanor Morin
American Red Cross
Civilian War Relief
G-5 HQ, 12th Army Group
April 7, 1945

Dearest Rose:

Well, I have two letters and a card for Easter to thank you for. The card arrived Easter Saturday. Very good timing. You got your wish, Easter was one swell day. In fact it boiled down to four and half "Swell Days." I'd been on a long trip to one of the armies to have our station wagon fixed, a good but tiring trip. We had been celebrating for a few days for lack of something better to do. The prospects of going to town depressed me as I had no clean clothes. However, I packed Saturday morning, just jammed everything in my cardboard box, and took off.

We made town in phenomenal time. In fact, just as all the kids were leaving the building for lunch. Jim Riordan had come down the day previously and was with Marg, Molly, Bill Giblin, and there must have been others. Lee, Molly, Jim and I went off for drinks and lunch. That afternoon the kids had a supper party for everyone in the world, including their servants.

John Dwyer, Jules Ortag, Jim, Capt. Emmons and Col. Smith went back to Jim's for dinner and later to a little bar near the kids' house. That folded so we went back to Marg's and Molly's flat. After they left, Margy and I sat up until about six in the morning drinking coffee and talking each other's head off. Molly had given all their food away to their borrowed servants and Marge had no dinner.

She had taken a nap after the party cleared out and woke up starving. The kids' apartment looked lovely. They had beautiful flowers everywhere. Next day we went to church in the neighborhood—can't think why we didn't go to Notre Dame, but I guess it was too late when we got up. Bill and the others met us there and we went back to the kids' place for a drink before going to a party that Bill had for all of us.

That was sensational. It was a lovely sort of inn out in the country. It was the best lunch in the most attractive surroundings you can imagine. We were supposed to have gone to the track after lunch, but dilly-dallied over lunch so long, there wasn't time. Bill had us all back to his apartment for cocktails. After dinner, Lee, Jim and I went to Montmartre. Jim was completely taken with the place and just sat absorbing the music and atmosphere, not to mind quantities of Cognac.

Everyone in the place but us was Russian and after all my experience with the Russians in the camps, I felt I had a bond with them. There was a wonderful violinist and two girls who sang extremely well. (I'm running out of adjectives.) During the evening we ran out of cigarettes and Lee went home and got some and some coffee—a large tin of Nescafe that made pitchers of the stuff.

We lost John Dwyer somehow or other. The phone connections are so terribly bad and with everyone dashing around it's no small wonder.

We finally caught up to him Tuesday. His hotel kept saying he wasn't there, but Molly beat them down. That night John D. and I went to the Lido. He met some of his friends and it was a good show. After, he had heard so much about our Russian place we decided to go back and see if it was as good as we remembered. We took a little horse and carriage. It seemed to me that we clopped around for hours before finding the place. I guess the horse knew where it was. The Russians were even better than I remembered. The proprietor bowed us to the best table, the musicians went to town and sent us in some of the most delicious cake I've ever eaten. And you know it's hard for me to wax enthusiastic about cake. It was vanilla in tiny layers with chocolate filling and icing. With that demitasse, the coffee kept being repeated and some fine old Cognac brought out. It seems the Red Cross did something for his family years ago and he had to spend all his gratitude on us.

So Pat is going to break down and get himself married? That's good. Be sure and send us all the news. Poor Mart. Is he still in that convalescent home? Give him my best.

I had just finished a letter to Billy and was kicking myself for not having asked about Sleepy because I thought he might be over here with the Canadians. I don't know for the life of me why Billy doesn't write me. He simply can't be that busy. Pull a chair out from under him for me next time he comes to the house.

Our moving has been on and off for centuries but—and there is nothing official about this statement, merely in inherited instinct from Cecilia Hickey to forecast the future—it may be pretty soon.

After existing in this barracks with outside latrines, foul lighting and drafty offices, anywhere they send us will be heaven. Someone said this would make a fine training ground for the Foreign Legion in the Black Hole of Calcutta.

I'm daydreaming of course, but I can see us now in a simple dwelling with a large sitting room, small library, medium dining room, glass-enclosed breakfast terrace, powder room in dusty pink with jade green fittings, old-fashioned garden in the back—filled with yellow tulips and scented stock—large sunny kitchen and four bedrooms with separate baths and built-in mirrors and lighted wardrobes, millions of windows with glass in them, and large ferocious dogs who can be relied on to eat anyone who tries to cross the threshold (with the exception of our staff and a select number of our military.)

Our offices will also be suitably simple—completely surrounded with Pittsburgh Plate Glass, carpeted, indirect lighting, bathroom and concealed bedroom—for when I work nights late.

I'm forgetting something I'm sure, I always do. Oh, by the way, let me know if the pictures arrived safely. Oh yes, Bob the bookie, is still missing in action and from reports of his friend who was with him just before there was some gunfire, there is little hope that he is alive. However, strange things happen and he may turn up among some of the prisoners they've uncovered. I hope so. He was an awfully good kid.

Lamet, or Fitzgerald's older double, is in the 9th Air Force. He writes, but distance and time seem to keep us apart. Anyway Molly doesn't think he's my type. My own opinion on that is—that makes him a good prospect—my own type and me would sink to an extremely low level in short order.

Well, Rose, I have an appointment to see about new living quarters for me and for all of our personnel, so I must dash.

I went to Mass with my old schoolmate Rowland Keating this morning. He is one of the wackiest characters it has ever been my privilege to work with.

Best of everything to you all, NELL

Margaret F. Morin
American Red Cross
Civilian War Relief
Continental Headquarters
April 10, 1945

Dearest Kids:

I'm sorry it has been such a long time since I've written you. I'm running around in a whirl most of the time and never seem to get much accomplished. However, Easter's come and gone and it was great fun. I'm sure Nell will give you all the gory details.

Rose I hope you got the note I wrote you about Bill G's gift—a very nice silk, lightweight dressing gown. I thought I could get a letter to you by courier but it didn't work. In any case, I'll tell him it's coming. I also asked for $150, which I do need badly. If in a few weeks you get a cable asking for more money, don't be frightened, it's just that I may have to settle my accounts here before taking a trip which will keep me away for quite a while. The Finance Office is a little sticky that way—poor dears!

I'm leaving tomorrow for Belgium. I'll be in Brussels for a few days and hope to see Marjorie.

Will write soon again. MARGARET

Rose Mary Morin
New York City
April 10, 1945

Dear John:

Pat Mente arrived back from West Point last Wednesday evening to have dinner with us, just raving about how attractive Lois and Bill's quarters are. To hear Pat describe them they are the nicest he has ever seen. He had a grand time up there and enjoyed seeing a lot of his friends, meeting Lois and her three-year-old "Jimpy." They went to Bear Mountain Inn in anticipation of having steak dinners, only to learn there were no steaks.

Pat was sure the professional team that was supposed to play the cadets baseball on Wednesday (game was called off on account of weather) had made way with the steaks.

The manager of the restaurant said that if they would say where they expected to be on Wednesday evening, he would provide steaks for the crowd. One of the men in the party said they'd be at his house in Pelham and they forget the incident.

The next afternoon while Pat was at Bill's for lunch the man who lived in Pelham telephoned and said, "Ten steaks had been delivered to his house," and would they be down?

Pat almost died and wondered when he knew he was coming to our house why he had not asked to send them to 425 East 86th. He said the manager had insisted he would furnish steaks, "for this wounded colonel by reason of those fighting he (the manager) was able to keep his business running," but they had not taken him seriously.

Pat left here for Washington Thursday to pick up his car and we have not heard further from him. I hope he arrived in Louisville safely after that long drive alone. In addition to the Purple Heart he also has a Bronze Star for action at Metz, which I forgot to mention in my letter last week.

The only other excitement we have had was Sunday afternoon when the man in the apartment adjoining ours jumped out the window and fell 11 stories to his death.

His motive, if anyone knew, has not been revealed. (Reason enough: He was a German native.)

Love, ROSE

Rose Mary Morin
New York City
April 18, 1945

Dear John:

The enclosed should keep you busy as well as amused for a while at least. Nell must be having a pipe dream thinking anyone going over would be able to take such a huge package as her requests would fill—but there is no harm in her dreaming I guess. I guess she does get rather bored with her uniform and being away from the bright lights, especially since Marg is right in the center of so much activity.

Biz spoke to Bill on Saturday. Natalja White was here and was trying to make plans for Lois and Bill to come into town this weekend so she and Jim (retired colonel now with the ARC) could see them. He had heard nothing more from Pat Mente, nor have we, except that Anne writes that he left Washington Sunday the 8th and apparently they heard that evening or the next (Mart's birthday) that he had reached Columbus safely Sunday night.

Anne had a birthday party for Mart and they had all gone out to celebrate Pat's homecoming at the Shoreham Saturday before Pat left on his trip to Louisville.

Honey and Nance don't think he is as well as he pretends to be, and I think he tries to accomplish too much for someone who has been laid up since December.

No one can figure out why you never write—you can't be that busy.

Love, ROSE

Lt. Col. Alvin L. Mente, Jr.
Ward 23-A. Kennedy General Hospital
Memphis, Tennessee
April 19 & 20, 1945

Dear Rose:

Just a few lines to let you know that we are back at Kentucky General Hospital and are doing quite well.

After I left you over a week ago I spent three days in Washington at Sybil's. I saw Anne and Bob and their children. They are both grand kiddies. Martin looked quite well (to me, who prefers thinness to obesity). Although he never mentioned his back, he favored it somewhat in rising and sitting, but he did look grand.

I drove to Columbus and spent a night with Janet, Pat and Molly. Pat was sick but he looked big and healthy to me. Molly is a cutie.

I arrived here two days ago. Jack removed the cast. My foot is grand, he says. I can move the ankle and I'm anxious to walk on it. He, of course, says wait a while. Tomorrow I get a shoe and he says I can put it on the ground but cannot put full weight on it for a few days. I've been to physiotherapy and I am really doing 100%. Jack's really marvelous.

(I ran out of ink, it is now 20 April.)

My foot is ready to walk on but Jack wants to wait a week of wearing crutches. Actually, I put more weight on it than he allows, but don't mention it to him, Amy or Helen.

How's Biz? Best to Bill and Lois if you see them.

Love, ALVIN

P.S. Received your cablegram of February yesterday. Mother's in Pittsburgh and Washington D.C. for a week. Nothing else new. No word from West Point.

Love, ALVIN

Mary Eleanor Morin
American Red Cross
Civilian War Relief
G-5 HQ, 12th Army Group
April 19, 1945

Dearest Rosebuddy:

The suit came today and it couldn't be nicer. I can barely wait until suitable opportunity comes along to wear it.

We had a christening for it before lunch today. My pal Keating, another sergeant and myself went over to my barracks and solemnly opened the package with cups of Scotch. I'd asked them over for a spot, but it has been nine months since they've tasted Scotch, so they decided to divide it three ways. They had some Cognac while I was finishing my first drink. It's a simple way to get rid of the one bottle of Scotch that the officers get a month.

Instead of being too small, the suit is just a bit large, but that is good because it is a simple matter to have it altered. That is if I can ever get off this silly post. I can't remember when my hair was last washed, and I was to go down for a fitting of a skirt, but can't get away from the place. I have a pile of washing at least six feet tall to do before we move. I'm down to my last shirt and that is a mass of wrinkles.

Before I go on. The furniture: One thing is for sure, you simply can't afford to go on paying storage for that stuff. I hate to think of losing it, but it just isn't practical. Since no one seems to want to buy it, why not just pick out the nicest things that will fit into a small apt. and give the rest to some nuns. They always want things to fill up some rooms for bishops or types of that sort. Too bad Mercy Hurst is so far away, Mother Borjia would have a field day with that bedroom set of father's.

Have you asked Aunt Mazie about it? She through her voluntary Social Service Work is bound to know someone within a stone's throw who might not only want it, but also need it badly.

I hope you won't give up that nice inlaid round table, and those chairs that used to have green plush seats, or the telephone table. I hate to think of that mirror-lined glass cupboard getting out of our clutches, or that cabinet with the leaded-glass panel in the front top.

But the rest of the stuff isn't going to twist my personality too awfully, if it shouldn't be there when we get back. Whatever else happens, don't lose the Lowerstoft bowls that Bill and Marion gave me, my electric clock, or that Japanese vase. That reminds me, the marble-top table, too, that's nice. Oh, and my forget-me-not china. That would kill something fine in me if it were not there when I got back.

I've had you send so much stuff, that I'm sure you've had to use your own money to get them in advance of my check, but I won't ask for anything else, so figure out how much that darn stuff has been costing you and start taking money out of mine until you've paid half of it. Everything we've been exposed to for a long time now is so entirely otherworldly that I'm sure we seem to be awfully selfish and unconcerned about you and Biz but in spite of appearances, I assure you, that is the furthest thing from the case.

I might do something very farfetched and get married, you can't tell. People get away from home for a long time, get stranded in a drab place like this, Sans Dames, and their standards change. Lord only knows what the non-fraternization will add to the currently desirable situations a gal finds herself in with this outfit.

So make your plans to suit your best convenience and don't worry about what we will think or feel. We will be quite numb for years, so it won't disturb us in the slightest.

April 24, 1945

The shoes arrived today. They are stunning. I'm going to save them until we get to someplace where we have sidewalks. The roads here are so bad that they ruin shoes in no time. They've put rocks down to fill the bad holes and cover the drives. You can imagine the result particularly late at night.

My hair was getting so long and ungainly that I decided to go to the G.I. barber on the post to have it cut. When I went to make the appointment the barber was standing with his back to the window and I couldn't see him. He assured me that he'd cut several ladies hair before so I went in fearlessly on the day of my appointment and told him to follow the way it was cut and make it three inches all over. Then I settled down to a good book. When I looked up he had it three inches in the front all right, but practically nothing on the sides or in back. He wasn't the regular barber, but was pinch-hitting for his friend who "didn't feel so good today." He's a mechanic or something. It will be months before it grows out again.

The other horrible thing that happened is the other night I was in a hurry to get to the R.C. tent and went to the latrine here. I didn't take time to find the light and put my purse down. When I reached for it, groped around for an eternity, and finally faced facts. It had fallen in.

I'd have left the wretched thing there, except that I'd just had my check cashed and it contained all kinds of things like glasses, identifications, cigarette lighters that I simply couldn't replace. So there was nothing for me to do but to call the Headquarter Commandant and ask them to get it out.

I tried to be very impersonal about it, but the officer who answered recognized my voice and became hysterical. He told me to wait for a half hour and call back. Meanwhile, my friends came to look for me and insisted that we were to go for a ride. I said I couldn't that I'd just developed acute appendicitis, but they weren't to be put off so easily, so I had to tell them.

I didn't dare leave the thing there over night because they burn out the darn things at dawn. I don't know what I thought their reaction would be, but they took it beautifully in spite of my embarrassment.

One of them got a radio antenna wire and a flashlight and we set out to retrieve it. Of course, we ran into a million curious people. I had to stand guard so no strange girl would come wondering in. We got so hysterical that it was hard to catch. But we finally managed.

Fortunately the inside wasn't affected, and all my things were okay, but I haven't the courage to carry the thing no matter how well it's cleaned. The tragedy is that we can't buy purses over here. They've been threatening to have them in the PX but that's as far as they get.

Meanwhile, I'm carrying my good black grosgrain purse and it is getting beat up rapidly, in addition to looking awfully silly with the uniform. Well, that is the worst thing that can happen, so I can relax now.

Well, Rosebuddy, there isn't much else to write about, so I'll wind this up. Give my love to everyone especially to you and Biz.

All the best, NELL

P.S. Marg had called me about Mart's promotion when she received your cable. In the next breath a friend of mine from our A.G. section called to ask if I had a brother, Martin J. Morin, and announced that he'd been made a full colonel. The papers had just gone over his desk. He's the one that worked on Mart's papers when he went home.

M.E.

On Saturday, April 28, Mussolini was hanged upside down by Italian militia. Two days later, April 30, Adolf Hitler, Eva Braun, Joseph Goebbels and Goebbels's wife committed suicide.

Lt. Commander T.H. Hanson
U.S.N. C.C.UNIT #1
NAVY 3142 c/o F.P.O. San Francisco, Calif.
April 25, 1945

Dear Rose:

All of our naval contingent arrived recently and this place is a beehive of activity. Typewriters were scarce before, and are almost nonexistent now, so you'll have to decipher my almost illegible script.

Both your airmail and the V-mail are at hand. You know how good it is to receive letters, so I'll say nothing but thanks for being so good. I marvel at your ability to keep up such a volume of correspondence.

The news of Martin's promotion was wonderful. Please extend him my heartiest congratulations, and tell him I'll drop him a line when I get his address from you. That's sample of my low cunning, now you'll have to write me again. News of the improvement of Pat Mente was also good to hear. It is my earnest hope that the both of them can finish out this war in the United States. They've done their share.

Patsy and the youngsters seem to thrive. Her letters to me continue cheerful and while I know she must have had some bad days, she has certainly kept me from knowing about it, and it helps no end. I'm very grateful to her for it. Little Rose is apparently progressing rapidly and Patsy tells me that she races around the floor like a squirrel playing tag with Paul. He, incidentally, if reports aren't too colored, is quite a precocious young man. They are all very dear to my people, who are doing everything in their power to make things easier for Patsy.

I continue to thrive and have no complaint except I'm away from those I love. My best to you and Biz, and may it not be too long until we are together again.

Love, as always, TOM

Rose Mary Morin
New York City
April 26, 1945

Dear John:

You will enjoy the enclosed news from Pat that he is showing such rapid improvement. I hope Nance will be able to get up here before she returns to Southern Pines.

Bill and Lois came down Saturday and with Biz had cocktails with Nat and Jimmie White, then they all went to the Stork Club for dinner. They didn't want to bring me in from New Jersey so didn't call me. Biz is going up to West Point tomorrow for the weekend. They also invited me but I had already written Anne that I'd go to Washington this weekend if I could get away. I hated to change the plans again since I have been promising to come since Easter and it will be a month or more before I can get away again.

Had a note from Dot saying the kids have both had chicken pox and as usual George had the worst case. Eleanor's was slight and she was completely over it. Jane is very busy in her two jobs. They were wondering if we had heard anything from you—to which I will have to say NO. As long as my letters don't come back I figure nothing is wrong, yet people think it is awfully funny we never hear from you.

Love from all, ROSE

Mary Eleanor Morin
American Red Cross
Civilian War Relief
G-5 HQ, 12th Army Group
May 3, 1945
Somewhere in Germany

Dearest Rose:

You're two up on me, but I haven't been able to write because things have been in a state of uproar over the moving. Since we've been here we've been consumed with getting offices put together.

We thought there would be office furniture, but arrived to discover there was furniture all right, but we had to go out and get it and drag it in. About four hours went by, people came to visit and marvel that we were organized so quickly and suddenly the branch chief arrived and said we were in the wrong place so we had to move down two flights of stairs into one room that had been the ghost closet of a tenement house.

By that time I was furious and everyone knew it—way beyond being tactful and polite. I began to brood about the real possibility of having to drag my enormous desk, chairs, metal cases, wardrobe, etc., when Lee came back and saved the day.

We enlisted some G.I.'s who were supposed to be doing something entirely different and got the stuff down and set up that night before dinner. I spent yesterday cleaning and polishing. I never knew a place could get so dirty. The dust just seeps in and you could sweep and dust every half hour and no one would be any the wiser.

I'm very pleased that in spite of all our moving around, we were the first office ready and it looks pretty good. We heaved all the old junk that was in it out, put up some pictures, and took down the blackouts. That will be a problem if we're still here next winter, but the chance of that is pretty slim.

As far as living quarters are concerned everyone is in temporary ones, and I think it will be a long time before that gets settled. Where I am is the most attractive I've been in ages. It is a small room in a hotel that has been pretty much beat up, but is clean, light and modern. It has a washstand and lights (electric). So far we have been allowed to have people in our rooms, they are fixed up like little sitting rooms, so it hasn't been lonely in the evenings. Someone pops in and we have a drink or so.

Last night Lee and I took the WAC captain to dinner with us and then we went up to my room and sat around and listened to some of the WAC difficulties. Believe me, ours are nonexistent in contrast. They gave her girls pretty bad living quarters and of course she was terribly upset. However, she said in a few choice words, that a more suitable place would be found today. I'm afraid to go home for fear they'll tell me to move out. I hope to stay where I am until Marg gets here. She'll only be in town a day or so, but it will be more fun as this place is centrally located. The office is about 6-8 blocks away. Next war I go to I'll take my own chauffeur.

I was relieved to get your V-mail. Not that I like the damn things, I had to read that with my glasses plus a little microscopic lens I have. I was afraid you'd have fits over all the requests and was greatly relieved to hear that you didn't think it too much. I hope the things will arrive in a month or so, so I'll have them for the warm weather. At the moment we are enjoying a very cold spell. It is bitter and no fun with no kind of heat at all. We have a good stove in our office and Lee managed to gather some bits of wood, but it is all burnt up and no more to be found. Strange that we should have a turn like this as we had weeks of really beautiful weather.

The only way to get warm is to take a mineral bath. Last night was the first time we were able to. I hadn't been washed beyond my face and hands since Sunday and was getting darned uncomfortable, so we all went down right after dinner and had a bath party. It's the devil's own work to get a lather, but the hot water felt good and made me feel clean. After the kids went home I read for a while and then went to sleep. I was awake a million times, itching like crazy and couldn't figure what it was all about. This morning I told the people at the breakfast table and they advised me that I was supposed to rinse with plain water. That's cold, though, and I would rather have the itch.

I just went out to the PX I thought if I didn't have a piece of candy I'd go mad. It is the first time I've been on the street by myself and it is the funniest feeling. It is particularly hard not to smile at the kids. There are some very cute ones. I felt like a big pig walking back with the bag of cigarettes and candy and not being able to give them some.

We developed such a habit of smiling at everyone wherever we've been, as it is expected by soldiers and civilians, it's hard to remember to look through people as though they weren't there. I don't know why that's such a problem since I roamed around Washington and New York for years without grinning at everyone I passed.

I'm feeling much better now, I've consumed an "Oh Henry" and part of a Nestle. It really does make you feel warmer. I wish I had a couple quick Cognacs, though. That's the most efficient quick warmer I've come across.

I'm just wondering who is going to eat with me tonight. If there is anything I hate it is to suffer though is a meal without someone to talk to. What I'd like to do would be to have a nice hot, fresh water bath, put on clean clothes and a skirt and go to a fancy place with soft music, martinis and delicious non-fattening food. I wonder where I get such ideas.

That was pretty good about the man who sent all those steaks in honor of Pat. Do you think it will still work when we get home? He won't know that we haven't been at the front picking people out of the trenches. I'm glad Pat is having such a good time. Be sure and tell us all about the wedding.

Give my love to everyone. I'll write soon again and hope by then I'll have something interesting to say.

Loads of love, NELL

P.S. Do you think you could find me some navy blue pumps? I really need them badly. My uniforms are so worn out after two years that I like to get into civilian clothes as much as possible to save what is left.

On May 6, German Admiral Karl Doenitz surrendered Germany and ordered all German U-boats to cease operations and return to port.

Margaret F. Morin
American Red Cross
Civilian War Relief
Continental Headquarters
May 6, 1945

Dearest Kids:

I'm in Germany with Nell at the moment. We're at her office, which she is trying to make look like a cross between a drawing room and an office. The effect is so far very pleasant, but definitely not military, which is a help. I came over here, further south, in the beginning of the week to do a job and came up here yesterday.

I got orders to be back in my headquarters tonight, but there are no planes out today. The weather has been lousy for the last two weeks. The other day I went through three snowstorms and two rainstorms in about four hours drive in an open jeep. Well enough of this griping.

Please do send the black high-heeled oxfords or black kid pumps. I love the ones you sent Nell. Perhaps you could get me a pair like that. Thanks for sending the robe. It hadn't arrived when I left last week. I'm sure Bill will like it. Thanks also for the jacket and I'll see that Nell's dress gets to her.

It was curious that you asked about Pat Morin. I didn't see his article that was in the "Coronet." He turned up at my place about a month ago all out of the blue, from Egypt. It was a great surprise. I surely was glad to see him.

The cable I sent sending congratulations to Mart was for his promotion, I had forgotten about his birthday. I am truly ashamed of myself, I swear I can't remember a darned thing anymore. One gets so involved in one's little world that weeks go buy in a fog.

Well, here I am filthy dirty and Nell is trying to discourage me from taking my things back to the hotel. This life certainly puts doubts in my mind about the legend of cleanliness that we once knew. Days go by in the same clothes, a quick wipe of the face, etc.

Goodbye for now and my love to everybody. Oh, I almost forgot, I received the money orders, thanks a million.

Love, MARGY

On May 7, German General Alfried Jodl signed the unconditional German surrender. On May 8, V-E Day, victory in Europe was celebrated in most of the world.

Mary Eleanor Morin
American Red Cross
Civilian War Relief
G-5 HQ, 12th Army Group
May 8, 1945

Dearest Rose:

The most disappointing thing has happened. I've been expecting Marg to visit for so long and looked forward to showing her a grand time, but as luck would have it, she arrived at the dullest possible time. Nothing here set up and people milling around not knowing where they were or what they're up to. It was cold and damp and hideous. I got so mad that I'm afraid that I wasn't worth visiting.

The day she left it cleared up and has been lovely since. We discovered that we'd been sitting up in our cold barn of a room all evening and three bars had been opened and everyone was out having a fine time. There's been something going on ever since. People are gradually settling down and getting together on things.

My friend Page found an adorable house for Civilian War Relief—green stucco with a nice garden that would have been perfect for us. Someone outranked him on the deal. That is the trouble. You find something and then have to get permission to have it and that spurs the powers into looking at what it is and they decide they have a friend it would be nice for.

Page also found quite an imposing house for himself. No damage to speak of with the exception of a couple broken windows and a couple of radiator tops torn off. We all had dinner together last night. He's having four other officers move in with him. I was carried along to make suggestions for furnishing it. We dream of what it will turn out to be, but there is a great possibility that someone will have a good laugh and not release the furniture. It will be a pity of that happens as the house could be a lot of fun.

Margy looked wonderful. She'd been on quite a trip and said she was tired but didn't look it at all. Everyone has been asking about her since. Even though there didn't appear to be a soul around, a great number of people saw her and were disappointed to hear that she'd just been visiting.

My office is more or less like Times Square. Practically everyone goes by sooner or later. I'm out of touch with all our people for one reason and another, so I just sit here peacefully and watch the passing show. I don't think the G.I.'s will ever be finished hauling cases and furniture around. They've more or less given up trying to utilize the displaced persons as very few people can get their wishes across to them. The G.I.'s have fallen into a wonderful habit of throwing anything out the window that isn't needed rather than cart things down four flights of stairs. The courtyard is a sight. They'll have the stuff to start a lovely fire out there.

I walked into a lot of barbed wire the night before last that had not been there at lunchtime. My best pair of stockings are torn to ribbons and my legs and hands are scratched as though I'd tangled with a tiger—a mad one. I twisted my ankle somehow in trying to retain my balance and it hurts like anything if I have to walk far. I thought I'd never get to the office this morning. There's a perfectly good car sitting in front of the hotel, but no one to drive it for me.

Give my love to everyone and please write. Had a nice letter from Father Ready. He said Pat had asked for an opportunity to meet him and couldn't make much sense of his aunts overseas.

Lots of love, NELL

Mary Eleanor Morin
American Red Cross
Civilian War Relief
G-5 HQ, 12th Army Group
May 13, 1945

Dearest Rose:

What a week this has been. Reminds me of Washington. It is the most terrific change from very cold, damp weather. In addition, we have been busy with some new personnel and I had to move from the hotel where Marg visited me to a little one nearby filled to the gunnels with WAC officers, nurses, and R.C. "Girls." The civilians were moved out one day, the place cleaned and we moved in next day. I hated to move and heard the gloomiest reports from the others about what a horrible place it was (there is only one bathtub in the house for 100 rooms), but it turns out to be old-fashioned and immaculately clean. In my room all the lights work, and there is a washstand with hot water. I have clean linen sheets, a nice pale green blanket and a big wardrobe for my clothes. In some ways it reminds me of country hotels in England.

We don't have a separate mess, thank God. We can eat at any mess we like. There are several mess halls open and now they all have lounges and bars.

I've been helping Colonel Page and Major Moffitt fix up their new house. Believe me, it is a job. For the last two days we've spent every free moment hauling furniture to the house and yesterday afternoon after lunch Col. Page asked me to go up and supervise the D.R.'s and G.I.'s in placing it.

The Russians were full of gusto and charged up and down stairs with huge pieces, but the lighting fixtures, walls and legs on several pieces took a beating.

They had to leave at 5:30 to go back to camp and I decided to stay on and fix up the downstairs a little. I finally collapsed on the davenport where the bar will be with my feet throbbing. There I was when the Naval liaison officer, who will live with them, and two other officers came in.

He talked me into getting washed and going to dinner. Otherwise, I'm sure I'd still be there. I don't know what has happened to my feet, but they have been acting up for over a week now. I thought I was getting fallen arches again, but I think it is the heat and walking on pavements, hills and stairs that I haven't been used to for a long time. They actually hurt when the sheets rub them. I can't stop walking, though. That's part of my reducing program. My weight is a source of amusement to everyone. I go up and down with no rhyme or reason. I'd gained an awful lot when Marg was here and in a couple of days was down to normal.

Rose, I've been waiting for mail every since we arrived here and finally your V-mail of May 2 arrived on the 11th. I hate the darned things. Even when they're clear I have to use a special glass to read them and it's never is as good as a letter you type or write long-hand. Yesterday I went at it again and made out that James Hickey had died. Poor kid, he surely had one hell of a life. I'll ask our chaplain to say a Mass for him. James had a miserable life and there didn't seem to be any kind of decent future for him.

I called Marg this morning. I hadn't been able to get through to the Paris office and asked her to have them call me. I'd barely gotten hello out of her when the wire faded and I had to hang up, very disappointing. I had so many things I wanted to talk to her about.

Just had a very nice thing happen. A G.I. wandered into the office carrying a large leather handbag and my heart sank. I had visions of a collection of requests to find relatives. They hear on the radio that someplace has been liberated and before the announcer has finished they are on their way to us to find out where and how their people are. There is no possible way for us to know and when you tell them that, they look crushed so that it's plain to see they think we're holding back.

Instead, the bag turned out to contain three bottles of Champagne that Jim Riordan liberated for me yesterday on a trip.

Something funny about Champagne happened the night before last. Four of us went to the house from the mess to work and brought a couple bottles of Champagne from the mess to have when we finished, as the bars close at 10. As we were walking back some officer stopped us at an M.P. station and asked directions. As we were telling him, there was a slight explosion. For a second everyone was rooted to the ground fearing snipers, then the G.I.'s started to laugh and we realized that the cork had popped out of the bottle that Page was carrying. There it was—wine running like water in the streets.

I haven't had a clean stitch of clothes to my name and can't send laundry out for several more days. I'm going to see if I can't get one of the maids in the hotel to do it. They are the help that worked there before and keep the rooms very well so I guess I can trust them with my clothes. I've learned the necessary words and only hope she'll say "yes" when I spring them on her. The sun streams into my room in the morning so I'll have no trouble drying. I have a little tiny balcony opening into the court so I can hang things out there.

Best love to all, NELL

Rose Mary Morin
New York City
May 9, 1945

Dear John:

Well, V-E Day has come and gone and things have gone back to normal and we're looking forward to final VICTORY!

Monday was most exciting when the first news came over. The spontaneous celebration was more enthusiastic than when the "official" news came yesterday. We celebrated Monday by having a nice dinner (steak) at Moriarty's. Biz was late for dinner because her office force quit work at 10 a.m. and proceeded to celebrate for the rest of the day. It was much more lively and gay downtown than in midtown. Those who were off Monday worked yesterday, and vice-versa.

Last night we had a second celebration with dinner at Betty Brown's, where we lived before getting the apartment on 86th Street. She got hold of a leg of lamb and wanted some friends to help her celebrate the great day!

Will it mean that you will come home or have you, like the girls, laid plans to go East? The papers mentioned before V-E Day that the 8th Army Air Force would be leaving England. I hope if you are coming this way and have an opportunity to see the girls on the Continent before leaving.

We were surprised at the news on Sunday that Mr. LaGuardia is not running for election as mayor come fall. I hate to see him stepping out but suppose he is entitled to a little bit of private life for a while. Some think he wouldn't have had a chance anyhow. I missed his radio address Sunday when he said that he could run on a laundry ticket and win!—but would give someone else the chance.

Love, ROSE

Rose Mary Morin
New York City
May 16, 1945
V-MAIL

Dear John:

We called Patsy on Sunday evening and had a chance to speak to young Paul. He wanted to know when we were coming out to see him swim. Patsy says he is remarkable in the water—not a bit afraid. He told her at breakfast one day last week that he'd be going off the board soon and on Sunday he had gone off. They keep a rubber tube on him at all times, but even with that he is doing pretty well for a two year old.

A letter from Pat Mente says that D-Day is to be June 5 this year—the day when marries Jane Robbins of Louisville, Kentucky. He was to be discharged from treatment at Kennedy General Hospital May 15, make a quick visit with Nance and Honey with a stopover in Washington to see Bill Mente, who is on furlough, and a short visit to West Point. He would like to be assigned up there and our Bill seems to think he has a good chance.

My friends Helen and Jackie Flanagan are both very fond of Pat and have been seeing a lot of him when he can get away from the hospital.

Jack is very much pleased with the progress he has made. He was going without crutches, but using a cane occasionally. He walks without support with a slight limp. I think that after thirty days he has to report back for final physical before assignment.

Let us know how you are getting along. What are your plans? The papers say the 8th Army Air Force is headed to the Far East.

Love from all, ROSE

On May 20, the Japanese began to leave China; and on May 25, the U.S. Joint Chiefs of Staff targeted November 1 for the invasion of Japan.

Lt. Commander T.H. Hanson
U.S.N. C.C.UNIT #1
NAVY 3142 c/o F.P.O. San Francisco, Calif.
May 19, 1945

Dearest Rose:

I'm just back from a three-day hurry up trip into the southern provinces, and have clipped a bit behind on my letter writing. Your V-mail of April 23 arrived a day or two before I left and as usual I was tickled to hear from you. While I was gone your VARGA calendar came, not too much the worse for wear after the five-month trip. Those gals are indestructible, I should think. Thanks much for it. It's a bright spot.

The death of the President was much of a shock for everyone out here and the sadness of the people was genuine. I'm sorry that he wasn't around for the finish, but he lived a full life and was a wonderful man.

Patsy is certainly a wonderful mother for those children, and gains praise even under the critical eyes of her in-laws, which is something. My Aunt Gussie wrote me the other day blowing her up to the skies, and my people have rave notices for her at each writing.

The rains are almost upon us, and I've been beating my brains out to get the detachment under cover—we need lumber for flooring badly, and my Navy ensign is doing yeoman duty for us—a good part of my time is spent hustling around the area beating the various Seabee outfits out of 2X4's with such success that I'm known as the greatest scrounger on the island—an enviable reputation in this den of super thieves.

We'll be well tented for the next ten days—the vagaries of war may boot us out of our house at anytime. There is better than an even chance that we'll occupy our present abode as long as we're here—but I'd rather not gamble.

That's all for now—my best to Biz, Martin, Bill, Anne and everyone else. Take good care of yourself, and let me hear from you as often as possible.

As always, TOM

Rose Mary Morin
New York City
May 22, 1945

Dear John:

Well, you'll probably be surprised to hear that Margy is home—for a conference. She flew into Washington Friday night at eleven and was on the phone from Anne's to say hello to us at midnight. She has to remain in Washington to give a few talks at the Red Cross but hopes to come to New York sometime tomorrow. Biz says Margy told her she would have thirty days. We are most anxious to see her. She saw Nell in Wiesbaden.

Mrs. Westwater wrote yesterday that Martin has succeeded in finding a furnished house in Alexandria for the summer, June 14-September-14, and he and Janet have a date for the Preakness. During the summer he will look around for something more permanent if he is to remain in Washington. Janet also hopes to rent their Columbus house for the same period.

Bill will be in to visit his tailor on Thursday and to say hello to Margy. He wants her to visit Lois and him at the Point over the weekend. The McKetricks are planning to take us all to dinner some evening while Margy is here and a lot of her friends are anxiously waiting to see her. I imagine after four days of talking in Washington she won't have much more to say here. Her biggest thrill so far seems to be in the well-fed-looking people and shops with merchandise to sell.

Patsy wrote that she had a slight accident on Mother's Day. She avoided crashing into her garage doors when the brakes didn't work, but tore down the fence. No casualties; and repairs have been made.

Love from all, ROSE

Lt. Commander T.H. Hanson
U.S.N. C.C.UNIT #1
NAVY 3142 c/o F.P.O. San Francisco, Calif.
May 27, 1945

Dearest Rose:

Your V-mail of May 16 arrived yesterday and I can get right to answering it since this is Sunday and comparatively quiet.

Patsy wrote me of your call to her, and all in all she must have had quite a picture. She must have had quite a Mother's Day for herself—she told me that she could not imagine that the day now applies to her also, and my comment was that under the circumstance I couldn't see how she could avoid the situation. She was delighted that you called and wrote me most of the conversation. She mentioned also that the little fellow did right proud when he talked to you and that you thought his voice was exceptionally clear. He must be a bright little guy. My brother Paul predicted once that Rosie would surpass him, but if she just matches up I'll be the world's most fortunate father. Patsy does wonderfully keeping me up to date with their progress so they won't be strangers when I get back.

That's rather speedy for Pat Mente isn't it? Hope that it isn't one of these war jobs that will peter out. Congratulate him for me. I'm glad that he's out of the hospital and will have no ill effects from his hurts—he's a lucky guy.

Much to do in the world news these days, but somehow we can't get very steamed up about it. There's still a whale of a job to do out here, and the general consensus is a hope that our bungling politicians won't mess things up with the Russians. We'd sure like to have them on our side—together we could wipe this thing up completely in about six months.

Not much in the way of personal news. We stay busy, have our share of fun and I'm in the best physical shape of my last ten years. So there is nothing to complain of except the heat.

Tell Martin that 100 Pardre Burgon has been gone for some time. The Filipino government took it over shortly before the war began, razed the premises and planned to build offices on it. The Japanese, of course, put a stop to that.

The fighting in and around the walled city knocked the ground around a bit, and even the tennis courts near there were destroyed. Tell him he'd have a hard time recognizing anything outside of North Manila, which was the worst part of the city apparently. I'm going to write him one day and try to give him an idea as to what actually happened, although I know he has access to all the G-reports and summaries.

Be sweet, take care of yourself and give my best to Biz and everyone.

Love as always, TOM

Mary Eleanor Morin
American Red Cross
Civilian War Relief
G-5 HQ, 12th Army Group
Germany, May 23, 1945

Dearest Rose:

I don't have a penny to put in the purse or maybe I do. I don't know whether the authorities will approve or not, but just so you won't think it's going to bring you bad luck, take the phony francs. Tell Anne, Pat and Janet that I'll try to get back to the place and get one for each of them, also wallets for the boys.

Again I am imposing on you by sending them lock, stock and barrel to you to send to the others. The first to arrive are for you, Biz, Lois and Mary M. I got two beautiful black ones for myself so don't feel sorry for me. Your box with the gum, cigarettes, stockings, a sachet from Aunt Mazie, New Yorkers and soap arrived yesterday. Thanks a million. One of my best friends was being married so I gave her the hose and Aunt Mazie's sachet. I'm sure neither of you will mind. I simply couldn't go empty handed. She's a southern belle, Louise Smart. I'll ask her to call you when she goes home.

I've been homesick for the first time! I suddenly realized that Mart, Pat and Marg had gone home and what the hell was I doing sitting around here on my oversized fanny?

Hope to see you soon and happy birthday. Give my love to all and tell Marg to hurry back. I miss her.

All my love, NELL

Germany, May 25, 1945

Dearest Rose:

I'd give anything to be home now. Molly and Marg must be having fun. Bill Giblin called me about it the other day, but I'd go by slow boat and would be away when a lot of important changes are being made and might lose out on my job. I'd love to have been there and all of us together. But unless Bill insists, I think I'll pass it up for the time being. Anyway, I couldn't stand the diet. From all I hear, it's impossible to get a meal. That touching story about having to go to the Stork Club and dine rather than eat the everlasting scrambled eggs at home was too much for me. I'm almost tempted to send that tin of mushroom soup that I've been hoarding back to you.

Your latest epistle reached me two days ago. Good time considering that it sat around here in our regional director's office for a couple days. Telephone communications being what they are, it's sometimes days before I find out there is mail for us. The maddening part is that the A.P.O. is in the building next door. I told them that it would be kind if they'd keep my one-a-week out for me and I'd pick it up with Lee's 21 or so. I think I convinced them.

Pat wrote me about getting married. I wrote back so the letter should reach them before the wedding. I addressed it to Kennedy General. Pat was lucky to fall into Jack's hands. I'm glad to hear that he has progressed so well. I'll also send a note to Louisville, just in case.

Ho-Hum, all these marriages. We had a humdinger here last week. It couldn't have been prettier. But it was a weird mixture of generals, G.I.s and assorted others with multitude of Clubmobile gals to lend tone. I felt like an old, beat-up clubwoman. There I was for the first time in ages with a cap and white gloves on, collar buttoned up and all, and they all turned up with flowers in their hair, collars open and charm bracelets.

It was a good reception and I personally wasn't put out by being late, because there's no satisfaction for me in kissing the bride, and people always offend me by getting my name wrong. Champagne, which is getting to be a bore, if you can imagine such a thing, flowed freely.

When the kids took off for the Riviera everyone went right on celebrating until all hours of the night.

Well, I guess you've had about enough of this. I'd love to have seen Molly before she left. I would have gotten to town by some means if I'd known sooner—probably the reason why they didn't tell me.

Well, goodbye for now. MAKE everyone write.

All the best, NELL

Rose Mary Morin
New York City
May 30, 1945

Dear John:

Margaret arrived in New York last Thursday evening and looks wonderful. I met her at the train and when we arrived at the apartment Biz had things looking very lovely with vases of blossoms (mountain laurel and peonies) and in addition the McKetricks had sent a large vase of giant-size peonies. (They lasted until yesterday when I broke down and disposed of the remains.)

Pat Mente had gone up to West Point Wednesday and he and Bill (Morin) came into town Thursday to see tailors, bootmakers, furniture dealers, etc. (Bill is getting furniture for the E.M. club.) They went to the party given for the West Point officers and men at the Lambs Club then came to the apartment later. The Moriartys came in for supper with Biz, Marg and myself. After Bill and Pat arrived the McKetricks came in, so it was a gay crowd but we got very little information out of Margaret with so many people talking all at once.

We didn't get to bed until about four o'clock because after the others had left Bill stayed to wait for his train at 2:50 a.m. He says staying up late doesn't bother him because he is always tired anyway.

Friday night Pat came up to wait for his plane to Cincinnati as he had to be in Louisville Saturday and could get no other reservation except one at 4:15 a.m.

He and Jane advanced their wedding date to Friday of this week, June 1. They are going to the Edgewater Beach Hotel in Chicago for their honeymoon and plan to be back in Louisville on time to attend the Derby. We will have a chance to meet the bride when they hit New York.

Margaret contacted a lot of her friends on Friday and went up to the Manhattan Music School where her piano is being cared for. Saturday morning she left early for the weekend at West Point and didn't arrive back until noon Monday. She had a cocktail and dinner engagement with one of her friends from Paris, and, yesterday at noon, left for Long Island to spend the holiday with Gerry McLaughlin.

She has to report to Washington June 18 but plans to go down about the 14th to spend the last weekend there with Anne, Mart, Janet, etc., and perhaps attend the Preakness.

The McKetricks are taking all of us to the Stork Club for dinner tomorrow night. I'll have to leave early as it is my night at the neighborhood Bond Drive office—much as I'd like to stay.

Saturday we hope to visit the LaGuardias and Sunday the Moriartys are having us for dinner. I suppose Marg has already made additional plans for next week. We've hardly had time to talk to her.

      Love, ROSE

Lt. Commander T.H. Hanson
U.S.N. C.C.UNIT #1
NAVY 3142 c/o F.P.O. San Francisco, Calif.
Sunday. June 3, 1945

Dear Rose:

Had a letter from Nell (mailed May 19 from Germany—how's that for speed?) in which she told me that she had given up her idea about this hemisphere, and told of the surprise trip to the U.S.A. that Margy made. Bet you were all thrilled to pieces, even though you more or less expected her to drop in unannounced. If she is still around, please give her my best love.

Was glad that Nell had decided against this place—it's no good for men, let alone girls, and I'd hate to think of her getting fouled up out here. Many of the ARC people are resigning for various reasons, and more are being evacuated with skin diseases that they can't seem to cope with—sanitary conditions are such that it is almost impossible to keep even reasonably clean.

Things go well here—the supply situation has improved immeasurably, and we now have fresh meat, eggs, potatoes, onions and, once in a while, fruit. Don't think we'll be without those items for any length of time from now on, and it helps.

The war moves on apace, and with the air power from Europe we'll have the Japs reeling in no time. I may fix it so I can come home after we wind things up here, sure hope so anyway.

Nell, incidentally, says that she'll be on rotation before very long, which I know will make you happy—she seems to have a very nice assignment for the time being, after taking rough going for the most of the time that she's been away.

Thanks much for writing me, you know how much I appreciate hearing from you. Patsy continues to thrive and the children seem to be more than one man deserves.

Be sweet, my best to Biz and the rest, and write when you can.

Love, as always, TOM

Rose Mary Morin
New York City
June 6, 1945

Dear John:

The enclosed correspondence about your "inheritance" is self-explanatory. Not knowing whether you could handle a check from the bank over there, I suggested that they pay yours in a money order.

Margaret has been having a gay time. She went up to the West Point graduation with the LaGuardia family yesterday and says the "hat" stole the show. Lois and Bill had them to a wonderful luncheon of roast turkey and all the trimmings with about six other people.

Tonight Margaret and Biz are going to see *Harvey*. It has been impossible for anyone to get tickets, but one of Marg's friends asked her to name the shows she wanted to see so she mentioned *Harvey*, *Oklahoma!*, *Carousel* and *Glass Menagerie*. He succeeded in getting two tickets for each of them except the *Glass Menagerie*—he's still working on that. He was to attend the performances with her but had to go to Washington today so is losing out on *Harvey*, much to Biz's good fortune.

Molly Ford has arrived in New York (she cabled her family she would be in on Sunday or Monday) but Margaret hasn't reached any of them by phone as yet.

Margaret is hoping to go to Pittsburgh to see Mrs. Simon, Uncle Bill and your family on Monday and hopes to stay about three days. When she returns to Washington depends on whether the brothers can get the box for the Preakness—in which case she'll go down for the weekend of the 16th. Otherwise she will remain here. We had a wonderful party at the Stork Club last Thursday night with the McKetricks.

Best love from all, ROSE

Rose Mary Morin
New York City
June 12, 1945

Dear John:

Margaret has been continuing her mad whirl and has been so busy she had to call off her trip to Pittsburgh because of lack of time so there won't be any first hand report for you about the children.

She went to Gerry McLaughlin's over the weekend after attending the matinee of *Carousel* on Saturday. This afternoon she is having a few friends in for a drink and to say goodbye. She has not quite decided whether to go to Washington on time to attend the Preakness (we listened to the Derby on Saturday—Biz and I—and it was most exciting). There is a letter from Martin at the apartment now so maybe he will have some news that may make her decide to join them. She'll probably be on her way back this time next week.

We are expecting Lois and Bill to come down this afternoon but are not sure. If they don't come, Margy is going up there to say goodbye to them—and to buy a traveling bag at the PX. She is finding it very hard to get the things she had on her list to buy while at home. Shoes are her biggest problem (no pun) because the supply of the larger sizes is limited and summer shoes seem to have been bought up by now.

She had hoped to serve Scotch at her party today but it is out of the question. To her amazement, she was served "domestic" Scotch at one of the most expensive dining places in New York. In Washington she had noticed a sale of Scotch and bought a bottle for Bob only to find on her arrival in Arlington that it was also "domestic" and no one liked it. I guess she is lucky to get rye and soda and have martinis (but without French vermouth).

We all went to 7:30 Mass this morning—Mother's anniversary. Mother's Mass was on the main altar this year as I had made arrangement after the holidays. Last year we had to take a side altar and even then didn't get the exact date. We go to the Jesuit church—St. Ignatius Loyola—and there are usually five Masses being read at the same time and since they have a 7:30 Mass every morning it is easy to attend and not be late for the office.

I left Margy and Biz to have breakfast together at the Croydon while I hurried down to grab a quick juice, toast and coffee near the office.

Gerry McL. thinks Bill McL. may be coming home soon. What are your chances? Have you gone on any of the "sightseeing trips" over Europe since V.E. day? I guess you know Nell is in Wiesbaden. It would be nice if you could get over there to see her. She seems to like it more and more and from her last letter has even given up on the idea of coming home for leave on rotation.

I guess the bride and groom—Pat Mente and Jane—are on their way back to Memphis for his discharge from the hospital. My friends the Flanagans there have a nice mess of "ribs" stored away in the freezer locker so they can give a barbecue in their honor.

Love from all, ROSE

Rose Mary Morin
New York City
June 20, 1945

Dear John:
Enclosed are letters from Tom and Nell. Margaret left here for Washington at 5:50 p.m. Sunday—and was it hot. She had a reservation on an air-conditioned train. She was due in Washington on the 18th and said she would telephone us when she had word on when she would be taking off. So far we have had no word whether or not she has already gone.

Mrs. Simon came in—most unexpectedly—last Friday. When Margaret was unable to make it to Pittsburgh, Mrs. Simon went down to Washington to visit Edna, thinking she would also see Margy there—but when Margy decided to stay here until Sunday, Mrs. Simon decided to visit her friends the Strausses near us on Park Avenue.

She looks wonderful and seems to be doing a good job in her antique business. We had lunch together on Saturday then went to have cocktails at the mayor's. He had two tickets for me to the Eisenhower festivities at City Hall yesterday so I took Mrs. S. along and she was thrilled as he is one of her heroes.

She was also thrilled to hear Marion Anderson singing the *Star Spangled Banner*. It was quite a celebration. The General and his party are at West Point today and I guess Bill is pretty busy as a result. Margaret suggested that Bill get hold of "Butch" who would likely want to duck into someplace and relax for a while and get away from the clamoring throngs—so the mayor agreed to tell Capt. Butcher yesterday to be on the watch for our Bill today.

Mrs. Simon says the last time she saw Dot all the children were well. I guess that was during Nance's last visit to Pittsburgh.

We had a little excitement at the apartment this morning, being awakened by firemen pumping water and ammonia gas out of the adjoining apartment where the electric refrigerator had gone up in flames! I was surely relieved to learn the old lady who lives there was not harmed.

Love, ROSE

Rose Mary Morin
New York City
June 27, 1945

Dear John:

Received a copy of the *Pittsburgh Bulletin Index* last week which carried a picture and announcement of Jane's having been selected the "Woman of the Week." She has been awarded a scholarship to an art school in Chicago. I haven't heard any of the details from her, but apparently her many hours of work with Outlines and Boggs & Buhl advertising has not been in vain.

Margaret left Washington Thursday and on Monday we received a cable announcing her safe arrival Friday afternoon. At that time we were attending a very nice cocktail party that Molly Ford's sister, Julie Pugh (Sun Oil), gave for her. It was at the Pughs' apartment in the Waldorf Towers—39th floor. Biz and I went without escorts but there were several unattached men—mostly "beaux" of Margaret and Molly, newspaper correspondents, etc., who were overseas with them. It was an interesting gathering.

Saturday evening my friend Isabel Pinard, who went to Poland with the Foreign Service in January 1938 and has been overseas ever since, arrived and is spending a few days with us before going to Washington and eventually to her family in San Diego. She really has some interesting stories to relate having been in Warsaw when it was bombed by the Germans and escaped from there to Romania and later to France. She was then assigned to the embassy in Madrid and from there went to Bern, Switzerland, where she has been since shortly before our invasion of North Africa.

Mrs. Simon left for Pittsburgh last Thursday afternoon so we did not have an opportunity to say goodbye. When she had dinner with us Wednesday she said she would not leave until Friday or Saturday although she was quite anxious to get back to Billy. Martin is reported to be 100% once more—his back cured.

Love, ROSE

Margaret F. Morin
American Red Cross
Civilian War Relief
July 2, 1945

Dear Kids:

I hope you received the cable saying that we arrived safely. We came on a super plane called the Continental. It carried 42 passengers; and we were served hot meals en route.

As you probably know by now, Russ Gray is no longer at the same airfield in the Azores. He had gone over to take over another one of the islands and I didn't get to see him.

We got to Paris Friday night around 8:30. Nobody was at home so Marj and I dejectedly got ourselves home to my place—to find that Dorothy

Reader and Godfrey had the place filled with flowers and two bottles of Champagne in the icebox.

The next morning we found that everybody had been at the same party the night before.

I spoke to Nell the other day. She thinks she will come down for July 14. Morty Simon is now stationed just outside of Paris so I've seen him quite often. In fact, I'm driving him back to camp tonight. Bill McLaughlin had called several times while I was away, but he is now on a trip to Germany. I don't know where his headquarters are, but I left word for him to call me as soon as he got back. Please call Jerry and pass that news along.

It's been as cold as the devil, with constant rain since I've gotten back. Everybody loves the clothes I got. I haven't found a solution about the apartment yet. I had a note here from Isabel Pinard, saying she would be through here on the 12th of June. She's probably here by now. John Boland was in the other day. He's awaiting transportation and discharge from the Army—honorable of course.

Bill, Ralph and Pat all liked the things I brought them. Bill hasn't worn the tie, yet, but I think he's waiting for an occasion.

I can't tell you all how much I enjoyed my visit home. Thanks a million one and all. Was Bob ever able to do anything about the gas coupons?

Best love to you all, MARGY

AMERICAN RED CROSS
IN GREAT BRITAIN AND WESTERN EUROPE
GENERAL HEADQUARTERS
APO #887
JULY 20, 1945

Miss Rose M. Morin
New York, NY

Dear Rose:

I know that in spite of the assurances I tried to put in my cable to you, you must still be worried about Margaret. I hope, however, that you have received a letter from her in today's mail so that your worries will have lessened.

Margaret had a very bad automobile accident (July 17), which occurred as a result of a blowout. It was completely unavoidable, and seemed to be one of those things in which the hand of fate had a part.

On the other hand, fate was good, as she could have been much more seriously hurt than she was. I saw her yesterday and she is in fine spirits and is in no pain. She had a couple of bones broken in her shoulder and is in a cast. She is in such good condition that they are moving her from Chartres to one of our American General Hospitals in Paris tomorrow.

Since she will have to be in a cast for a while, I am afraid she will be evacuated to the United States. I doubt if she will like the idea of this at first, but I know that it will be more pleasant for you and also for her.

I have been given every assurance that there is no cause for worry and that for all practical purposes she is completely recovered now. All that is necessary is the time for the breaks to heal.

It looks now as if Nell will be going home on rotation shortly, so you may have all of your family together again much sooner than you anticipated.

You may be assured that Margaret is getting every attention and there is nothing she requires.

My best to you and the entire Morin clan.

        Sincerely,

        BILL

        W.H.G. GIBLIN

(Hand written note)
John: Margaret cabled this morning, which Biz read over the phone, says she is all right and will see us soon. ROSE 7/28/45

Lt. Commander T.H. Hanson
U.S.N. C.C.UNIT #1
NAVY 3142 c/o F.P.O. San Francisco, Calif.
July 26, 1945

Dear Rose:

The machine is busy but I have a little time so I'll see if you can decipher my hieroglyphics. Yours of July 9th has been here for ten days or so, but this is the first chance I've had to answer it. Our Chief Yeoman, Stanley Knecht, who has been with me since I was sent to San Diego is down with a bad bronchitis and my C.O. Ripley, whom I've mentioned to you before, is also under the weather, so routine has kept me fairly busy.

Patsy writes that John is with you now so the "Mary" hunch must have been correct. You must have been tickled to see him. If he goes on with the 8th Army Air Force he'll wind up on Okinawa, as General Doolittle is already there, and the air force is expected soon. Tell him hello for me, and that if he gets to the place, I'm in the GHQ, AFPAC telephone directory.

You're about half right on the confirmed Californians score—I am, but I'm not sure Patsy can be classed in that category. She likes the place well enough, but that's as far as it goes I'm afraid. Doesn't make any difference as we'll be happy wherever we wind up. I don't think, however, that I'll go back to the White House unless I go as assistant to the man in charge.

Everyone here is optimistic about an early end of hostilities, and so am I, as it doesn't seem possible that they can go on much longer even if there is no capitulation. If there is a quick peace we'll hurry to Japan, set up our machinery, get the job going, turn it over to the occupation, and head for home—I can dream of being there at Christmas, but that's just an outside possibility and Easter is more like it—but hope for me anyway.

Guess we won't know what Nell and Margy are going to do until they do it—but I'll say again that this is no time to see this part of the world.

I'm still healthy as a horse and managing to keep my weight down, for which I'm right proud. We continue to do very well and have about everything we can reasonably expect in the way of creature comforts, thanks to my making friends with a couple of men who just happened to be Navy supply officers.

Patsy and the youngsters seem to thrive. She's certainly doing a wonderful job for us and any fears I may have had about her handling the situation were laid to rest long ago.

That's it for now, so my best to everyone, and thanks again for writing to me.

Love, as always, TOM

## Chapter 35

### Now We Know

Winning the war in Europe was no surprise. The newspapers were filled with maps every day with arrows showing how American, Russian and British armies were closing in on Germany from all sides. When the surrender news finally came in early May, pictures in the paper showed people in New York celebrating in the streets, even holding on to lamp posts because the streets below were so crowded.

About a mile up Craig Street, down the hill from Bigelow Boulevard, Immaculate Heart Church celebrated Germany's surrender like no other place in Pittsburgh. Almost everyone who lived there was Polish and had relatives in Poland when the Nazis invaded two years before Pearl Harbor. So when the news finally came on May 8, Immaculate Heart's church bells were heard down Heron Hill to the Lawrenceville and Bloomfield neighborhoods and to the corner of Centre and Craig. Wieners's boys hawked, "Nazis surrender, next stop Tokyo, read all about it."

In Oakland all anyone talked about was now we had to beat the Japs. "Remember Pearl Harbor" was still a top song on the *Hit Parade*. And no one thought that part of the war would be easy. Me and my friends knew how bad it would be from seeing movies like *Wake Island* and newsreels showing battle scenes from Guadalcanal and Iwo Jima.

Now we were fighting on Okinawa. The newspapers said it was the last island we had to conquer before invading Japan. They printed pictures of marines using flamethrowers to flush Japanese soldiers out of caves.

All Jane could think about was Father. She telephoned Aunt Rose in New York to see if she knew when he would be back from Europe. Aunt Rose hadn't heard from him but, "Undoubtedly he'll be back in Pittsburgh soon," she said.

Mike Trent's father arrived home in June as school let out for the summer. When I met him he still wore his British Red Cross uniform and looked the way British Army officers looked in the movies. He was tall and thin with streaks of gray in his light-brown, close-cropped hair. He spoke softly and said to me, "I'm very pleased to meet you."

A week later Mike's grandfather came from England to visit. He was a heavy man with a head of thick white hair and wore a loose-fitting gray suit. I shook hands and sat in the living room as everyone talked – you know, like grown-ups do. Then Mike's grandfather pulled out of his suit coat pocket what I thought was a fountain pen. He held it up and said, "This is going to change the way you write."

He took the top off and instead of having pointy tip like a fountain pen, it had a little ball. He wrote Mike's name on a piece of paper and passed it around. It was amazing. No filling up a fountain pen, no ink well, no bottles of ink. Just a pen with a little ball on the tip.

I asked him how much it cost. He said five pounds. I asked how much was a pound worth. He said about five dollars. *"Whew,"* I thought, *"I'll never have one of those."*

That summer we found a way to get into every day game the Pirates played at Forbes Field. Sometimes, instead of climbing up the right-field stands, we snuck in the left-field bleachers under the truck entrance's metal gate. When the gate was locked down, it could be lifted high enough for kids to squeeze under. There were always men around who liked to lift up the gate to help kids sneak into a ball game.

The other way to get in was to beg while looking as helpless and pitiful as possible, "Hey, mister, you have an extra ticket please, mister, an extra ticket?"

When we weren't watching baseball we were playing it. We had worn away the grass where the batter and pitcher stood on Schenley High's lawn and in spots around the bases. I had learned how to catch the ball in my undersized, hand-me-down glove – and to pivot and throw it at least in the right direction.

Because it was still light out after dinner, we took to playing catch or just loafing in front of Rodger's Dairy on Centre Avenue between Craig Street and

Melwood. The rule was still to come home when the streetlights came on, but as we grew older we stayed out later.

One really hot night in August, I went home sometime after dark, and Mother was ironing in the kitchen, listening to the radio. As soon as I shut the apartment's door she called down the hall, "Wait till you hear what's happened."

I went to the kitchen and she said, "The war should be over soon. We dropped a new kind of bomb on Japan."

I sat at the kitchen table and listened to the news on the radio while Mother adjusted the shirt on the ironing board and stroked the wrinkles out of the collar.

The radio said it was an atomic bomb that wiped out almost an entire city. Mother turned the shirt over and said she knew what an atom was, but didn't know how anything that small could make a bomb powerful enough to level a city.

Three days later we dropped another one.

Wieners's boys hawked, "Extra, extra! Second Jap City A-bombed, read all about it."

Six hot August days after that it was done: Japan surrendered. The official news came early in the evening. Church bells and car horns made music together.

Jimmy Leighman's uncle offered to drive us downtown to see the celebration. The sun was low in the sky and cast a warm orange light. Jimmy's mother got in the front seat next to her brother. Jimmy, Danny and Mike piled into the back. Gordo hopped on the driver's side running board and I took the passenger's side.

I pulled my olive drab Army fatigue hat down tight and held on as the green 1938 Dodge sedan puffed up Dithridge Street to Bigelow Boulevard, joining the honking parade of cars, trucks and busses heading downtown. On the sidewalk, people hiked in the same direction carrying American flags and hand-painted signs. One sign announced, "It's V-J Day in the USA." Another declared, "We still Remember Pearl Harbor!" And my favorite said simply, "America, We're Beautiful!" I waved my hat at the signs as we drove by and the crowd cheered back.

By the time we reached downtown it was almost dark. Cars turned on their headlights and kept honking. The church on Smithfield Street rang its bells, as if answering all the church bells that were echoing off the hillsides along the rivers.

It took what seemed like an hour to drive two blocks down Smithfield Street and three blocks over on Wood. People clogged the sidewalks and street – strolling, singing and dancing. Police watched from doorways. Older boys and girls were sitting on the roofs of parked cars. As we crawled past, most saluted us with beer bottles or small flasks of whiskey.

Finally, the Dodge turned up Fourth Avenue and headed to Bigelow Boulevard for the return home. We parked on Bellefield Avenue. I was cold from the night air and my arm was stiff from holding on, but I didn't mind. There was no other place I would have rather been than on that running board driving through the heart of Pittsburgh celebrating the end of World War II.

I remembered the night after Pearl Harbor when I asked my mother, "What does *war* mean?" Now I knew why she didn't answer.

# Chapter 36

## P.S.

Rose Mary Morin
New York City
August 28, 1945

Dear John:

I received your wire last night giving your new address and am enclosing herewith mail and a cable that I have held awaiting word from you.

I will get your uniforms out of the cleaner this afternoon and send them at once—also a blouse and pants and a pair of shoes you left in the closet. Elizabeth has had the shoes stitched.

Nell went to Washington on Friday and thought she would come back today. She promised Lois she would go to Lake George with her for the horse show and also told Molly she would spend a few days with her and her mother at Spring Lake as well as a few days with the McKetricks at Long Beach. I don't see how she can fit it all in unless she has her leave extended, as the 30 days are over next week.

Margaret had a cable from Bill Giblin saying he would be home this week and would be in Washington next. She spoke as though he were coming home permanently so it doesn't look as though there is any chance of either Nell or Margaret returning to Europe. Nell was to have an interview with Mr.

Ryan at the Red Cross yesterday so she will likely know what she is to do when she returns home.

I ran into Martha Bolger on the street yesterday and she was so sorry to have missed you. I told her when you returned from Pittsburgh you had only a few hours Sunday afternoon with us. She looks younger every day. I had told Martha after you left for Pittsburgh that we'd go over to see her on your return.

If you should be in Los Angeles, Patsy's address is Mrs. T.H. Hanson, 214 East Haven Avenue, Arcadia, California—Telephone Monrovia 9321.

Keep us advised of your whereabouts.

Love, ROSE

Also a very Happy Birthday and many more. R.

# Chapter 37

## Ball Hawk

It was a Sunday night after dinner and I was in my room listening to *The Shadow*, a radio program about an out-of-this-world detective who can read men's minds and uncover their crimes. Every episode started with a sinister-sounding voice that said, "Who knows what evil lurks in the minds of men? *The Shadow* knows."

Just as the program finished, Jane opened the door and asked to come in. She had that I've-got-a-secret look again. I was lying on my bed with my feet up on the wall. She closed the door behind her and sat next to me, keeping her feet on the floor.

"Father's home," she said.

I didn't say anything, not sure how that would affect me.

"He would like to see you."

I didn't know what to do. I lowered my feet from the wall and rolled over. Tears blurred my eyes. I held my breath. Then I erupted with sobs and tears. I couldn't stop.

Jane hugged me until the crying faded. Tears also smeared her face and we looked at each other without words.

We took the 71 Negley streetcar downtown. As we passed St. Paul's Cathedral and the Cathedral of Learning, I watched men strapped to the sides of the buildings steaming off the blackness, revealing a light-gray stone that looked as clean as the Church of the Holy Innocents in Sheraden.

When we reached downtown, we transferred on Liberty Avenue to another streetcar going across the Allegheny River to the North Side. We got off in front of Boggs & Buhl, the department store where Jane worked.

The restaurant, across the park from the store, had high dark wooden booths along one wall and a long shiny bar along the other.

As we walked in, a man popped up from behind a booth and said, "Hello there." He wore a dark blue suit, a white shirt and a red-and-blue striped tie. His lapel sported a gold veteran pin. "Did you have any trouble finding the place?" he asked, looking at me.

"No, we took streetcars," I said.

"Well, you were in good hands, wasn't he, dear?" He leaned past me and kissed Jane's cheek.

In the booth Jane and I faced him, me on the outside with a view of the bar and front windows.

When the waiter appeared, Father said, "William, I'd like you to meet my son and daughter."

William was large and bald with thick glasses and a big smile. He gave us a little bow and said, "How do you do, folks? What are we having today?"

Father read off a list and soon the table was filled with rolls, butter, coleslaw and salad.

"We'll forgo the wine today, William," Father said. "Georgie, what do you like to drink?"

"Do they have Coca-Cola?" I asked.

"Yes, sir," William said and took the other orders and was off.

As we waited for our drinks, Jane and Father talked about I don't know what. I watched the colored neon lights inside the glass columns on each end of the bar. The lights would spiral up and then down, changing to red, blue and yellow as they twirled.

Eventually, Father turned his head to see what mesmerized me so. He turned back and said, "Well that's a good business to get into – your grandfather did good by it."

I knew he didn't know what I was looking at, but I couldn't explain it, so I didn't say anything.

My lunch was topped off with two scoops of vanilla ice cream covered with hot fudge and whipped cream. When I finished digging out the last spoonful Father said, "I hear you're becoming quite a baseball player."

"We just play roundsies," I said.

"How are you doing with your grandfather's glove?"

"It's okay," I lied.

He reached under his seat and pulled out a cardboard box with SPALDING in big red letters printed on all sides. I think my heart stopped.

He opened the box and took out a dark-brown fielder's mitt and handed it to me. "I thought you could use a glove that's a little more up to date," he said.

The moment it touched my hands I knew what it was: a Frankie Gustine Ball Hawk! I rubbed my fingers over the dark, soft leather and deep pocket between the glove's thumb and fingers. The Ball Hawk was the best fielder's glove there was. Frankie Gustine's signature was written in silver on the glove's palm.

Jane and Father both beamed at me with every crinkle in their face. Seeing them like that, I realized Jane looked a lot like Father.

After I calmed down, Father said, "You know I've played a bit of baseball myself – your grandfather taught me. If you'd like, on Saturdays, we could drive up to the Schenley Park Oval and toss the ball around. Maybe give you a few tips."

My eyes started to blur. I looked down and punched the Ball Hawk's pocket and said, "Okay," without looking up.

# *Acknowledgments*

If it hadn't been for that crushed cardboard box in the corner of my father's garage, this book would not have been born. The box contained over 400 crinkled, yellowing onionskin pages jammed with single-space typewritten words that my father had kept for almost 50 years.

My aunt Rose took the handwritten letters she received from her relatives serving in World War II (two brothers, two sisters, a cousin and a brother-in-law) and typed them in quadruplicate on a circa 1935 Remington to distribute to all.

So topping my thank you list are Aunt Rose Mary Morin, for typing the letters, and my father, John M. Morin, Jr., for saving them,

Next are those who wrote them, aunts Margaret Fleming Morin and Mary Eleanor Morin, uncles Martin J. Morin and Thomas H. Hanson, and cousin Alvin J. Mente, Jr.

All the family members serving overseas in World War II thrived, maybe even survived, by receiving Aunt Rose's constant flow of onionskin. In return she received news of fears, hopes, prayers and – shopping lists.

Without the help and support of my wife, Kathie Gordon Morin, I could not have turned those pages of onionskin into digitized sentences and paragraphs. She not only delivered encouragement, but also contributed generously with ideas and suggestions.

Our daughter, Elena Sara Morin, a gifted writer of prose and poetry, also guided my hand as I strived to capture the voice of a six-to-nine-year-old storyteller. She had patience for neither corn nor cliché.

I also thank my aunts Anne Morin Brown and Patricia Morin Hanson for sharing with me their memories of their sisters and brothers.

I'm indebted to my cousins Patrick Morin, Molly Morin Merrill, Alvin J. Mente, III, Robin Brown, Eleanor (Nunsey) Brown, Kate Brown DeFore, Paul Hanson, Rose Mary Hanson Posey and Helen Hanson for their approval and support of my effort to relate our family's wartime story.

I found the Internet a gold mine of information. At the History Place I found the timelines that synched my family's letters with the progress of the war. Other sites from which I checked facts and refreshed my memory were GlobalSecurity.org, Wikipedia, Historic Pittsburgh, the American Red Cross World War II scrapbook, the 323 Bomb Group 454th Bomb Squadron history, the 2nd and 7th Armored Divisions histories, the Fraternal Order of Eagles and the histories of the 8th and 9th Air Forces.

My memories of my childhood friends remain vivid, but I haven't been in touch with any of them for many decades – and wouldn't dream of using their real names without permission.

My writing and journalism skills received invaluable fine tuning through Laurel Touby and her brainchild, Mediabistro, where I learned from some of the most capable authors in New York: Tom Zoellner, Steve Friedman, Susan Shapiro and Kimberlee Auerbach.

I first studied writing at Duquesne University on my way to a B.A. in English Literature. I began in the Journalism Department but soon transferred to the English Department, lured by the creative writing courses of Professor Ida Collura whose warmth and wisdom I'll always remember. There I strove to turn a phrase and capture a mood from sophomore through senior years, producing essays and short stories. I don't know if I could have stayed the course without the encouragement and friendship of my colleagues in the effort: Bob Carter and Ron Semler.

Saving the best for last: I profess my lifelong appreciation for my sisters, Jane Morin Snowday and Eleanor Morin Davis (Nellie in these pages), my mother Dorothea Wilson Morin and my grandmother, Jane Neal Wilson. What would I have been without them?

And thank *you* for your interest in and, hopefully, enjoyment of *Love & War As Never Before.*

# Index

323rd Bomb Group, 42, 75, 252

## A

Allies, 52, 63, 70, 109, 114, 133, 194, 197, 286, 297
American Legion, 79, 92-93, 269
American Red Cross Social Services, 34
Anne (store manager), 48
Annie (Eddie's husband), 206
Armstrong, Jack, 158
Aunt Maizie, 99
Aunt Rene, 206-7
Aunt Ruth, 12, 14-15, 22, 80, 183

## B

Baker, Betty, 233, 286, 296, 302
Barden, Judy, 262
Barker, Fred, 240
Battle of the Bulge, 34-35, 249, 261, 265
Baumberger, Marjorie, 177

"Bell Bottom Trousers," 80
*Bell for Adano, A*, 137, 227
Benedictine Monastery, 144
Benny, Jack, 126
Blair (Sue's brother), 206
Boland, John, 114, 127, 129, 335
Bradley, Bobby, 23, 47, 78-81, 92-93, 213
Bradley, Tommy, 23-24, 31, 47, 78-81, 92-93, 213
Broder, Ralph, 16
Bromberger, Marje, 263
Brown, Betty, 99, 239, 322
Brown, Bob, 36, 90, 187, 190
Brown, Nunsey, 76, 82, 90, 101, 138, 154, 160, 168, 191, 252-53, 286, 348

## C

*Catherine Was Great*, 204
Chartiers Avenue, 12, 22, 48, 58, 80, 211
Churchill, Winston, 171, 177
Civic Center, 183, 211-13

Connors, Patricia, 16
Cosgrave (Betty Baker's beau), 280
Cullen, Mike, 96
*Curtain Rises, The* (Reynolds), 131

**D**

Dahlgren, Eva, 189
Dan (uncle), 99, 124, 150, 203
Dangerfield, Binx, 256
Darr, Anne, 171, 176, 178
Darr, Bess, 54, 175-76, 178, 216
Darr, Jack, 15, 171
Daschbach, Mary Lou, 71
Davidson, Bill, 208
Davis, Norman, 62, 161
Doenitz, Karl, 316
Dolan, Rose, 177, 185, 189, 239
Donut Dugout, 137, 142, 150, 161, 179
Dorothy Reader, 250, 279, 287, 334
Dot. *See* Morin, Dorothea Wilson
Dravo Corporation, 13, 359
Dwyer, Bijou, 237, 287
Dwyer, John, 61, 67, 100, 136, 142-43, 172, 193-94, 240, 290, 302-3
Dyer, John, 50

**E**

Eddie (husband of Annie), 206

**F**

Fairbanks, Douglas, Jr., 55
Father Keefer, 147-48

Fields, Sid, 119
Fitzgerald (major), 99-100
Flanagan, Jack, 277, 289-90
Ford, Molly, 238, 331, 334
Foster, Dave, 15, 176, 216, 232
Fraternal Order of Eagles, 33, 348
Fredette Street, 23

**G**

Gallagher, Jim, 77, 141
Gallagher, Kash, 141
Giblin, Bill, 41, 74, 84, 97, 113, 134, 263, 265, 274-75, 285-86
Godfrey, Skippy, 255
Goering, Hermann, 176
Goodman, Gordo, 246-47

**H**

Hanson, Tom, 33, 36, 167, 261
Harmon, Ernest T., 208
Harris, Johnny, 210, 237
Hayes, Gerry, 131
"Hell on Wheels," 34, 105, 163, 180
Hickey, Cecilia, 304
Hickey, James, 320
Hilda (Mrs. Simon's sister), 42
Hinckly, Al, 196
Hitler, Adolf, 148, 172, 311
Holesworth, Ernie, 70
Hope, Bob, 53, 55, 62, 66, 72-73, 119, 192
Howard, Barbara, 193, 239
*How Green Was My Valley*, 137

## I

Immaculate Heart Church, 338
Iwo Jima, 261, 282, 289, 338

## J

Jamison, Minor, 86
Jamison, Rita, 86
Jed, Tennessee, 158

## K

Keating, Rowland, 256, 305
Kimmy, 206-7
Kirkman, Donnie, 93
Kirkpatrick, Helen, 125
Knecht, Stanley, 336
Kuhn, Jim, 207, 256
Kulp, George, 195

## L

*Lady Luck II*, 33
LaGuardia, Fiorello, 21, 33
Langford, Frances, 73
Langley High School, 58, 64
Langman, Dulcie, 35, 45
Lee (supervisor), 190, 250, 255, 274, 285, 287, 302-3, 314-15, 327
Leidecker, Charlie, 204
Leighman, Jimmy, 246-47, 340
letters
  Dunlop, 264
  Giblin, Bill, 336

Hanson, Tom, 262, 277, 293, 312, 324, 326, 330, 337
Mente, Alvin, 188-89, 200, 209, 234, 243, 265-66, 289
Mente, Alvin, Jr., 264, 268, 277, 308
Morin, Margaret Fleming, 40-41, 46, 53, 55, 62, 66, 75, 83, 86, 90, 96, 99, 107, 135-36, 139-40, 291-92
Morin, Martin J., 41, 43, 52, 61, 74, 76, 84, 88-89, 107, 113, 118, 121, 128, 132, 138, 150
Morin, Mary Eleanor, 45-46, 51, 55, 61, 63, 69-70, 73, 77, 91, 98, 100, 109, 111, 129-30, 168-69, 193
Morin, Rose Mary, 42, 67-68, 70-71, 95, 110-12, 123-26, 134-35, 160, 180-81, 187, 194-95, 232, 251-52, 275, 322-24, 331-34
Rant, Edith, 143
Longman (lieutenant), 111
Louie (waiter), 224-25

## M

MacArthur, Douglas, 92-93, 261-62, 276
Major Lamet, 208, 239-40, 305
March, Fredric, 96
Margy. *See* Morin, Margaret Fleming
Market Garden, 191
McCormack, John, 112
McGuire, Liz, 175
McKetricks, 71, 83, 87, 90, 123, 151, 154, 219, 324, 328-29, 331, 342
McLaughlin, Bill, 70, 97, 100, 123, 125, 127, 131, 140, 143, 151, 195, 288, 332, 335

McLaughlin, Gerry, 195, 231, 329, 331
McVickers, Johnny, 276
Mente, Alvin, 33, 35, 38, 60, 85, 96, 105-6, 120, 124, 142, 188, 347
Mente, Alvin, Jr., 33, 35, 38, 96, 105-6, 120, 142, 164. *See also* letters Mente, Alvin, Jr.
Mente, Bill, 85, 95, 180, 322
Mente, William Basil, Jr., 169
Mercy Hurst, 136, 154, 309
Monahan, Donny, 64-65
Monahan, Jim, 64-65
Monte Cassino, 109, 144, 149
Moriarty, Mary, 56, 86, 141, 235, 239, 284
Morin, Anne Patricia, 135
Morin, Dorothea Wilson, 12, 15, 20, 54, 58, 67, 84, 101, 106, 215-16, 232
Morin, George Wilson
  as a baseball player, 298-300
  Christmas experiences, 15-16, 31
  first day at St. Paul's Cathedral, 244-45
  with friends at Pritchard Street, 12, 23, 34, 96, 106, 160, 162, 239, 244-45, 256, 264, 273, 328, 335
  given a baseball glove, 346
  grandfather's death, 19
  with his wagon, 48-49
  at Jim Monahan's funeral, 64-65
  meeting his aunts, 20
  memories at Citadel Street, 12-13
  memories of grandfather, 33
  memories with the Bradleys, 73, 79-80, 279
  with Mike Trent, 245, 247
  moments with grandmother, 13
  playing Gen. Macarthur, 92-93
  playing war games, 24
  singing at Sheraden Tavern, 80
  time with his father, 29-30
Morin, Jane, 12-16, 21, 29, 58, 64, 94, 239, 328, 333
Morin, John M., 12, 33, 347
Morin, John M., Jr., 33, 347
Morin, Margaret Fleming, 20, 33-34, 123, 125, 336, 347. *See also* letters: Morin, Margaret Fleming
Morin, Martin J (*see also* letters: Morin, Martin J.), 34, 40, 43, 52, 74, 76, 84, 87-88, 107, 112, 118, 120, 127, 132, 137, 149
Morin, Mary Eleanor, 20, 34, 72. *See also* letters: Morin, Mary Eleanor
Morin, Mary Elizabeth, 21, 36
Morin, Nellie, 12-16, 20-22, 30-31, 48, 57-59, 64-65, 80, 157, 175, 348
Morin, Patsy, 21, 36, 181, 191
Morin, Rose Mary, 20, 32-33, 36-37, 39, 100, 107, 142. *See also* letters: Morin, Rose Mary
Morin, William A. M., 34
Mr. Clancy, 23, 31, 211
Mr. Keegan, 252
Mr. MacLennon, 110
Mr. McKetrick, 87, 123
Mr. Meyer, 90
Mrs. Simon, 42, 331, 333-34
Mrs. Westwater, 137, 190, 232, 277, 324
Musial, Stan, 246-47, 298
Mussolini, Benito, 42-43, 66-67, 148, 311

## N

Newgarden, Paul, 171
Newman, Frankie, 23, 31, 47, 64, 78-80, 92-93, 158, 204, 211, 247, 298, 346

## O

Oakland, 44, 212-13, 244, 272, 338
O'Brien, Janet, 256
O'Donnell, Jack, 256
*Oklahoma!*, 14, 51, 85, 175, 178, 198, 297, 330
O'Neill, Barbara, 175
*One Touch of Venus*, 178, 204
Opening Day, 299
Opera House, 41, 46, 53
Ordinance Ground School, 95
Ortag, Jules, 302
Oxford, Edna, 152, 179

## P

Paris, 185-86, 218
Pat. *See* Mente, Alvin
Patterson, Margie, 47, 49, 65, 211
Paul (Patsy Morin's son), 61, 68, 88, 124
Pearl Harbor, 14, 33, 187, 297, 338, 340-41
Pidgeon, Walter, 229
Pinard, Isabel, 334-35
Pittsburgh Plate Glass, 33, 185, 304
Pope, Alexander, 87
Pritchard Street, 22, 29, 47-48, 157, 183, 359
Pugh, Julie, 334

## R

Rant, Edith, 143
Ray Earhardt, 171
Ready (bishop), 229, 237, 241, 254, 256, 281, 319
Red Cross Clubmobile, 30, 38, 174
Relman Morin, 154
Reynolds, Quentin, 55, 126, 131, 266
  *Curtain Rises, The*, 131
Riordan, Jim, 240, 286, 302, 321
Ripley, K. T., 262
Robbins, Jane, 302, 322
Robbins, Peggy, 93
Roberts, Dickie, 23-24, 31, 47, 64, 78-80, 92-93, 158, 211
Roberts, Ozzie, 291
Robinson, Bill, 266
Roosevelt, Franklin Delano, 15, 93, 99, 193, 200, 220, 275, 297, 299
Rosewell, Rosy, 245

## S

*Searching Wind*, 175
Semple, Sleepy, 296
Serger, Danny, 246-47
Shair, Janet, 115
Simon, Morty, 130, 173, 335
Sister Bertha, 272
Sister Fredette, 244, 272
Skinner, Cornelia Otis, 175
Slaff, George, 135
Smart, Louise, 326
Sottle, Mary, 144

*Stage Door Canteen*, 110
Stalin, Josef, 275
Steinbeck, John, 45, 72
*Strike a New Note*, 119, 127
Sue (Blair's sister), 206
Sullivan, Mary, 98
*Sweeter and Lower*, 122, 127
Sybil, 95, 169, 307

**T**

Tebbett, Lois, 221
*There Shall Be No Night*, 123
Tiley, 119, 133, 135, 144
*Tomorrow the World*, 120
Trent, Mike, 245-46, 339

**U**

Uncle Charles, 14-15, 58-59, 211-12, 214, 245
*Up in Central Park*, 290
U.S. Fifth Army, 110

**V**

Variety Club, 210, 237
Veterans of Foreign Wars, 79
Vilsack, Carl, 256
Vincent, Agnes, 16, 147, 182

**W**

Wallace, Robert, 160
West Point, 14, 20, 30, 33-35, 38, 95, 112, 131, 142, 222, 288, 296-97, 302, 306, 308, 328-30
*While the Sun Shines*, 122, 127

Edwards Brothers,Inc!
Thorofare, NJ 08086
01 December, 2010
BA2010335